MESSIAH AND TEMPLE

SOCIETY OF BIBLICAL LITERATURE
DISSERTATION SERIES

edited by
Howard C. Kee
and
Douglas A. Knight

Number 31

MESSIAH AND TEMPLE
The Trial of Jesus in the Gospel of Mark

by
Donald Juel

SCHOLARS PRESS
Missoula, Montana

MESSIAH AND TEMPLE
The Trial of Jesus in the Gospel of Mark

by
Donald Juel

Published by
SCHOLARS PRESS

Distributed by

SCHOLARS PRESS
University of Montana
Missoula, Montana 59812

MESSIAH AND TEMPLE

The Trial of Jesus in the Gospel of Mark

by

Donald Juel
Princeton Theological Seminary
Princeton, New Jersey

Ph.D., 1973   Advisor:
Yale University   Nils A. Dahl

Library of Congress Cataloging in Publication Data
Juel, Donald.
  Messiah and temple.

  (Dissertation series - Society of Biblical
Literature ; no. 31)
  Bibliography: p.
  1. Jesus Christ—Trial. 2. Bible. N.T.
Mark—Criticism, interpretation, etc. I. Society
of Biblical Literature. II. Title. III. Series:
Society of Biblical Literature. Dissertation
series ; no. 31.
BT440.J8   232.9'62   76-46397
ISBN 0-89130-120-8

Printed in the United States of America
1   2   3   4   5
Printing Department
University of Montana
Missoula, Montana 59812

TABLE OF CONTENTS

CHAPTER 1

THE TRIAL IN THE HISTORY OF MARKAN SCHOLARSHIP

In the last several decades biblical scholars have devoted considerable attention to Jesus' so-called trial before
the Sanhedrin. One obvious reason for the interest has been
the problem of anti-Semitism so forcibly thrust into the fore-
ground during the Nazi years in Germany. The Gospel accounts
have been used by some scholars to prove that the traditional
characterization of Jews as the murderers of Jesus is baseless,
that in fact anti-Semitism begins in the New Testament. Men
like Hans Lietzmann, Paul Winter and, most recently, Haim Cohn,
have argued that the account of the trial in Mark is a Christian
fiction, that for various reasons Christians found it convenient
to blame the Jews for Jesus' death.[1] The trial account has
been used for other purposes as well. Scholars like S. G. F.
Brandon have insisted that the trial narrative as it appears in
the Gospels is part of a concerted effort on the part of early
Christian apologists to conceal Jesus' involvement in the burn-
ing political issues of the day, most notably the revolutionary
movement against Roman occupation.[2] Today there exists a vast
literature dealing with the trial, and it is beyond the scope
of this dissertation to survey more than a fraction of that
literature. A recent publication by David Catchpole provides
a survey of at least some of the pertinent literature.[3]

In addition to obvious historical and theological concerns, one of the reasons the trial before the Jewish council
has received so much attention is that the various Gospel
accounts admit of no simple explanation. Luke reports no such

---

[1]Hans Lietzmann, "Der Prozess Jesu," Sitzungsberichte
der preussischen Akademie der Wissenschaft, phil.-historische
Klasse (1931), 313-322; Paul Winter, On the Trial of Jesus
(Berlin: Gruyter and Co., 1961); Haim Cohn, The Trial and
Death of Jesus (New York: Harper and Row, 1971).

[2]S. G. F. Brandon, Jesus and the Zealots (Manchester:
Manchester University Press, 1967); idem., The Trial of Jesus
of Nazareth (London: Batsford, 1968).

[3]David Catchpole, The Trial of Jesus: A Study in the
Gospels and Jewish Historiography from 1770 to the Present
Day (Studia Post-Biblica 18; Leiden: Brill, 1971).

1

nocturnal trial, only a hearing before the Jewish authorities on the morning after Jesus' arrest (Lk 22:66-71). Yet the Gospel of Mark, Luke's principal source, contains a clear report of a trial on the night of Jesus' arrest at which Jesus is condemned to death by Jewish authorities (14:55-65). In Matthew's version of the story the Jews are even more clearly responsible.[4] And in the Fourth Gospel, the only reason Jesus is not executed by the Jewish leaders is that they do not possess the requisite authority (Jn 18:31).

There are also serious problems within the individual Gospel accounts. Mark's version of the story is no exception:

a) The whole account of the trial is sandwiched between the story of Peter's denial (Mk 14:53-54 and 14:66-72), betraying literary activity on Mark's part.

b) Although the task of reconstructing the legal procedures in effect in Israel before A.D. 70 is extremely difficult, it is striking that the trial as Mark reports it violates almost every regulation we know from the Mishnah.[5]

c) After the account of the trial in chapter 14, 15:1 is surprising. There is no indication that any trial has taken place,[6] or at least there is no clear connection in Mark between the trial before Pilate and the trial before the Sanhedrin. There is even a difference in titles at the two trials.[7]

d) Although Jesus is convicted of blasphemy (14:64) and on that basis condemned to death, he is crucified, not

---

[4]This is especially clear in Mt 27:25: "And all the people answered, 'His blood be on us and on our children.'" Cf. Nils A. Dahl, "Die Passionsgeschichte bei Matthäus," NTS 22 (1955-56), 27.

[5]Cf. below, 59-63.

[6]R. Bultmann (History of the Synoptic Tradition [tr. J. Marsh; New York: Harper and Row, 1963], 272) argues that 15:1 is a reference to the trial itself; Sherwin-White (Roman Society and Roman Law in the New Testament [Oxford: Clarendon Press, 1963] 44-45) argues that the phrase συμβούλιον ποιεῖν cannot mean "held a council meeting," but must mean "taking a decision" or "forming a plot" - in which case the text presents no problems regarding two separate formal meetings.

[7]Numerous commentators have argued that the difference between "King of the Jews" and "the Christ, the Son of the Blessed" is considerable. This is probably not the case in Christian tradition. See below, 43-52.

stoned. And Mark makes no effort to explain the
discrepancy as does the author of the Fourth Gospel
(Jn 18:31).

e) From all we can determine from extant Jewish Legal
sources, nothing Jesus is reported to have said at
the trial could have been construed as blasphemy in
the legal sense.[8]

f) One of the two charges at the trial seems to presuppose a specific threat made by Jesus against the
temple (Mk 14:58). But this charge presents numerous
problems:

1) Nowhere in Mark does Jesus make such a statement.
He predicts the destruction of the temple in 13:2,
but this is spoken to his disciples (actually to
one of them), the verb "destroy" is in the pas-
sive, and nothing is said about rebuilding.[9]

2) Mark notes before and after the specific charge
that those presenting testimony were unable to a-
gree (14:56 and 59). Yet the actual charge is
quite specific (14:58), and it is not at all clear
in what way the witnesses were unable to agree -
particularly when the threat (or a version of it)
appears to be public knowledge in chapter 15 (15:
29, the taunt at the cross).

3) Verses 57-59 look very much like an interpola-
tion.[10]

4) Mark twice characterizes those giving testimony as
false witnesses (14:56 and 57). Yet the charge in
14:58 appears to have been carefully formulated,
especially the terms "made with hands/not made
with hands," and there are literary indications
that Mark intends the statement to be viewed by

---

[8]According to the Mishnah Sanhedrin 7:5, blasphemy is
simply pronouncing the ineffable name of God: "'The blasphemer'
is not culpable unless he pronounces the Name itself." (All
translations from the Mishnah are taken from H. Danby, The
Mishnah [Oxford: Clarendon Press, 1933].)

[9]The Western reading in MSS D and W would appear to be
an attempt to link the prediction of destruction with the
charge at the trial by the addition of the saying about
rebuilding.

[10]Bultmann, History, 270.

his readers as true in some sense.[11]

5) The question of the High Priest in 14:61 seems to assume some relationship between the charges (esp. πάλιν), that there has been some preparation for the claim to be "the Christ, the Son of the Blessed." Yet no relationship is spelled out, and the temple issue is not raised again at the trial, where the sole issue seems to be Jesus' Kingship.

6) No allusion is made in the testimony to the event reported in 11:15-17, the so-called cleansing of the temple. In the Fourth Gospel the link is clearly made (Jn 2:17). But although Mark notes that after the incident the chief priests and scribes "sought a way to destroy him" (11:18), no link is made to the trial. The witnesses report only a statement made by Jesus that he would destroy the temple made with hands. There is a considerable difference between "cleansing" the temple by overturning tables and threatening its destruction (as his own act!).

7) The precise meaning of the terms "made with hands/ not made with hands" is unclear. The phrase "in three days" (δια τριῶ ἡμερῶν) is also problematic.[12]

g) Jesus is pointedly silent in the face of the numerous false accusations (14:60-61). Yet he answers without reserve in the following verses the question about his identity, thus revealing a secret jealously guarded throughout the rest of the story.

h) The High Priest's question and Jesus' reply feature three christological titles and a somewhat puzzling combination of (at least) two references to Scripture. There is little agreement about the relationship among the titles or about the exact picture intended by the scriptural references.[13]

---

[11]See below, 117ff on 14:58.

[12]See below 143-44 on the phrase "in three days."

[13]With regard to the titles, many German commentators believe that the use of Son of Man in 14:62 is a signal that what follows is to be interpreted as a correction of the question of the High Priest, despite Jesus' positive answer to the

Many attempts have been made by commentators to explain these difficulties in Mark's version of the trial. Considering the importance of Jesus' death both for the historian and theologian, it is not surprising that study of the trial has focused on the historical realities behind Mark's Gospel and that solutions to the difficulties in the story have been sought at this level. Nor is it surprising that in the last decades form critics have attempted to solve the difficulties on the level of pre-Markan Christianity and by examining Mark's use of sources. The literary character of Mark's Gospel invites such study; the story is sometimes composed of bits and pieces of prior tradition joined together rather artlessly. Yet it is nevertheless astonishing how little attention has been devoted to an examination of Mark's account as a piece of literature, with its own literary integrity. Not even redaction criticism, a recent movement concerned to lay bare the theology of the individual evangelists,[14] has shifted to a study of the Gospels as literature.[15]

It may be the case that Mark's Gospel is literature of a peculiar type.[16] He apparently did not have a free hand in composing his Gospel. It seems most probable that he did not have direct access to the events he reported but was dependent upon tradition. Even with regard to tradition he was probably limited in his freedom to compose his Gospel. There seems to be a growing consensus that traditions reached Mark in the form of

---

question. For a discussion of the various views and my own interpretation, see 85-94 below. For the scriptural references in 14:62, cf. Norman Perrin, "Mark 14:62: The End Product of a Christian Pesher Tradition?" NTS 12 (1966), 150-155, and below.

[14]The three "classical" works in redaction criticism are H. Conzelmann, The Theology of St. Luke (tr. G. Buswell; New York: Harper and Row, 1961); G. Bornkamm, G. Barth and H. J. Held, Tradition and Interpretation in Matthew (tr. Percy Scott; Philadelphia: Westminster, 1963); W. Marxsen, Mark the Evangelist (tr. D. Juel et. al.; Nashville: Abingdon, 1969). For an excellent account of the movement, see N. Perrin, What is Redaction Criticism? (Philadelphia: Fortress, 1969).

[15]Cf. 24-36 below on redaction criticism.

[16]The question of literary antecedents of Mark and the precise genre of his work has been receiving considerable attention recently. A special task group within the Society of Biblical Literature has been formed to study "The Gospel as Genre." Thus far results are preliminary.

6

complexes, and most scholars are agreed that the passion story
in particular came to Mark in somewhat fixed form.[17] But Mark
still deserves to be viewed as an author in some sense. There
is some evidence that Mark made some selection among traditions,
at least with regard to Jesus' sayings.[18] But even if this is unde-
monstrable elsewhere in the Gospel, even if we were to accept
the theory of an Urmarkus, the present text of Mark deserves to
be examined as a piece of literature, as a literary whole with
an integrity of its own. We should begin with the assumption
that Mark was at least capable of telling a coherent story, that
there is a certain structure and cohesiveness to his Gospel.
Only when every attempt to determine the place of a text within
the whole has failed to account for its presence or to provide a
reasonable account of its function within the story are we justified in seeking explanations for the text based on Mark's un-
thinking use of prior tradition.[19]

It would seem reasonable, therefore, to begin a study of
the trial before the Sanhedrin in Mark on the literary level,
i.e. by examining the function of the trial in the story, by

[17]This was a rather standard opinion among form-critics:
R. Bultmann, History, 275-84; M. Dibelius, From Tradition to
Gospel (tr. B. L. Woolf; New York: Scribner's, 1935), 178-183;
K. L. Schmidt, Der Rahmen der Geschichte Jesu (Berlin:
Trowitzsch, 1919), 303-306. Even more recent redaction-critics
who insist that much of the passion story is due to the activity
of Mark believe that there were at least traditional complexes
prior to the writing of the Gospel: E. Linnemann, Studien zur
Passiongeschichte (Göttingen: Vandenhoeck and Ruprecht, 1970),
127-134; J. Schreiber, "Die Christologie des Markusevangeliums,"
ZTK 58 (1961), 157-158, note 5 (a summary of his dissertation).
For the most recent discussion of the problem of pre-Markan passion traditions, see the report prepared for the Markan Task
Force at the 1971 meeting of the SBL, "Reflections on the Question: Was There a pre-Markan Passion Narrative?"

[18]See esp. Nils A. Dahl, "The Purpose of Mark's Gospel."
This essay originally appeared in Norwegian ("Markusevangeliets
sikte," SEA 22-23 [1957-58], 32-46). Because the article was
available to me only in English and because it will soon appear
in English in a volume of Prof. Dahl's essays, I will refer to
the article in translation and cite pages in the typewritten
manuscript. - Ms Linnemann (Studien, 130) seems to assume that
Mark was bound to include in his Gospel any prior tradition he
encountered.

[19]Recourse to such a low estimate of Mark's abilities is
apparent, for example, in Ms Linnemann's Studien, 130-131, where
she argues that in composing the present account of the trial,
Mark has twice mentioned the false witness to leave no doubt a-
bout Jesus' innocence - without observing that it did not at all
fit with 14:60. No real attempt is made to penetrate the logic
of the text.

noting Markan themes present in the account, and by examining
the function of the various components of the trial narrative
within the whole. If there are difficulties in Mark's story,
we should first ask if these are literary difficulties capable
of literary solutions. By "literary solution," however, I do
not mean what most form critics mean by the terms,[20] i.e.
source reconstruction. Isolating sources may be of help in interpreting Mark, but it must be subordinate to literary study in
the broader sense and it should not be the first question asked
of the text.[21]

Such a literary approach to the account of the trial in
Mark is all the more essential if it can resolve some of the
persistent problems in the account that other approaches have
failed to resolve. Thus before proceeding to the examination
of the trial, a brief survey of other approaches to the material
is appropriate. What follows is a selection of several rather
distinct ways of interpreting the account of the trial in Mark.
There is some overlapping, but the choice of scholars has been
made to highlight significant ways of approaching the text.
The survey is obviously not a thorough review of all literature
written on the trial of Jesus in Mark, nor can it consider all
of the problems in his account mentioned on pages 1-2. Since
from the point of view of this study the crucial problem in Mark
is the temple charge in 14:58, the survey will focus on the
various attempts to explain this verse in Mark's account. The
review is not strictly chronological, although the most recent
works on the trial will be considered at the end of the chapter.

For those who view the Gospel of Mark as a reasonably
trustworthy historical account of the events reported, it is
most reasonable to study the trial on its historical level.
Such study will pay little attention to problems of historical
criticism, particularly the problem of the transformation of the
story of the trial during the period of oral tradition. If
there are problems in the account, the attempt will be made to
resolve them on the historical level - often by supplying information not in the text that must be presumed to exist, or by

---

[20]Ms Linnemann, for example (Studien, 110), insists that
the first task of the interpreter is to write the history of
the development of a text, to separate tradition from redation.
This is a "literary" approach in a peculiar sense.

[21]Cf. below, 43-44.

psychologizing. There are numerous such studies that deserve little attention from the serious scholar. There are also, however, serious scholars whose work on the trial follows these lines and merits consideration.

One of the clearest examples of such an approach is the short study done by G. D. Kilpatrick.[22] His essay was written as an alternative to the views expressed by Hans Lietzmann in his important essay reviewed below,[23] according to which the whole account of the trial before the Sanhedrin in Mark is a Christian fiction (a view that Kilpatrick considers a "drastic conclusion"[24]). With one important exception, the account of the trial is trustworthy, according to Kilpatrick, and can be explained on the level of the events themselves.

Many of the legal difficulties in the story can be explained if the story can be traced to a man unfamiliar with the intricacies of the law:

> We cannot imagine that it went back to a witness who understood the legal implications of each stage of the proceedings or that it was shaped to answer the questionings of the nineteenth and twentieth centuries. Consequently, if it leaves us questions and problems, this is neither surprising nor disquieting.[25]

Yet some of the most serious difficulties in the story can be explained. The first has to do with the two, apparently unrelated charges. Why are these two charges reported by Mark and what do they have to do with one another? Kilpatrick believes that the problem disappears when we understand the tactics of Jesus' opponents. The story makes sense if it was necessary first to convict Jesus in the eyes of his fellow Jews before drawing up a political charge and handing him over to Pilate. This would be necessary if, as Mark seems to indicate, Jesus' popularity was a problem for the High Priest and his followers.[26] The first problem was thus to convince Jews that Jesus deserved to be put out of the way:

---

[22]G. D. Kilpatrick, The Trial of Jesus (Oxford: Clarendon Press, 1952).

[23]See below, 16-18.   [24]Kilpatrick, Trial, 7.

[25]Ibid., 21.

[26]Kilpatrick (Ibid., 8) cites the execution of James the brother of Jesus by Ananus (Jos Ant 20: 200ff) as evidence that it was unwise for the Sanhedrin to act without popular support.

There was one way in which this might be done and that was by showing that the prisoner was guilty in Jewish law of an offence punishable by death: and this was the course, I think, Caiaphas took. The charge was that Jesus had spoken blasphemy against the Holy Place, the Temple.[27]

This presumes, of course, that it was blasphemous to speak against the temple in Jesus' day. Kilpatrick discusses the point briefly, citing Wellhausen's arguments[28] and citing the examples of Micah and Jeremiah in the Old Testament. His principle for reconstructing the first-century legal code is:

Where the Old Testament requires the death penalty for an offence, we may expect that Jewish law in the time of Jesus would sanction its infliction.[29]

But this must imply that there is something wrong with Mark's version of the story. For according to Mark, the testimony was given by false witnesses, and because no two witnesses could agree, the testimony could not be entered as evidence. At this point Kilpatrick makes a "correction" in Mark's account.[30] The charge was not false testimony. Although in Mark's Gospel Jesus never makes a statement quite like the one reported in the trial, he does predict the destruction of the temple in 13:2. By studying Matthew and John, Kilpatrick argues, we can see that the saying or some form of it was viewed as true. He therefore concludes that this must be the case for Mark as well:

Let us proceed on the assumption that Jesus did say either what the witnesses charged him with at Mark 14:57-59 or something substantially the same.[31]

But then why does Mark report that the charge was uttered by false witnesses? At this point alone Kilpatrick is willing to consider influences on the developing story during its pre-Markan stage.

If...as we think probable, the Gospel according to St. Mark was written before A.D. 70, the Temple was still standing and the saying might seem false. Further, it would not be surprising if one of those who had handed down this tradition had taken the view that all witnesses against Jesus were false witnesses. Considerations such as these will easily explain Mark's treatment of the saying.[32]

---

[27] Kilpatrick, Trial, 9.

[28] J. Wellhausen, Das Evangelium Marci (2nd ed; Berlin: G. Reimer, 1909) on 13:2. Cf. below 14.

[29] Kilpatrick, Trial, 11.

[30] Ibid., 10.   [31] Ibid., 11.   [32] Ibid., 10.

Despite the apparent connection between the messianic
confession in 14:61-62 and the charge of blasphemy, Kilpatrick
argues that the charge of blasphemy could have applied only to
the temple charge. The second issue, the question of Jesus'
identity, reflects the further stage in the plot of the High
Priest. It represents an attempt to trick Jesus into a statement that could incriminate him in the eyes of Pilate.[33] The
need for a political charge indicates for Kilpatrick that the
view of the Fourth Gospel is to be preferred: the Jewish court
did not have the right to inflict the death penalty in capital
cases.[34]

There is one more problem in the account to be explained,
namely the difference between the title "the Christ, the Son of
the Blessed" in the question of the High Priest, and "King of the
Jews," the title used in the trial before Pilate. Mark does not
indicate how the change was made and he does not even mention
a direct report from the Sanhedrin to Pilate. Here Kilpatrick
argues that we can understand the story by filling in the gaps.
He theorizes either that the High Priest asked Jesus about
numerous messianic claims and that 14:61 is the one that "stuck
in later tradition," or that in addition to the question in
14:61, the High Priest later asked Jesus explicitly if he was
the "King of Israel."[35] By such hypotheses Kilpatrick is able
to avoid the assumption of any non-historical influence on the
account in Mark and is able to make sense of the story as it
stands:

> Thus we have two possible interpretations of the inconsis-
> tency between the High Priest's question at Mark 14:61 and
> Pilate's question at 15:2. Whichever we choose the incon-
> sistency disappears and our narrative becomes coherent.[36]

Whatever merit some of the historical arguments may have
in their own right, they do not explain the text of Mark.
Kilpatrick does not deal seriously with the Gospel. This is
clear with regard to the titles. He insists that "'King of the
Jews' and 'son of the Blessed' are not interchangeable,"[37] and
thus insists that the only way the story makes sense is to assume that the title in 15:2 depends upon a different question

---

[33]Ibid., 14.   [34]Ibid., 16-20.

[35]Ibid., 14-15. He assumes that there are decisive
differences between the titles.

[36]Ibid., 15.   [37]Ibid., 14.

by the High Priest. But this simply ignores the clear relationship among the titles in Mark, a relationship important for
understanding not only Mark but perhaps also Jewish and
Christian messianic imagery at Mark's time.

The failure of Kilpatrick's historical arguments is even
clearer in the case of the temple charge. He is unconcerned
about the precise wording of the charge and is satisfied to view
it as authentic "in some form." But there is a considerable
difference between Jesus' prediction in 13:2 and the charge in
14:58. In the trial it is Jesus who is the alleged destroyer,
and the enigmatic saying about rebuilding at the trial is still
without parallel in Mark. The saying in 14:58 is too carefully
formulated to ignore the differences between it and 13:2.
Kilpatrick can account only for the saying about destruction in
the charge. But the saying also includes a promise (another...
in three days...not made with hands) which cannot be unimportant
for Mark. What sense do these words make on the lips of "false
witnesses"? Kilpatrick never examines the problem on the
literary level, to determine, for example, if Mark is making
deliberate use of irony. His own attempt to account for the
"falseness" of the testimony is too imprecise and oversimplified
to be taken seriously. And whatever basis there may be for
viewing the temple problem as the crucial issue at Jesus' historical "trial" before the Jewish authorities, there is absolutely no justification for linking the charge of blasphemy in
Mark with anything but Jesus' reply to the High Priest's question in 14:61-62. Kilpatrick employs improper methods to study
the Gospel of Mark as a piece of literature; psychologizing,
inventing material to fill alleged gaps in the story, and
harmonizing the Gospels are methods rightly rejected by most
scholars. But perhaps the most telling criticism of Kilpatrick's approach is that it is unable to account for the
temple charge as it appears in Mark's Gospel.

It may seem that Kilpatrick's study is too convenient a
foil, that such methodology is not typical of contemporary scholarship. Yet the work of P. Benoit, published as recently as
1969, reflects most of the same methodological weaknesses.[38]
Benoit too is ready to explain the text by recourse to Jesus'
intentions; he displays the same willingness to harmonize the

---

[38]P. Benoit, The Passion and Resurrection of Jesus Christ
(tr. B. Weatherhead; New York: Herder and Herder, 1969).

Gospel accounts, with a preference for the version of the story
in the Fourth Gospel; and he likewise fails to take the wording
of the temple charge in Mark seriously. And at least with
respect to the temple charge in Mark, one of the classic works
on the passion, that of Josef Blinzler, belongs in the same
category.[39]

Blinzler also accepts Mark's account as reliable. And he
too attempts to solve the problems in the text on the historical
level. Unlike Kilpatrick, he believes that the temple issue
was not the reason for Jesus' conviction; the real basis for the
verdict of the Sanhedrin was Jesus' claim to be the Messiah.[40]
The temple charge was, as Mark indicates, an attempt to incriminate Jesus that failed.[41] But Blinzler is thus forced to view
the actual charge reported in 14:58 as the confused testimony
of false witnesses, an interpretation difficult to square with
the careful wording in Mark. The saying is not completely
false, according to Blinzler: "Actually, Jesus did once say
this or something like it."[42] But he is convinced that the
whole point of the charge at the trial was false:

> for whatever the original meaning of His words about the
> Temple may have been, during His public life Jesus quite
> definitely never had any intention of destroying the
> Temple building or permitting it to be destroyed.
> According to His own clear words, He expected the destruc-
> tion of the city and the Temple to come to pass as
> judgment of God (Mk 13:1f.). But the words about the
> Temple definitely did not form the reason for the final
> death sentence.[43]

If there was an original saying, and Blinzler seems to
assume there was, it is difficult to understand why the statement about rebuilding should have become an issue--if, as
Blinzler argues, the point of the saying was its threat to the
temple building.[44] He does suggest later that the saying about
destroying and rebuilding the temple "had a messianic tone for
the Jews of that time, because they looked foreward to a renewal
of the glory and magnificence of the Temple when the Messias

---

[39] J. Blinzler, The Trial of Jesus (tr. from 2nd ed. by
I. and F. McHugh; Westminster, Md.: Newman Press, 1959).

[40] Ibid., 103-104. [41] Ibid., 100-101.

[42] Ibid., 99. [43] Ibid., 100.

[44] He surmises (Ibid., 100), in light of Jn 2:19, that the
false witnesses have changed an original "destroy this temple"
to "I will destroy this temple," and thus give "false" testimony.

should come."[45] But he makes no attempt to find a link between
the two charges at the trial. The temple charge must be viewed
simply as false testimony. It is thus not at all clear why
Blinzler even mentions the supposed messianic implications of
the charge, implications that have to do particularly with the
statement about rebuilding. Arguing on the historical level, he
insists that the temple charge was an abortive attempt to incriminate Jesus on the basis of an alleged threat against the
temple and that the statement as it appears in Mark is a dis-
tortion. But appealing to Jesus' own attitude toward the temple
as a way of interpreting the charge in Mark is simply to ignore
the author of the Gospel and his own beliefs. Furthermore,
Blinzler's interpretation is unable to account for the precise
wording of the charge in Mark. He unfortunately makes nothing
of his own suggestion about messianic implications in the
statement, and it is thus not clear in his work what the statement about building the temple means and why it was included in
the charge. His study does not explain the place of the temple
charge in Mark's account of the trial.

Most scholars have rightly insisted that in studies of
the trial in the Gospels, some account must be taken of the
problems raised by historical criticism. Since the advent of
form criticism, considerable attention has been devoted to study
of the oral stages of tradition and the various influences operative prior to the writing of the Gospels. Before attempting to
determine what really happened, most studies begin with some
consideration of the dogmatic and/or apologetic concerns that
have contributed to the shaping of the passion tradition. The
degree to which this affects method of study, however, varies
considerably among scholars. In many studies there is some
attempt to examine critically the forces that shaped tradition
combined with simple historical speculation of the type already
discussed. The works of Wellhausen and Lietzmann provide
interesting examples of the combination of critical and rather
uncritical method.

Wellhausen's study certainly represents a step forward
when compared to the work of Kilpatrick and Blinzler, even
though he wrote decades earlier.[46] He recognizes that there are

---

[45]Ibid., 102.

[46]Wellhausen, Mark. (All commentaries, regardless of
titles, will be cited in this manner.)

concerns other than purely historical in the accounts of Jesus'
trial. He argues first of all that the confession attributed
to Jesus in 14:61-62 reflects the beliefs of the community
rather than Jesus' own view of himself:

> Jesus bekennt sich also nicht einfach als den Messias,
> sondern er nennt sich den Menschensohn und weissagt seine
> Parusie. Es ist wenig glaublich dass er das überhaupt
> getan hat, und am wenigsten dass er es vor dem Synedrium
> getan hat. Dieses hätte auch in dem Ausspruch nur einen
> locus communis erkennen und keine Beziehung auf Jesus
> heraus hören können...Entscheidend freilich sind andere
> Gründe, welche beweisen, dass die beiden Verse 14:61
> (von πάλιν an) und 62 nicht zur ältesten Überlieferung
> gehören, sondern eingelegt sind.[47]

Wellhausen's decisive arguments, however, are not based
on literary considerations but on historical reflection. The
account cannot be reliable in its present form because it was
not blasphemous to claim to be the Messiah in the first century.[48] The way to explain the present text is simply to assume
that verses 61-62 were later inserted into the story. With this
exception, Wellhausen views the account as reasonably trustworthy. The original issue at the trial must have been a statement Jesus made against the temple which, if the rest of the
trial narrative is to be followed, must have been considered
blasphemous. Wellhausen argues that this was actually the case,
that is was considered blasphemous to speak against the temple.
He cites the cases of Jeremiah and Micah in the Old Testament,
insisting that things had not changed by the first century.

> So etwas sahen die späteren Juden wie die älteren als die
> schrecklichste Blasphemie an, wie bereits zu 13:2 gesagt
> und belegt ist.[49]

The important point for Wellhausen is the apparent link
between Jesus' prophecy in 13:2 and the charge at the trial:

> Daran ist so viel richtig, dass die Anklage sich in der
> Tat auf die von Jesus 13:2 getane Äusserung über die
> baldige Zerstörung des Tempels bezieht. Diese mag
> ursprünglich schroffer gelautet haben, denn unsere
> jetzige evangelische Überlieferung sucht in diesem
> Punkt zu mildern.[50]

The whole tendency of the present accounts of the trial,
Wellhausen suggests, is to play down the importance of the
temple issue. The tendency is present in Mark and explains
both the characterization of the charge as false testimony, as
well as the inclusion of the messianic confession in 14:61-62.

---

[47]Ibid., 124.   [48]Ibid.   [49]Ibid.   [50]Ibid., 123.

Die evangelische Überlieferung, wie sie uns gegenwärtig
vorliegt, trägt sichtlich Scheu, eine Lästerung Jesu
gegen den Temple als den Grund für seine Verurteilung
durch das Synedrium zuzugeben. Sie sucht in Abrede zu
stellen, dass eine solche Lästerung wirklich gefallen, und
namentlich, dass sie einwandsfrei bezeugt gewesen sei: Mc
und Matthäus erklären die Zeugen für Lügner, Lukas lässt
das ganze Zeugenverhör radikal aus und gar noch Mc 15:29s.
dazu. Und sie behaupten übereinstimmend, dass vielmehr
das Messiasbekenntnis den Ausschlag für die Verurteilung
gegeben habe.[51]

At this point, however, it becomes clear that despite his
willingness to take the concerns of the Christian community into
account, he has not taken the text of Mark seriously. Wellhausen's reconstruction of the events is historically plausible,
but his proposal does not help to understand either the place of
Jesus' confession in Mark's account or the function of the
temple charge. It is clearly impossible to remove the confession (14:61-62) from Mark's account without destroying the
whole structure of the trial narrative, and even such a correction in the account would not explain the temple charge. The
relationship between 13:2 and 14:58 is not at all clear. Even
if Jesus' original prediction is harsher, it still says nothing
about rebuilding the fallen temple or replacing it with another
of a different order. Wellhausen simply ignores the second
half of the charge. Nothing is said about the precise wording
and its obvious importance for Mark, the difference between
14:58 and 13:2, and the statement about building another temple
not made with hands. His suggestions that the confession in
14:61-62 derives from the community of believers and that there
appears to be some sensitivity about the temple issue are valuable. His proposal, however, does little to interpret the text
of Mark, and whatever other criticisms are made of his method,
for our purposes this is the most decisive.[52]

The important paper delivered by Hans Lietzmann in 1931
before the Prussian Academy of Science belongs methodologically
with the work of Wellhausen.[53] It exhibits the same peculiar
combination of critical study and historical speculation. The
purpose of the paper, according to Lietzmann, is to get behind
the Gospel accounts of the trial to firm historical ground.

[51]Ibid., 125.

[52]Cf. Bultmann's criticisms of Wellhausen in History,
270.

[53]H. Lietzmann, "Der Prozess Jesu"; cf. note 1.

16

The trial before the Sanhedrin is superb literature but poor history.[54] Lietzmann believes that it is possible to recognize throughout the trial concerns of the Christian community that have significantly altered the real story. He believes it is possible to prove that the trial before the Sanhedrin is a Christian fiction, that Jesus was crucified by the Romans for political reasons after having been tried according to Roman law. His major concern in the article is to prove his contentions and to indicate why the story has been altered to its present form.

The reason for Lietzmann's view of the trial is both literary and historical: the trial is a disruption in the section of the passion story in which Peter is always present--a section in whose historical reliability Lietzmann has great confidence.[55] Even according to Mark, there were no Christian witnesses at the trial, which must make the report suspect. Closer examination of the account simply confirms the unhistorical character of the narrative. Jesus' silence at the trial is a motif taken from Isa 53:7. The term "Son of the Blessed" is thoroughly unjewish and could not have been used by the High Priest as a designation for the Messiah; the expression must, therefore, be a Christian formulation and a later development in tradition. Finally, the temple charge in 14:58 does not reflect the ideas of Jesus but of Hellenistic Christianity epitomized by Stephen.[56]

> Das Wort stellt den auferstandenen Jesus als Meister des neuen Lebens dem ausser Kraft gesetzten mosaischen Gesetz gegenüber, wie es Johannes 2:19-22 richtig interpretiert; es atmet den Geist der bekehrten Hellenisten von der Richtung des Stephanus, die nach dem Bericht der Apostelgeschichte (6:14) in solcher Gesinnung die Bedeutung des Tempelkultes bezweifeln...Von solchen Anschauungen aus ist das Wort geformt und auf Jesus übertragen, der so zum Vorbild des Märtyrers Stephanus wird.[57]

Lietzmann's suggestion that there is a relationship between Mk 14:58 and Acts 7 deserves some attention, particularly because the expression "made with hands" is used of the temple in both places (Mk 14:58 and Acts 7:48).

But the decisive consideration, according to Lietzmann, is the fact that Jesus was not stoned but crucified. He argues

---

[54]Ibid., 313. [55]Ibid., 315 and 319-320.

[56]Ibid., 316. [57]Ibid.

that if Jesus had really been tried by the Jewish court and
found guilty of blasphemy he would have been executed in the
manner prescribed by law (Lev 24:14).[58] Since this was not the
case, the account of the trial in Mark must be viewed as
unhistorical:

> Jesus ist nicht nach jüdischem Recht gesteinigt worden;
> also hat ihn auch nicht nach dem jüdischen Gericht wegen
> Gotteslästerung verurteilt, und der Bericht des Markus
> 14:55-56 ist unhistorisch. Alle die aus den verschiedensten
> Einzelheiten erwachsenen Bedenken werden durch diese
> abschliessenden Entscheid bestätigt. Der Bericht über die
> Nachtsitzung des Synedrions ist wirklich ein Fremdkörper in
> dem grossen Petrusbericht, der nur eine kurze Beratung des
> Synedrions in der Morgenfrühe kannte (15:1).[59]

Lietzmann even believes it is possible to explain why
the account of the trial was added to the passion story. It is
part of an observable tendency to absolve Pilate of any blame
in Jesus' death and to increase the responsibility of the
Jews.[60]

The weaknesses of Lietzmann's paper are obvious. He is
far too uncritical in his evaluation of the so-called Petrine
material in Mark. He is unable to appreciate, for example,
the clear literary relationship between the denial of Peter and
Jesus' trial in Mark because of his preoccupation with historical questions. He is simply uninterested in the literary
function of the trial in Mark. He is too ready to harmonize
all sayings about the temple in Mark, John and Acts. Even in
Mark he does not concern himself with the problem involved in
the characterization of the charge as false testimony as well
as the problematic relationship of 14:58 to Jesus' prediction
in 13:2.

But this is perhaps best viewed as an indication of
Lietzmann's real concern. He is principally interested in historical questions. It is as an historian that Lietzmann
examines the account of the trial in Mark and pronounces it un-
reliable historically. And for his study the historical
question about the juridical competence of the Sanhedrin is
decisive. Depending heavily on the work of Juster,[61] published

---

[58]Ibid., 317.   [59]Ibid., 319-320.   [60]Ibid., 321.

[61].J. Juster, Les Juifs dans l'empire Romain (Paris:
Guenthnen, 1914), esp. vol. II, 127-156. Through the accidents
of history, Lietz. was the first to apply the work of Juster
to the study of the trial due to the author's untimely death
and the outbreak of WWI.

18

in 1914, he insists that those who want to view the Gospel
accounts of the trial as historical must take serious account
of the status of the Jewish court within the legal structure
of the Empire. He agrees with Juster that Jn 18:31 is simply
wrong, that the Sanhedrin did possess the authority to execute
criminals convicted of capital offences according to Jewish
law.[62] If the court could execute capital offenders and did
not, the only reasonable inference is that Jesus was not tried
according to Jewish law, as Mark reports, but according to
Roman law. The trial in Mark can thus not be explained on
historical grounds because there never was such a trial. The
task of the interpreter of early Christianity and of the Gospels
is to determine the motives for the development of such an unhistorical account. Although Lietzmann makes a few suggestions
about such motives, this is not his real interest in the paper.

Historically, Lietzmann's application of Juster's research to the study of the trial has perhaps been his most
important contribution. But there are several other valuable
insights in his study more relevant to literary study of the
Gospels. His characterization of the trial as Christian
apologetic has proved to be correct.[63] Several scholars have
come to similar conclusions following different avenues of
approach. His specific suggestions about the temple saying
also deserve consideration. But it is his concern with historical questions, most notably the juridical competence, that
has received most attention from other scholars.

A few comments on the response to Lietzmann's paper are
in order, although we need not pursue the legal discussion
through the history of scholarship. His paper elicited immediate response from fellow scholars like F. Büchsel,[64] which in
turn occasioned two replies by Lietzmann.[65] The legal discussion initiated by Juster continues to be prominent up to the

---

[62]The cases cited as evidence by Juster are discussed
by Lietzmann (Ibid., 318-319).

[63]See 36-37 below.

[64]F. Buchsel, "Die Blutgerichtsbarkeit des Synedrions,"
ZNW 30 (1931), 202-210.

[65]H. Lietzmann, "Bemerkungen zum Prozess Jesu I, " ZNW
30 (1931), 211-215, and "Bemerkungen zum Prozess Jesu II, " ZNW
31 (1932), 78-84; Buchsel, "Noch einmal: Zur Blutgerichtsbarkeit des Synedrions," ZNW 33 (1934), 84-87.

the present. J. Blinzler devoted considerable space to the problem;[66] J. Jeremias wrote a short piece of his own and provided a summary of some of the important literature that had already appeared on the subject.[67] The massive volume written by H. Cohn provides an exhaustive if somewhat one-sided discussion of legal matters.[68] Sherwin-White, who approaches the whole problem of the trial from the perspective of Roman law, insists that the question of the Sanhedrin's competency is decisive for interpreting the Gospels.[69] And in the most recent book to appear on the trial, David Catchpole summarizes much of the history of the discussion with his own survey of the evidence and appraisal of the legal arguments.[70]

It is unnecessary to retrace the course of the debate here, both because that has been done by Catchpole and because the question is to a certain extent irrelevant for our purposes. Even if the historical question regarding the authority of the Sanhedrin to try capital crimes and execute capital sentences can be settled, it does not settle the problem in Mark. Mark, unlike the author of the Fourth Gospel, makes no attempt to explain how the two "trials" are related. He does not say that representatives from the Jewish court went to Pilate to have a sentence confirmed. The text never says that Jesus is accused before Pilate for offences against Jewish law. The claim to be the "King of the Jews" would be as legitimate a political charge as a religious. Mark says simply that the Jewish leaders accused Jesus πολλά (15:3). It is not immediately apparent why Mark makes such an obvious effort to describe Jesus' appearance before the Jewish court in chapter 14 as a trial, when in chapter 15 it seems that Jesus is simply handed over to the Roman authorities to be tried according to Roman

---

[66]Blinzler, The Trial of Jesus, esp. excursus VII, 157-163.

[67]J. Jeremias, "Zur Geschichtlichkeit des Verhors Jesu vor dem Hohen Rat," ZNW 43 (1950-51), 145-150. The bibliographical information is provided on 145, note 1.

[68]H. Cohn, The Trial and Death of Jesus.

[69]A. N. Sherwin-White, Roman Society and Roman Law in the New Testament, esp. 35ff. See the critical review of Sherwin-White's arguments by T. A. Burkill, "The Condemnation of Jesus: A Critique of Sherwin-White's Thesis," NovT 12 (1970), 321-342.

[70]David Catchpole, The Trial of Jesus, 221-260.

law. The problem in Mark cannot be solved on the historical
level, even if the juridical questions about the legal status
of the Jewish court can be settled.

With the advent of form criticism, there have been significant changes in the study of the trial in Mark. More attention has been focused on the oral stage of tradition, and more
precision has been achieved in the study of its development.
Nowhere is the shift clearer than in the approach to the Gospels
as literature. They are examined far more as sources for reconstructing the beliefs of the early Christian community than
as sources for reconstructing the actual events reported. The
Gospel writers are not principally historians but "collectors,
vehicles of tradition."[71] Although Wellhausen and Lietzmann
made important contributions to the study of the Gospels, suggesting that in order to understand the present text it was
necessary to take into account the motives for development of
tradition within the early church, their lack of clarity regarding the distinction between historical and literary questions necessitated a restudy of the trial by form critics.
According to Bultmann, the first question is "not what can be
thought of as historical but: what is intelligible as tradition
in the Christian Church."[72] The proper approach to the Gospels
is to isolate prior units of tradition, the forms in which
tradition circulated within the early Christian communities,
the units whose formal characteristics reveal something about
their setting in the life of the community and whose development
reveals a great deal about the beliefs and concerns of the
church. Before the Gospel of Mark can be used to reconstruct
the actual trial of Jesus, it must first be examined as a piece
of literature--in this case meaning a collection of traditions
that tell us less about Jesus' trial than they do about the
early church.

What is strange is the course form-critical study of the
trial actually took. The approach of Bultmann,[73] with its almost complete disregard for the Gospels as literature, has come
to be the dominant "literary" approach among form-critics. But
this might not have been the case. Far more promising

---

[71]M. Dibelius, _From Tradition to Gospel_, 3.

[72]Bultmann, _History_, 270.

[73]See the discussion of Bultmann below, 22-24.

beginnings were made by G. Bertram and M. Dibelius, both
form-critics but both also capable of literary appreciation of
the Gospels in the proper sense.[74] Both men were more interested in pre-Markan tradition than in Mark; both were more interested in the development of the passion tradition within
the life of the church than in the outcome of that development
in the four Gospels. Yet both men made extremely perceptive
remarks about the literary dimensions of the trial narrative
within the context of the Gospel of Mark.

Bertram, for example, who viewed the trial as a convenient setting for early Christians to work out problems important
in polemics and to provide material useful for exhortation,[75]
could still appreciate Mark's place in the history of tradition
and his unique contributions. He insists, for example, that
the place of the temple charge in 14:58 reflects a common embarrassment about a sensitive issue discernible throughout
early Christianity.[76] But Mark's attempts to defuse the po-
tentially dangerous issue are unique. First, he inserts "made
with hands/not made with hands," thus relating the statement
to the founding of the Christian community.[77] He also characterizes the testimony as "false witness." Further, the failure
of the witnesses to agree should be viewed as an attempt by the
evangelist to dissociate the eventual verdict from the temple
charge and to motivate the decisive question and answer in
14:61-62:

> mit seiner Behauptung, dass sich jetzt noch nicht die
> Zeugen in ihrer Aussage übereinstimmten, lässt er den
> ersten Teil abruptschliessen und setzt dann unvermittelt
> mit etwas gänzlich Neuem ein.[78]

Dibelius makes similar comments about Mark's concerns in
the trial narrative. Despite his obvious concern for the
setting of the developing traditions within the life of the
church and the concerns apparent in that developing tradition,
despite his famous characterization of the evangelists as mere
"collectors of tradition," he can insist that the trial must be
understood as the work of an author. Although the present unevenness of the text is due to the combination of distinct

---

[74]G. Bertram, _Die Leidensgeschichte Jesu und der
Christuskult_ (Gottingen: Vandenhoeck and Ruprecht, 1922).
M. Dibelius, _From Tradition to Gospel_, esp. 178-217.

[75]Bertram, _Leidensgeschichte_, 55.

[76]_Ibid._, 56-57.   [77]_Ibid._, 57.   [78]_Ibid._, 58.

traditions, an "interfusion of motives,"[79] he insists that nowhere in the Gospel is the concern of the author as apparent
as in the account of the trial. The narrative represents the
"first high point of Mark's Passion Story."[80] And here Mark
uses "contrary means" such as hostility and mockery to point,
paradoxically, to Jesus' majesty. The peculiar place of the
temple charge in 14:58 is explained not simply by insisting
that Mark is using prior tradition but by appeal to the concerns of the author:

> Perhaps occasioned by the old record Mark brings in a
> threat of Jesus against the Temple, but does not
> wish it to be decisive, and so explains that the
> witness was not sufficiently confirmed.[81]

The work of Dibelius and Bertram might have resulted not
only in the study of pre-Markan tradition as a way of interpreting the trial and explaining the text of Mark, but also in
study of the trial within the context of Mark's Gospel, that is,
in literary study of the Gospel in the proper sense. But that
was not to be the real heritage of form criticism. The
approach most influential in subsequent scholarship has been
that of R. Bultmann in his History of the Synoptic Tradition.[82]

Bultmann insists that the way to account for the difficulties in the present text of Mark's Gospel is not to attempt
a reconstruction of the events reported but to isolate the prior
units of tradition that Mark has combined in the present
account.[83] He believes there is clear evidence that the story
has been produced by the evangelist using only fragments of
tradition. He cites the following:[84]

a) After 14:59, the question of the High Priest in v.
   61 is unmotivated.

b) The two charges are doublets; and since witnesses
   are not called to substantiate Jesus' messianic
   claim--i.e. there is no stylized parallelism--the two
   charges apparently circulated independently prior to
   their inclusion in Mark's story.

c) "But, since vv. 57-59 is a particularization of v. 56,
   and since v. 59 is a feeble and senseless repetition
   of the motif of v. 56, I hold that vv. 57-59 are
   secondary, and believe that the story originally was
   intended to record that Jesus was condemned on account
   of his Messianic claim."

---

[79] Dibelius, From Tradition to Gospel, 192.

[80] Ibid., 193. [81] Ibid., 213. [82] History, esp. 269-284.

[83] Ibid., 270ff. [84] Ibid., 270-271.

There is further evidence that the whole account of the
nocturnal trial is an intrusion in the passion story and consequently should not be naively accepted as historical: Luke's
Gospel contains no account of such a trial, and even in Mark
the account is "inserted into the close context of the story of
Peter."[85] There are, Bultmann agrees, historical improbabili-
ties in the story, but the literary characteristics of the
account are far more decisive for interpretation. Because the
account appears to have been composed of independent traditions,
one must first look to the setting of the individual tradition
for its interpretation. The most important result for the
study of the trial, according to Bultmann, is that the temple
charge and the messianic confession must be interpreted independently. The temple charge must be viewed as an insertion
into a closely-knit account whose point, as noted above, was
that Jesus was condemned for claiming to be the Messiah.[86]
Wellhausen's proposal that the messianic confession is an insertion into the story cannot be defended on literary grounds.

Bultmann's comments on the trial scene in Mark appear in
his History of the Synoptic Tradition. Thus he cannot be overly
criticized for not providing a thorough interpretation of Mark.
The importance of his comments lies in his rigorous attempt to
understand the account as the product of the early church and
in his insistence that literary questions are primary. He takes
the text seriously. But there are weaknesses apparent in his
method. His view of literary investigation is extremely narrow;
he is really interested in source analysis. His principal concern with Mark's text is to explain one glaring feature: its
unevenness. By viewing the account as a collection of originally separate sources, he argues that he can account for some
of the peculiarities of the literature. But he is not really
interested in interpreting the present text of the Gospel. He
shows little interest in literary questions in the broader
sense; questions about the function of a scene in the story, a-
bout the development of the plot, etc. Even if Mark has woven
his account from separate strands of tradition, we should be

---

[85]Ibid., 270.

[86]The original story of Jesus' condemnation based on his
messianic claim also belongs to a "later stage of the tradition," (284), however, and represents one of the principal dogmatic motifs present in the whole passion story, the "idea that
Jesus suffered and died as the Messiah" (284).

able to expect some unified pattern in the final tapestry. It
may even be that there are other ways to explain the unevenness
in the account than to postulate sources or to identify seams.[87]
The greatest danger Bultmann's approach poses for the interpreter is that it provides too convenient an escape from the
text of the Gospel. If the story does not appear to cohere,
one simply attributes the problems to artless juxtaposition of
independent traditions rather than attempting to penetrate
deeper into the logic of the story. An interpreter of Mark interested in the trial can hardly be content with explanations
like those offered by Ernst Haenchen, who insists that the
double mention of false witnesses in the trial is simply due
to Mark's combining of similar traditions, the purpose of which
is "die Szene mehr zu füllen."[88] We may reasonably assume that
Mark was capable of a bit more sophistication and that a bit
more sophistication may be expected of his interpreters.

It was concern to correct this neglect of the individual
evangelists among form critics that gave rise to the new
"school" of redaction criticism in Germany in the 1950's.
Scholars like Willi Marxsen, Hans Conzelmann and Günther
Bornkamm clearly demonstrated that the evangelists are more than
mere collectors of tradition and that there are considerable
differences even among writers using similar traditions.[89] Ad-
vocates of redaction criticism did not propose to displace
form criticism but to employ its literary tools to study the
individual Gospels. In some respects, however, the shift in
scholarship has done little to alter the approach to the trial
in Mark.

Two important studies of the passion story in Mark, by
Eta Linnemann[90] and Johannes Schreiber,[91] have recently appeared
in Germany. In both works the methods associated with redaction

[87]See below, note 108, and 30-35.

[88]E. Haenchen, Der Weg Jesu (2nd ed.; Berlin: de
Gruyter and Co., 1968), 509.

[89]See the works cited in note 14 above.

[90]Eta Linnemann, Studien zur Passionsgeschichte.

[91]J. Schreiber, "Die Christologie des Markusevangeliums."
The article summarizes the more important results of Schreiber's
dissertation: "Der Kreuzigungsbericht des Markusevangeliums"
(unpublished Ph.D. dissertation for theological faculty at U. of
Bonn, 1959).

criticism are employed. Schreiber's work is more than redaction criticism in the narrow sense,[92] but both he and Ms Linnemann insist that study of the passion in Mark must begin with literary and not historical questions.[93] And by literary study they mean first of all source analysis, the separation of tradition and redaction. The major difference from the approach of form critics like Bultmann is that the emphasis is on the final stage of redaction. Ms Linnemann's intent is to examine literary-critical, form critical, redaction critical problems and problems dealing with the history of tradition in Mark's account of the passion not resolved by prior scholarship.[94] She insists, however, that her study of prior tradition is simply to help understand the present text of Mark:

> Der einzelne Text mit seinen Verstehensschwierigkeiten
> steht jeweils im Mittelpunkt. Der Rückgang auf seine
> Urfassung und die Verfolgung seiner Traditionsgeschichte
> sollen seine jetzige Gestalt durchsichtig werden lassen.[95]

Her major criticism of previous attempts to interpret Mark is that no one has really succeeded in explaining the text in its present form.[96] It soon becomes apparent, however, how Ms Linnemann conceives the literary task and what constitutes an explanation of the text. Her conception of the literary task coincides with that of most form critics: the first task is to locate sources, to separate tradition from redaction. To interpret Mark, what is first necessary is to locate his particular literary contributions, particularly to determine where he is joining traditions. Problems in the narrative should first be examined to determine whether sources are being combined:

> Störungen in der Logik der Erzählung kann man nicht mit
> der Frage begegnen, was historisch und was unhistorisch
> ist, sondern nur mit der Überlegung, ob der vorliegende
> Text mit seinen Unstimmigkeiten die ursprüngliche Fassung
> ist oder ob diese Unstimmigkeiten auf spätere Bearbeitung
> zurückgehen.[97]

Her conception of a literary explanation of the text is extremely narrow and almost completely defined by form

---

[92]See below, e.g., 127-28.

[93]Schreiber, "Kreuzigungsbericht," 2-3; Linnemann, Studien, 110.

[94]Linnemann, Studien, 9.

[95]Ibid.   [96]Ibid., 110ff.   [97]Ibid., 110.

criticism. And despite her claim to be interested in the text
of Mark, her real concern in the book is to prove that there was
no coherent pre-Markan account of the passion.[98] Yet her book
deserves consideration, in the first place because it clearly
reflects some of the weaknesses of redaction criticism. But
it is also important because her criticisms of prior scholarship
are so incisive. She reviews the work of numerous scholars who
have interpreted Mark's passion story and finds most of them
deficient. Most of her criticisms are justified, and at the
very least her book poses some clear challenges for anyone
attempting to interpret Mark.

She isolates five problems in the account of the trial
that must be explained if an interpretation is to be considered
adequate:[99]

a) The summary statement in 14:56 does not anticipate the
continuation in 57f.

b) The statement in v. 59 that the witnesses could not
agree does not fit with the unambiguous charge in v. 58.

c) The high priest's question in v. 60 is unmotivated
after the statement in v. 59 that the testimony was
unusable as evidence.

d) Jesus' pointed silence in v. 61a agrees poorly with his
willingness to answer the question of the high priest
in vv. 61-62.

e) There is a striking difference in titles between the
high priest's question and Jesus' reply (61b and 62b).

She proceeds to argue that the only sufficient explanation for these difficulties is that Mark has composed the
present account by combining two originally independent versions of the trial. Not only does her source analysis explain
the unevenness in the present text, thus providing justification
for the approach; the resulting sources are shown to be two coherent but independent accounts of the trial, each with one
consistent point:[100]

a) The first tradition is composed of vv. 55, 57, 58, 61b,
60b, 61a (in this order!). The point of this version
of the trial is Jesus' silence in the face of false
accusations. Here are to be found the first reference
to false witnesses, the temple charge, and the first
question of the high priest, followed by Jesus'
silence. The silence motif that characterizes this
tradition is rooted in Isa 53:7 and Ps 38: 13-16 (?).

---

[98]Ibid., 171-177.   [99]Ibid., 109-110.

[100]The following is taken from the discussion of the
trial narrative on 129-134.

b) The second tradition is composed of vv. 55, 56, 60a, 62, 63 and 64. It narrates Jesus' condemnation by the Jewish court on the basis of his messianic claim. Here we find the second statement about false witnesses (a feature common to both traditions), the second question of the high priest, and Jesus' reply, followed by the charge of blasphemy. This version of the story is concerned to show that Jesus was condemned by the Jews because he was the Messiah.

The composition of the present text of Mark's Gospel is explained as the joining of these two traditions. This explains, for example, the double reference to false witnesses:

Der Evangelist konnte entweder annehem, dass in 14:57f. genauere Angaben zu 14:56 nachgeholt wurden, oder aber, dass diese Verse die Fortsetzung des in 14:65 berichteten erzählten.[101]

The addition of v. 59 is one of the few things to be credited to Mark:

Offenbar lag ihm sehr daran, an der Unschuld Jesu keinen Zweifel zu lassen, Deshalb trug er die Aussage von 56b auch hinter 14:58, ohne zu merken, dass sie 14:60 störte.[102]

Mark may also have added the terms "made with hands/not made with hands," although if he did he was simply bringing out what was already implied in tradition. It is interesting to observe that after her careful literary (source) analysis of the trial scene in Mark, only two short paragraphs are required to summarize Mark's contribution, while four pages are devoted to the meaning of the trial in pre-Markan tradition.

The logic of Ms Linnemann's arguments is very strange. She is concerned to carry on the study of Mark on the literary level, without recourse to historical speculation. But there is an almost complete absence of any real literary investigation. Her interpretation of Mark is based almost solely on an extremely hypothetical reconstruction of sources. Despite her insistence that her literary analysis is a controlled, scientific enterprise, it is interesting to observe that Emmanuel Hirsch arrived at similar conclusions about the sources of the trial scene in Mark using, according to Ms Linnemann, "psychological arguments." The agreement is obviously of some embarrassment to her, since she spends almost two pages justifying it. There is an almost complete lack of the broader literary concerns common to the study of literature outside New Testament circles. Mark is credited with few of the characteristics of an author in any sense. His work is almost

---

[101] Ibid., 130.   [102] Ibid., 130-131.

28

exclusively confined to the combining of prior traditions;
little attention is paid to possible selections among various
traditions:

> Wir hatten bereits an der Perikope von der Verhaftung
> Jesu gezeigt, dass Markus Einzelperikopen vorlagen, die
> er am Faden des natürlichen Handlungsablaufs aufgereiht
> hat. Lagen zu einer Station des Leidens Jesu mehrere
> Erzählungen vor, musste er versuchen, sie miteinender zu
> verschmelzen. So auch in diesem Falle.[103]

The temple charge is an excellent test case for her
method. She insists that the meaning of the charge must be
sought in prior tradition. Mark's only real contribution is the
addition of v. 59, which must indicate his agreement that the
charge is false. The point of the specific temple charge in
the prior version of the trial, she argues, is clear from other
literature. It is a well-known "Märchenmotiv"; the hero is
charged with making an impossible boast. The charge at the
trial must mean that Jesus is accused of being a magician. The
accusation itself is simply a specific example of the false
charge raised against Jesus, whose "absurd character" Mark's
readers would readily have recognized. Anyone would recognize
that a new temple could not be constructed in three days!
Ms Linnemann does observe that the temple charge appears again
in the mockery at the foot of the cross in 15:29 and that it is
probably a conscious allusion to the trial that Mark has
added.[104] But she makes nothing of the observation, and when
she examines chapter fifteen to determine Mark's views, she
focuses only on the expression "come down from the cross."[105]

There are other reasons for Ms Linnemann's views about
the temple charge that will have to be taken more seriously
below.[106] She argues that attempts to do anything more with
the temple charge--to view it as positive in any sense or to
find messianic overtones or to relate the "temple not made with
hands" to the church--have failed to provide the requisite
history-of-religions parallels. They have failed, in other
words, to prove that such interpretations would have been
possible in the first century.[107] But her own approach to the
text is no real alternative. She reverses what should be a

[103] Ibid., 130.

[104] The observation is made on 116-117, where her exclusive concern is to prove that the saying could not have originated with Jesus.

[105] Ibid., 170. [106] See 38-39 below. [107] See esp. 122-126.

reasonable method of investigation. Even if her source analysis
of the trial scene were valid, which is unlikely, it is clear
that Mark has repeated the temple charge in the crucifixion
story, in 15:29. The first question should be why he has done
so. Is the charge of any special importance to him, either
positively or negatively? Ms Linnemann never bothers to ask.
Nor does she ask what function the charge serves in Mark's version of the trial. The reason is perhaps her low estimate of
Mark's literary abilities. But such a question would seem to
be far more answerable on the basis of an analysis of the
present text of the Gospel. It is at least legitimate to oper-
ate with the working assumption that Mark had a reason for including the temple charge in the trial, that the charge has
some function in his version of the story, and that there is
some reason for the repetition of the charge in 15:29. If we
can explain the function and meaning of the temple charge in the
present context of the Gospel, on the basis of Markan themes and
style, and if we can account for the difficulties in the text by
studying Markan style elsewhere in the Gospel without resorting
to source analysis, our interpretation would have some obvious
advantages.[108] The chief advantage would be simplicity, for
Ms Linnemann's view of the composition of the story by Mark--
combining two independent stories with the necessary rearrange-
ment of several verses, without any real awareness on the part
of the author of problems raised by such a combination--is almost as unreasonable a view of the process of composition as
Bultmann's view of the production of the Fourth Gospel. I hope
to show later that Ms Linnemann's interpretation of the charge
as having nothing to do with the frequent references to the
temple in Mark is untenable. At this point it is sufficient to
observe that her approach to the text does not explain Mark's
placement of the temple charge in his account of the trial nor
his repetition of the charge in 15:29.[109]

_____

[108]In the most recent study to appear on the trial in Mark
(Are You the Christ? The Trial Narrative in the Gospel of Mark
[SBLDS 10: Missoula: SBL, 1973]), Fr. John Donahue argues that
some of the "disruptions" in the flow of the narrative noted by
Ms Linnemann are occasioned by Mark's compositional technique
observable elsewhere in his Gospel and may not be viewed simply
as evidence of unassimilated tradition. For a review of this
important book, see below, 30-35.

[109]Schreiber, on the other hand, comes to a different conclusion following a somewhat similar approach. He argues that

In every respect the recent study of the trial Are You the Christ?, by Father John Donahue, represents an advance in scholarship. It is a compliment to his work that it cannot easily be categorized. There are new dimensions of his approach that represent important modifications of standard redaction-critical methodology. Nevertheless, Father Donahue insists that he is a redaction critic, which makes this the appropriate point in our survey to consider his work.

It is immediately clear that Donahue uses the term "redaction criticism" in a broad sense. One of the useful features of his dissertation is the brief review of the development of the movement in Germany and his characterization of the approach to the study of the Gospels.[110] He argues that redaction criticism, as it has evolved, must be viewed as an "umbrella concept which involves many different approaches to a gospel, and many different ways of finding the author's intent."[111] What characterizes the movement is the desire to identify the theology of the individual authors of the Gospels. But the methods by which this is accomplished include not only source criticism, the separation of tradition and redaction, but also "composition criticism,"[112] and the analysis of themes and motifs in a particular work. Donahue agrees with his teacher, Norman Perrin, that redaction criticism should be viewed less as one particular method of study than as a goal of scholarship. In Donahue's work, "redaction criticism" is thus a term for study the methods of which have subsequently been devised. The usage suggests that "redaction criticism" may be used to characterize studies that employ widely divergent methods.

It is equally clear, however, that Donahue shares one basic methodological concern with those who consider themselves redaction critics: the primary task of the student of the Gospels is to distinguish between tradition and redaction. His work reflects far greater appreciation for Mark's literary abilities than that of scholars like Eta Linnemann, but for

there is a clear relationship between statements made about the temple in Mk 11-15, and in particular among 14:58, 15:29 and 15:38. See esp. Theologie des Vertrauens (Hamburg: Furche Verlag, 1967), 41.

[110]Are You the Christ?, 31-51.   [111]Ibid., 31.

[112]The expression was coined by Haenchen in his Der Weg Jesu.

Donahue study begins at the same point:

> The first major problem is therefore to define as exactly
> as possible Mark's redactional and compositional activity
> in the trial narrative.[113]

This concern is reflected in the structures of the dissertation. The chapter that follows the history of research
is entitled "Tradition and Redaction in the Markan Trial
Narrative," a chapter of almost 50 pages in length. Further,
study of each of the major problems in the trial begins with
such considerations. Donahue immediately points out, however,
that this method of study has strict limitations. Interpreters
cannot hope to achieve the precision claimed by scholars like
Schreiber and Linnemann, who insist that they can identify
individual verses and even parts of verses as traditional or
redactional:

> As form criticism has definitely shown, the material ex-
> isted in a fluid state prior to its fixation by writing
> in a gospel text so that it is impossible to delineate
> exactly the form and content of traditional material.[114]

That means that the separation of tradition and redaction can only provide a "limited entree to the total theological
enterprise of Mark."[115] It must be supplemented by study of
Mark's compositional activity, focusing on techniques familiar
from the Gospel as a whole, and by study of themes and motifs
that relate a particular passage to the rest of the work. He
believes, in other words, that one should bring to Mark's Gospel
methods and questions familiar from the study of literature
proper. He recognizes that there has been a difference between
the kind of "literary criticism" practiced by biblical scholars
and that familiar to students of other literature. He suggests
that study of Mark might well employ "criteria taken from
secular literary criticism,"[116] though he indicates this will
not be a feature of his work.

Donahue's book is stimulating and suggestive. There will
be opportunity later to consider some of his specific proposals.
At this point it is important to locate his work within the
broader context of scholarship and to determine at least in
preliminary fashion the efficacy of his approach.

The problems Donahue identifies in the first portion of
the trial narrative are similar to those we have observed in

---

[113]Ibid., 30.   [114]Ibid., 40-41.

[115]Ibid.   [116]Ibid., 44.

the studies of most recent scholars:

> In a short narrative of twelve verses, four are devoted to
> material which has no apparent relevance to the rest of
> the narrative, since the charge about the temple is not
> taken up again in 14:60. There is a burdensome repetition
> of the falseness or inadequacy of the witnesses (14:55,
> 56a, 56b, 57, 59). Coupled with this is the problem of
> the presence on the lips of false witnesses of a threat of
> Jesus against the temple which Mark, in other places, does
> not record as false (13:2, 15:29), and which, in other
> traditions, is recorded as a true saying of Jesus.[117]

Donahue's intent in his study is to determine the meaning
of the temple charge in its present context. There is a whole
section in his dissertation entitled, "The Anti-Temple Theme in
Mark," indicating a considerable advance over the study of Eta
Linnemann. Yet Donahue's initial approach to the solution of
the difficulties in the trial narrative is similar to that of
Ms Linnemann. He surveys the views of scholars like Schweizer
and Bertram and rejects their attempts to resolve the tension
between the "falseness" of the testimony and the "truth" of the
charge as "harmonizations of content" which take "little cog-
nizance of Mark's purpose in allowing such a problem to exist
in the final redaction."[118]

Donahue proposes that the first step in solving the
problem posed by the tension between the false witnesses and the
true charge should be to examine the whole passage in light of
Mark's compositional techniques. He insists that before using
unevenness in the narrative as an indication of seams or of unassimilated traditions, it is necessary to have made a thorough
study of Mark's literary habits. When such a study of the
Gospel is made, and when the verses in the trial are examined
in light of the author's style, the complexion of the passage
changes considerably. The "burdensome repetition" of the falseness or inadequacy of the witnesses bracketing the temple
charge follows a pattern encountered elsewhere in the Gospel
that Donahue terms an "insertion technique."[119] The passage
must therefore be viewed as thoroughly Markan, and the very use
of this insertion technique provides a decisive clue to the
author's interpretation of the temple charge and the meaning of
the trial. Such an approach explains why Mark has permitted
such a tension to exist in the final edition of his work.

Yet in the last analysis, Donahue's explanation of the
text, as Ms Linnemann's, is based on a reconstruction of the

---

[117]Ibid., 71-72.   [118]Ibid.   [119]Ibid., 77-84.

history of the four verses in Mark. And at the level of par-
ticulars, his reconstruction is just as problematic. He argues,
first of all, that the references to false witnesses who testify against Jesus must be viewed as traditional. Mark interprets
this tradition by means of insertions. His major contribution
is the insertion of the temple charge into the context of the
trial.[120] This indicates how important the charge is for the
author. The charge, however, is bracketed by references to the
failure of the witnesses to agree. This peculiar feature of
the text follows a pattern Donahue sees elsewhere in the Gospel.
The earmarks of this insertion technique are the use of tauto-
logical statements both of which feature close verbal relationship (in this case, the statements in v. 56b and v. 59). The
temple charge is the major interpretive addition; the references
to the lack of agreement among the witnesses serve to modify the
initial "falseness" of the testimony to inadequate testimony,
thus leaving the truth of the charge open to question.

To support this reconstruction of the history of the
four verses in Mark, Donahue first attempts to demonstrate the
traditional character of the references to false witnesses.
The image is to be located in early Christian apologetic use
of Scripture; to be more precise, the image of an innocent man
being accused by false witnesses derives from Ps 27:12 and Ps
35:11. This derivation is not absolutely clear at first glance
and requires further support. There exists, for example, no
exact verbal parallel between Mark and the psalms. The witnesses in the psalms are called μάρτυρες ἄδικοι; the verb used
to describe their testimony is ψεύδεσθαι (in Ps 27 only). To
explain the difference in wording, Donahue reconstructs a history of this tradition that is extremely tenuous.

> Therefore, the earliest allusion to the innocence of Jesus
> before his accusers used Pss 27:12 and 35:11 as part of a
> Passion apologetic in a circle familiar with the Hebrew
> text, where the verbal allusions to the psalms would be
> clear, but the traditions were handed on in a Greek speaking
> milieu which allowed variant translations of the Hebrew.[121]

He makes no attempt to determine the context in which
this tradition might have circulated, which is somewhat problematic since allusions to psalms elsewhere in the passion story
generally use the language of the Greek Bible. Nor does he
offer proof that the image of an innocent man being falsely
accused is unusual enough to demand its origin in the apologetic

---

[120]For what follows, see pp. 71-84.   [121]Ibid., 76.

use of Scripture. He himself comments that the presence of the
tradition in narrative form without any direct allusion to the
text of the psalms may tend to "militate against this conclusion;" but he believes that study of pesher methods of exegesis has demonstrated that "historicization of Old Testament
texts on the basis of verbal allusions was a common practice in
early Christianity."[122] Whatever the validity of such a general-
ization, it hardly constitutes proof in particular cases.

What is even more damaging to Donahue's argument is his
observation that in the initial reference to the false witnesses in v. 56 there are clear indications of Markan style: the
introduction of a sentence with an unmodified πολλοί and a
characteristic use of γαρ. Donahue views this Markan half-verse
as the first real clue to the interpretation of the trial: this
particular use of γαρ is intended to prepare the reader for an
allusion to the Old Testament![123] The reference to the false
witnesses who testify against Jesus in v. 57 must therefore be
understood as a biblical allusion! It is hardly necessary to
point out that Mark's use of γαρ is an insufficient basis
for such an interpretation. The more serious problem is that
Donahue has not recognized the view of the evangelist his interpretation assumes. He argues, on the one hand, that Mark
inserts into the context of the trial a temple charge he believes to be true in some sense. Since the trial includes a
traditional description of Jesus before false accusers, Mark is
obliged to modify the reference to false testimony by inserting
two comments about the witnesses' failure to agree. On the
other hand, Donahue argues that Mark reworks the traditional
image of false witnesses. Mark himself repeats the reference to
false witnesses but must then immediately modify the impression
he has created. If the author does not view the charges as
false in any sense, if he takes pains to modify that impression,
it is difficult to understand why he even made use of the traditional image, not to mention repeating it himself at so prominent a point in the narrative! This would have to be viewed as
a major editorial blunder. One would be forced to view Mark
either as incompetent or as hopelessly bound to whatever material
was provided him by tradition.

Donahue's own question remains unanswered: why has the
author permitted this tension to exist in the final edition of

---

[122]Ibid.   [123]Ibid., 73-74.

his work? Even if we assume that Donahue has correctly identified Mark's compositional activity, the most natural interpretation of 14:56-59 is that no tension exists in the present
text. Mark permits the two references to false witnesses to
stand because he believes the temple charge to be false. Nowhere in Mark does Jesus ever make such a statement, and the
other evangelists reflect some sensitivity about the charge.
Mark's insertion of the charge into the context of the trial
would indicate the importance of discrediting this charge in the
eyes of the author. The references to the lack of agreement on
the part of the witnesses would be additions necessary to permit
the trial to move on to the decisive issue, Jesus' response to
the question of the high priest. If the witnesses had been able
to agree, presumably the verdict could have been reached and the
trial concluded. The strength of this explanation is that it
can account for the double mention of false witnesses without
having to postulate the existence of an apologetic tradition
that the author is forced to include in his account of the trial.

I will argue that this interpretation of the temple charge
is incorrect. But the issue cannot be settled by seeking to
delineate the compositional process. It will be settled only by
a proper literary examination of the charge within the context
of the trial and of the Gospel as a whole. Donahue is certainly
aware of the importance of such an approach. He does attempt to
relate the temple charge to other statements made about the
temple in the last chapters of Mark's Gospel. But this comes
at the wrong place in his dissertation. Donahue insists that in
order to determine what the temple charge means in Mark it is
first necessary to separate tradition from redaction. But as we
have seen, this cannot determine the author's view of the charge,
which is the real point of exegesis. Donahue reverses what would
seem to be the most reasonable approach to the text.

The most striking feature in Mark's account of Jesus'
trial and execution is the repetition of the temple charge at
the foot of the cross as part of the mockery to which Jesus is
subjected (15:29). No less significant is the description of
the tearing of the temple veil at the moment of Jesus' death
(15:38). For one interested in the author's view of the temple
charge, the first question must be what these three verses have
to do with one another. And before attempting to explain the
relationship between the false witnesses and the charge, basic
questions must be asked about the author's style and intent,

questions dealing with far more fundamental aspects of style
than compositional techniques.

From the brief examination of various approaches considered thus far, we may conclude that a satisfactory explanation of the trial scene in Mark and the place of the temple
charge should begin with a careful literary study of Mark, i.e.
literary study in the proper sense. The problems in the text
have not been resolved by historical reconstructions of the
events nor by appeal to Mark's sources. Redaction criticism,
although more concerned with the individual evangelists than
form criticism, has not provided tools sufficient to interpret
the trial. There is a certain methodological superiority
apparent in the work of three British scholars: R. H. Lightfoot,
D. E. Nineham, and especially T. A. Burkill.[124] These scholars
have been able to combine critical appreciation for the development of tradition with greater literary appreciation for Mark's
work. They are less preoccupied with the problem of sources
and more interested in tracing the logic of the story.

This is particularly true of Burkill. In his article
"The Trial of Jesus," he is concerned almost exclusively with
literary questions and with Mark's view of the proceedings. He
first delineates the influences operative in the shaping of the
trial narrative:

> Accordingly, the report which St. Mark presents in 14:55-65
> ought perhaps to be understood as a piece of Christian
> interpretation rather than as a plain statement of fact;
> the Jews condemned Christianity because of its affirmation
> of the Messiahship of Jesus, and, reasoning by analogy,
> certain sections of the apostolic church came to suppose
> that the sanhedrin condemned Jesus to death simply because
> he made claim to messianic dignity.[125]

This conclusion is justified, Burkill argues, because it
explains the charge of blasphemy in Mark's account of the trial,
a charge that can only refer to the messianic confession. This
interpretation of Mark is possible even it it was not considered

---

[124] R. H. Lightfoot, History and Interpretation in the
Gospels (New York: Harper Bros, 1934), esp. 130ff; The Gospel
Message of St. Mark (Oxford: Clarendon Press, 1950). D. E.
Nineham, The Gospel of St. Mark (Pelican Gospel Commentaries;
Baltimore: Penguin Books, 1963). T. A. Burkill, "St. Mark's
Philosophy of the Passion," NovT 2 (1957), 245-171; "The Trial
of Jesus," VC 12 (1958), 1-18. The essay "The Trial of Jesus"
appears intact in Burkill's book Mysterious Revelation (Ithaca,
N.Y.: Cornell U. Press, 1963).

[125] Burkill, "Trial," 2. Lightfoot, History and Interpretation, 130; Nineham, The Gospel of St. Mark. 402-403.

blasphemous to claim to be the Messiah. Throughout the article,
Burkill seeks to relate the trial to the rest of the Gospel and
to clearly Markan themes. He is particularly concerned about
the relation of Jesus' confession to the theme of the messianic
secret.[126] Here, however, we shall concentrate on his discussion of the temple charge.

Burkill's approach to the temple charge in 14:58 is to
examine the charge in light of what is said about the temple
elsewhere in Mark's Gospel. He argues, on the basis of its
context in the trial, that the charge must have a positive
meaning and that the repetition of the charge in 15:29 as well
as the tearing of the temple veil in 15:38 must be interpreted
together with 14:58. The first task is thus to explain why the
charge is characterized as false testimony. It is, he argues,
part of Mark's attempt to portray the trial as illegal:

> hence he reports that the witnesses testify falsely and
> that their evidence proves incoherent (14:59), not because
> their allegation is a misrepresentation of what they
> actually heard, but because they are opposed to the
> prisoner and are unable to grasp the mysterious import of
> his words.[127]

He also believes that in order to understand Mark's
version of the trial, it is necessary to appreciate Mark's use
of irony. In 15:29, scoffers at the foot of the cross repeat
the charge made at the trial that Jesus would destroy and rebuild the temple in three days (with some modification), a claim
they obviously consider absurd. In v. 38, there is the strange
report that at the moment of Jesus' death, the veil of the
temple is torn:

> and now in supernatural fashion the temple itself sets
> the scoffers at naught by bearing witness to the doom to
> which it is condemned.[128]

Burkill also pays close attention to the literary relationship between verses in Mark:

> Thus by the juxtaposition of vv. 37 and 38, the evangelist
> apparently means to imply that the Messiah's death and the
> destruction of the old religious order of Judaism are in-
> separably bound up together.[129]

There will be an opportunity later to assess the validity

---

[126]"Trial," 1-2.

[127]Ibid., 8. Burkill argues that Mark makes use of misunderstanding by Jesus' opponents in a way similar to the use in
the Fourth Gospel, esp. Jn 2:18ff.

[128]"St. Mark's Philosophy of the Passion," 267. [129]Ibid.

of his conclusions.[130] Here it is important to examine his
approach to the text. He tries to understand the trial within
the context of the passion story and the Gospel as a whole,
and he attempts to explain the temple charge by examining it
in the same context. However one understands the relation between tradition and redaction, the questions Burkill raises
must be answered. Interpretations must be tested by study of
the verses within the context of the Gospel. They must take into account Markan themes, the place of the scene in the development of the plot, and Mark's literary style. My own approach to
the text is very similar to Burkill's, even if there are some
differences in conclusions.

There is one important matter, however, that Burkill has
left relatively untouched: the problem of background studies.
Eta Linnemann has put the question most forcefully. She rightly
insists that any interpretation of the temple charge in Mark
must be intelligible against the background of Jewish tradition
to the extent it can be reconstructed. But here John Donahue
voices a protest. He agrees that consideration of the conceptual background of the New Testament is necessary, but he insists that this is not the task of the redaction critic:

> Analysis of such contacts represents a valid field of in-
> quiry, but it is not directly the redaction-critical
> field of inquiry, since it goes beyond the literary
> product, the gospel.[131]

There is some further indication that the enterprise itself is somewhat suspect in Donahue's eyes, for he seems to
agree with those modern literary critics who would reject any
such study as necessary for understanding Mark, since it "seeks
the meaning of a literary work outside the internal dynamics of
the work."[132]

But to suggest that this is all that is involved in the
reconstruction of the conceptual world of which the New Testament is a part reflects a basic misunderstanding. What Ms.
Linnemann suggests is that there must be some control exercised
over the ingenuity of interpreters, some way to limit the free
play of imagination in identifying Markan themes and interests.
And certainly statements about Mark's use of Jewish Scripture or
about messianic traditions in his Gospel must be made in light
of what is known about the use of Scripture and about traditional

---

[130]See below, 138-42.

[131]Are You the Christ?, 34.   [132]Ibid., 34, note 2.

messianic beliefs in Jewish circles contemporary with early
Christianity. An interpreter must at least attempt to demonstrate, by appeal to the conceptual background of the New
Testament, that a particular idea or the development of a particular tradition would have been conceivable. The difficulty
involved in such background study and the possibility of meager
results do not exempt one from the task.

As I hope to demonstrate, consideration of such matters
is by no means peripheral to study of the trial in Mark. That
is true even in Donahue's dissertation. Despite his insistence
that history-of-religions questions are outside his field of
concern, he makes decisions about such questions that decisively
affect his interpretations. In his discussion of the temple
charge, he makes reference to the view held by several commentators that the destruction and rebuilding of the temple somehow
reflect messianic expectations. He rejects this view because,
he insists, there never was such a tradition within the complex
of Jewish messianic beliefs. He cites as his authorities Lloyd
Gaston and Eta Linnemann, both of whom have studied the relevant
material in Jewish sources and have come to similar conclusions.

> Therefore Mark 14:58 cannot be explained as a piece of early
> Christian messianic expectation which Mark or the pre-Marcan
> tradition has adapted from contemporary Jewish thought.[133]

What is first of all noteworthy is that this statement
about Jewish traditions has a significant impact on the interpretation of Mark. It rules out any material relationship between the two charges at the trial even when there are indications in the Gospel that such a relationship is intended. Of
course any counter-proposal would have to be defended by appeal
to the same Jewish sources; it would be necessary to demonstrate
that the Messiah and the temple are related in messianic traditions. I believe this can be demonstrated, which suggests that
the assessment of the data by Gaston and Linnemann is inadequate. But we must at least recognize that study of the conceptual background of ideas and traditions in Mark is an indis-
pensible feature of any complete interpretation of the trial.
Proposals must be tested not only by their ability to explain
the text of Mark but also by their conceivability in light of
what is known about first century traditions and expectations.

---

[133] Ibid., 111-112.

CHAPTER 2

THE TRIAL IN THE CONTEXT OF THE GOSPEL

> The literary understanding of the synoptics begins with
> the recognition that they are collections of material.
> The composers are only to the smallest extent authors.
> They are principally collectors, vehicles of tradition,
> editors.[1]

The famous remark of Dibelius typifies a view of the
Gospel writers, especially of Mark, among many students of the
Gospel prior to the 1950's. Even the advent of redaction
criticism has done little to alter the view that Mark's literary
abilities are modest at best. The awareness that the earliest
Gospel does not represent the pinnacle of literary style and
form is not new. If we can accept the arguments of J.
Kürzinger,[2] even Papias and some of his contemporaries were
aware of the aesthetic shortcomings of the Gospel. The qualities that have led to this low estimate of Mark's literary
abilities are apparent even to the untrained eye. The story is
disjointed; the relationship among individual episodes is often
unclear. Transitions are frequently unmotivated and abrupt.
There is a tiresome repetition of phrases like "and immediately."
And the evangelist does not provide a good deal of information
that readers would like to have, e.g., what happened to the
disciples after Jesus' death, what the meetings between Jesus
and the disciples in Galilee were like (if there were such
meetings).

To the careful reader even more becomes apparent. Some
stories can be removed from their present context with relative
ease, with little effect either on the progress of the story or
the meaning of the individual unit. Material frequently appears
to have been gathered together on the basis of similarity in
form (parables, controversy stories), not a particularly sophis-
ticated style of composition. Even if the evangelist was
dependent upon traditional complexes or in a few cases on isolated traditions, one might have expected a bit more artistry

---

[1] M. Dibelius, From Tradition to Gospel, 3.

[2] J. Kürzinger, "Das Papiaszeugnis und die Erstgestalt
des Matthäusevangeliums," BZ, n. f. 4 (1960), 19-38.

in composing the story. Further, any student of the Greek language knows that Mark's usage does not represent the language's highest form. A few remarks from Vincent Taylor's commentary may suffice to characterize Mark's Greek:

> Mark's Gospel is written in a relatively simple and popular form of Greek which has striking affinities with the spoken language of everyday life..In this respect it differs profoundly from the masterpieces of Attic prose and even from the more cultured language of certain parts of Luke and Acts...Perhaps the most obvious characteristic feature of Mark's Greek is his frequent use of καὶ paratactic, and correspondingly his failure to use the longer Greek period with its particles, conjunctions, and subordinating participles.[3]

As Taylor himself notes, there is some literary justification for viewing Mark as the "interpreter of Peter," or, in more contemporary terms, as a collector, a vehicle of tradition.[4]

But a closer look at the Gospel provides some surprises. More than a half-century ago William Wrede argued that Mark had at least imposed a theme on his material, that the author had carried through a specific concern in his composition.[5] K. L. Schmidt showed that the evangelist was responsible for the framework of his story, the outline of Jesus' ministry.[6] But more and more, particularly since the 1950's, students of Mark are discovering that there is more to the author's concerns than meets the eye. An imposing corpus of works on Mark has appeared in which scholars are attempting to rediscover the teaching of the first evangelist. Redaction critics have at least shown that Mark's outlook cannot be explained simply by appealing to the traditions he used in composing his Gospel. Whether or not Mark's work is absolutely unprecedented as a story of Jesus,[7] his achievement represents more than a minor interruption in the history of the gospel tradition.

Particularly since the advent of redaction criticism, there has been a burgeoning interest in the enigmatic personality behind the earliest Gospel. Today most scholars view Mark

---

[3]V. Taylor, _Mark_, 52-53.   [4]_Ibid._, 53.

[5]W. Wrede, _Das Messiasgeheimnis in den Evangelien_ (Göttingen: Vandenhoeck and Ruprecht, 1901).

[6]K. L. Schmidt, _Der Rahmen der Geschichte Jesu_.

[7]Marxsen, _Mark the Evangelist_, 18-19, 28, and 209. According to Schneemelcher (_New Testament Apocrypha_ I: _Gospels and Related_ Writings [tr. R. McLean Wilson; Philadelphia: Westminster Press, 1963], 79) Mark is the creator of the literary form "gospel."

as an author/theologian of some sophistication whose "theology" is worth careful scrutiny.[8] Such scholars hail redaction criticism as a method whose literary tools are invaluable for recovering the thought of the evangelist. But as has already been suggested, the method is somewhat one-sided. It is misleading to picture Mark as a "theologian" who does theology by making subtle modifications in traditions he has received. Mark did employ traditions in composing his work, though the precise form of these traditions is difficult to determine with precision. What is more important, however, is that the result of his work is a story; Mark can perhaps best be viewed as a story-teller. His work has a popular quality; it was not written for scholars as, for example, much of the rabbinic corpus. He has a "theology"--definite views about God, Jesus, and the human condition. But his Gospel is in form a narrative about Jesus, and whatever theology Mark has emerges from his story.

It would seem reasonable, therefore, for students of the Gospel to employ categories appropriate to the study of such literature. Knowledge of the precise genre of the work would be helpful, but in its absence there are certain elementary methods that are suitable. We may assume that the story has a structure and a plot; we can examine the structure, observe the development of the plot, noting obvious high points in the story. We can isolate themes that run through the narrative. We can study the literary style of the author. The advantage of approaching the Gospel from this perspective is that we can work with obvious literary phenomena for which a literary explanation must be given in any case. Such a study is necessary and valid however one views pre-Markan tradition and its use; it is valid even if the Gospel has undergone successive stages of redaction.

---

[8]Marxsen, Mark the Evangelist, 216 (although he prefers the image of "preacher"); J. Schreiber, Theologie des Vertrauens; Q. Quesnell, The Mind of Mark: Interpretation and Method through the Exegesis of Mark 6:52 (AB, 38; Rome: Pontifical Biblical Institute, 1969); E. Schweizer, "Anmerkungen zur Theologie des Markus," Neotestamentica (Zürich: Zwingli, 1963), 93-104; T. Weeden, "The Heresy that Necessitated Mark's Gospel," ZNW 59 (1968), 145-58 and Traditions in Conflict (Philadelphia: Fortress, 1971). Norman Perrin (What is Redaction Criticism? [Philadelphia: Fortress, 1969], 53) is typical. He can describe Mark's compositional activity reflected in the Caesarea Philippi narrative as designed to "introduce his particular theology of the cross." Mark, he insists, should not be viewed as a historian but as a "theologian."

We may reasonably assume that the final story can be examined
as a literary whole. And if such an examination of the whole
solves problems in the narrative on the literary level, without
recourse to hypothetical source reconstruction or psychological
analysis of the characters in the story, the proposed solution
will be more credible. This approach takes seriously the
reasonable assumption that Mark, the final redactor of the
story, can at least be credited with the ability to tell a coherent story.

We will begin our study of the trial with some general
observations about Mark's literary style, observations about
the nature of his composition. Several interesting studies of
Mark's style have been attempted, one of which is devoted to
an analysis of the trial.[9] Here we shall consider only two
characteristics of the evangelist's style that have a direct
bearing on the interpretation of the trial. The first is what
may be termed the double level of the narrative.

One of the most interesting and perceptive studies of
Mark has been written by someone outside the field of biblical
studies. Erich Auerbach, in his epic work Mimesis,[10] devotes a
small portion of one chapter to the Gospel of Mark and makes
some important observations about the literary character of
Mark's work. Coming to the Gospel from the perspective of
classical literature, Auerbach sees some things in the work that
many biblical scholars, exclusively concerned with reconstructing
the actual course of events or with detection of sources, have
missed. Auerbach deals with the Gospel as a piece of mimetic
literature, literature attempting to represent reality. He
studies the Gospel with the works of Homer, Petronius, and
Tacitus. He recognizes that, when compared with other literature of the period, Mark's work is far less polished. It does
not respect aesthetic traditions; it represents a mixture of
styles. There are abrupt movements in the story--a characteristic of other biblical literature.[11] The features do not simply

---

[9] See the reference to Father Donahue's dissertation,
chapter 1 note 108.

[10] E. Auerbach, Mimesis: The Representation of Reality
in Western Literature (tr. W. Trask; Princeton: Princeton
University Press, 1953).

[11] Ibid., 23.

indicate Mark's lack of literary ability, however, but a different conception of the literary presentation of reality.

A characteristic of almost all literature of antiquity,
Auerbach argues, is its preoccupation with the external level
of events or persons to be described.[12] Whether in the epic
of Homer, in Petronius' description of a segment of Roman
society, or in Tacitus' account of a revolt, the author's interest is focused on the surface events. His intention is to
present a thorough sensory impression of the events or persons
to be described. Little attempt is made to relate the events
to broader historical forces or movements or to view the meaning
of the events as related to such forces. There is an important
difference in Mark's Gospel. His goal, according to Auerbach,
is not to provide a thorough sensory impression of the story
of Jesus or of the various characters who appear in it. His
goal is to relate the events and persons described to the profound change in the human situation that has come about as a
result of Jesus' life, death, and resurrection, and correspond-
ingly, to describe this profound historical movement by narrating the story.[13] Mark's lack of descriptive detail and information that may seem essential to the story signal his interest
in this deeper dimension of the reality he is representing:

> Here we have neither survey and rational disposition, nor
> artistic purpose. The visual and sensory as it appears
> here is no conscious imitation and hence is rarely com-
> pletely realized...The author of the Gospel according to
> Saint Mark has no viewpoint which would permit him to
> present a factual, objective portrait of, let us say, the
> character of Peter. He is at the core of what goes on; he
> observes and relates only what matters in relation to
> Christ's presence and mission; and in the present case it
> does not even occur to him to tell us how the incident
> ended, that is, how Peter got away. Tacitus and Petronius
> endeavor to give us a sensory impression, the former of his-
> torical occurrences, the latter of a specific stratum of
> society, and in doing so they respect the limits of a spe-
> cific aesthetic tradition. The author of the Gospel
> according to Saint Mark has no such purpose and knows no
> such tradition. Without any effort on his part, as it were,
> and purely through the inner movement of what he relates,
> the story becomes visually concrete. And the story speaks
> to everybody; everybody is urged and indeed required to take
> sides for or against it.[14]

---

[12]Ibid., chapter 2, 24-49.   [13]Ibid., 43-44.

[14]Ibid., 47-48. Auerbach can make such observations a-
bout the literary character of the narrative while believing
that the source of the story is "Peter, whose personal account
may be assumed to have been the basis of the story" (41).

Auerbach's observations are relevant for any study of the
Gospel. He is saying not that Mark's work is a collection of
symbols or allegories, pointing to a reality other than itself,
but that there is a dimension to the story beyond the obvious
one. The events are important because they belong to a deeper
reality, to the movement that traces its origin to the crucified
and risen Jesus Christ. And it is to this interior level of the
story that Mark directs the reader's attention, the level at
which the meaning of the story as Mark conceives it emerges.

A specific example may make the point clearer. Since
Wrede, scholars have recognized the so-called messianic secret
as a literary device of the author.[15] What many have failed to
recognize, however, is that the secret is not a secret for the
reader of the Gospel, nor did Mark intend that it should be.
The reader knows from the opening sentence of the work that the
story is about "Jesus Christ, [the Son of God]." He is never in
doubt that this Jesus is the Christ, God's Son with whom He is
well pleased, the Holy One of God, the stronger one who has come
to despoil Satan, the Son of Man who has come to give his life
as a ransom for many, the crucified Messiah who was raised after
three days, who is now enthroned at God's right hand and will
soon return with the clouds of heaven. But for the characters
in the story, Jesus' identity is a secret or mystery. Even his
most trusted disciples do not understand who he is, and they all,
even Peter, fail in the moment of crisis. We may assume that
most readers of the Gospel knew about appearances of the risen
Lord to the disciples and Peter after the story Mark tells, at
which time Jesus' identity was no longer a mystery.[16] But
during the story, the only ones who know who Jesus is are the
demons, a blind man and a handful of others.

The character of the secret as a literary device cannot
fully be appreciated until it is recognized that it is not a
secret for the reader. Nor can one properly describe Mark's use
of the device without such knowledge. Throughout the story, the
reader has access to a dimension of reality obscured from the

---

[15]One important exception was A. Schweitzer, Quest of the
Historical Jesus (tr. W. Montgomery; New York: Macmillan, 1964),
esp. 330-397. The following comments about the "secret" have
been suggested by Dahl in his essay, "The Purpose of Mark's
Gospel."

[16]The passion predictions indicate that Mark is quite a-
ware of the place of the resurrection within Christianity.

characters in the story. The reader is expected to interpret
the events in light of what has come afterward, and he is
able to understand the events at a different level. The important point for interpretation is that Mark makes conscious
use of this second level of the story·throughout his Gospel.

If one of the characteristics of Mark's style is the
double-level narrative, it is not unimportant to ask if this
stylistic feature can be detected in the passion story. In
fact, there are clear signs that the author utilizes this
particular stylistic possibility and that the use of the double-
level narrative makes possible the use of the most prominent
literary feature of the passion story: irony. It is not simply
that the events Mark narrates in the passion story are ironic,
though for the Christian they certainly were. Mark quite consciously tells the story to bring out the irony for his readers.
They know something the characters in the story do not: they
know that God raised Jesus from the dead. And Mark focuses
attention on the interior level of the story he is narrating,
the level at which the events he reports are viewed in light of
the resurrection and as fulfillment of Scripture and as visible
in the life of the church. The author of the Fourth Gospel
was a master of irony, but Mark proves to be not completely
lacking in literary ability. A few of the more obvious examples
will suffice to make the point.

There can be little doubt that Mark intended the reader
to understand the ironic significance of the mockery to which
Jesus is subjected by the Roman garrison (15:16-20). Jesus is
led into the praetorium, dressed in a royal robe,[17] a crown of
thorns on his head, and is hailed as "King of the Jews." The
reader knows, however, that the soldiers are really testifying
to a truth beyond the level of their understanding: Jesus is
king. Three times Pilate uses the title "King of the Jews"
(15:2, 9, 12), and the title appears in 15:26 as the inscription
of the charge. The kingship theme is even more obvious in the
Fourth Gospel's account of the passion (esp. the account of the
inscription of the charge in 19:19-22), but the ironic use of
the imagery is present in Mark as well. The author intends the
reader to understand the events at a deeper level: Christians

---

[17]The term used by Mark is πορφύραν, less accurate a
term for the soldier's robe than Matthew's χλαμύδα κοκκίνην .
This suggests not that Mark was uninformed but that his interest was clearly the royal imagery. Cf. Taylor, Mark, 585.

know that the mockery and the inscription of the charge point to
truth about Jesus. Even more important for our purposes is the
mockery to which Jesus is subjected while he hangs on the cross
in 15:29-32. The irony of the mockery is no less apparent here.
Jesus, who came "to give his life as a ransom for many " (10:45),
is taunted with the words, "He saved others, he cannot save himself! Let the Christ, the King of Israel, come down now from
the cross, that we may see and believe." To Jesus' enemies,
the idea that he can save anyone seems absurd; he cannot even
help himself. And the helpless figure on the cross hardly looks
like the Messiah-King! But Mark's reader knows that Jesus must
die as a "ransom for many," that he goes "as it is written of
him" (14:21 and 49); he knows that Jesus is the "Christ [the
Son of God]" (1:1), attested as Son by God himself (1:11 and 9:
7). The reader knows, in other words, that the mockery is
simply another testimony to the truth. The mockers are made unwitting confessors to Jesus' true identity.

There are two other observations that may be made at this
stage of our investigation, however. First, if Mark makes consistent use of irony throughout the passion story, and if the
mockery at the cross in 15:31-32 serves to point up truth about
Jesus at a second level of the story, it is possible that the
same is true for the mockery in 15:29: "Aha! You who would
destroy the temple and build it in three days, save yourself,
and come down from the cross." Perhaps Mark intends the reader
to appreciate the irony of this statement as well, or to put it
another way, perhaps Mark views this statement about the temple
as true in some sense at another level of the story. It is at
least important to ask how the first account of mockery, as
well as the second, functions in Mark's passion story in light
of Mark's use of irony. The second observation has to do with
the relationship between the two accounts of mockery in 15:29-
32 and the charges raised at the trial in 14:55-62. Both charges
at the trial (14:58 and 14:61) are repeated in the mockery. Even
at this early stage of our study, it is possible to suggest that
awareness of the dual-level narrative and the use of irony may
be important for interpreting the trial as well as the account
of the mockery and crucifixion in chapter 15.

Thus far it has been suggested that certain aspects of
Mark's style may be important for interpreting the account of
the trial as well as the passion story as a whole. Another way
of approaching the trial and its function within the passion

story is to ask if there are any major themes tying the account
of the trial to the passion story and to the rest of the Gospel.
Perhaps the best place to begin such a study is with the dominant theme in the passion story in Mark's Gospel, the royal
motif. But since this is an issue about which there are differences of opinion, some attention must be devoted to the
problem.

There have been numerous scholars who have suggested
that the dominant theme in the passion story is that of the suffering servant of Isa 53. Its most ardent proponent in recent
years has been Chr. Maurer,[18] although scholars like Dodd,
Dibelius, and Lindars, to name only a few, have made similar
proposals.[19] But there is a theme far more fundamental to the
passion story in Mark and a theme whose importance for interpreting the trial has not been sufficiently appreciated. The
theme unifying the passion story is the royal theme: Jesus is
tried, mocked, and crucified as King.[20]

The theme is clearest in chapter 15. We have already
surveyed briefly some of the evidence. Jesus is arraigned before Pilate as one alleged to be "the King of the Jews." The
term is used three times by Pilate, once by the soldiers, and
once in the inscription of the charge.[21] But the theme recurs
also in 15:32, in the mockery of the high priests and scribes.
Jesus is mocked by his Jewish opponents as well as by the Romans
as "King." But this verse may also provide a bridge between the
account of the crucifixion and the trial. As we have observed,
the two charges at the trial are repeated in the mockery at the
foot of the cross. At the trial Jesus is charged with having
made a statement about the temple (14:58), which is repeated (in
somewhat altered form) in 15:29; and he is condemned for a

---

[18]C. Maurer, "Knecht Gottes und Sohn Gottes im Passionsbericht des Markusevangeliums," ZTK 50 (1953), 1-38, and "Das
Messiasgeheimnis des Markusevangeliums," NTS 14 (1967-68),515-25.

[19]C. H. Dodd, According to Scriptures: the Substructure
of New Testament Theology (London: Nisbet, 1952), 91; B. Lindars,
New Testament Apologetic (London: SCM, 1961), 135-137; Dibelius,
From Tradition to Gospel, 184-185 and 187.

[20]See Bultmann, History, 283-284.

[21]The title is in all probability not a product of early
Christian theology, as Bultmann suggests (History, 284). For a
convincing argument for the historicity of the charge, see W.
Meeks, The Prophet-King (Leiden: Brill, 1967), 79, note 1, and
Nils A. Dahl, "The Crucified Messiah," The Crucified Messiah and
Other Essays (Minneapolis: Augsburg, 1974), 10-36.

messianic claim (14:61), which is repeated in 15:32. Here we
will focus on the second of the charges and the corresponding
taunt.

It seems clear that the taunt in 15:32 is a conscious allusion to the trial. Even Jesus' opponents are the same,
opponents who are important only within the context of the passion story.[22] But there is a difference between the terms used
in 14:61 and in 15:32. In 14:61, the high priest asks Jesus if
he is "the Christ, the Son of the Blessed"; in 15:32, Jesus is
mocked as "the Christ, the King of Israel." We will have to
examine the various terms with some care in chapter 4. But even
without detailed study of the terms, 15:32 indicates that Mark
knows "Messiah" is a royal title. The use of Messiah to mean
the king of Davidic descent is also found in Mk 12:35-37. But
the synonymity of "Christ" and "King of Israel" in 15:32 suggests that the term "Christ" in 14:61 is used with at least some
awareness of its royal connotation.

"King of the Jews" and "the Christ, the King of Israel"
are both used to describe the same reality; but they describe
that reality from different perspectives. "King of the Jews" is
a Roman, i.e., a non-Jewish formulation. As Wayne Meeks has
noted,[23] the title appears in Jewish literature only twice in
the works of Josephus, and it is never used as a designation for
the Messiah. "Jew" is the term used for members of the nation
Israel almost exclusively by non-Jews.[24] In time Jews of the
dispersion came to adopt the term as a self-designation to con-
form to the usage of their non-Jewish neighbors.[25] Mark's
account, however, is appropriate for a Palestinian setting. The
term "Jews" is used in the story when non-Jews are speaking. It
is the Romans who call the King of Israel "King of the Jews."

On the other hand, "King of Israel" is the appropriate
Jewish formulation. "Israel" was the self-designation of the
Jewish nation in Palestine and among the Rabbis.[26] "Israel"

---

[22]See the arguments of Paul Winter, On the Trial of Jesus,
111-153, especially the charts on 121-123.

[23]Meeks, The Prophet-King, 79, note 1. The two references are Jos Ant 14:34-36 and Ant 16:311. Neither text is
eschatological and neither in any way refers to the Messiah.

[24]Karl Kuhn, art. Ἰσραήλ , TDNT III, 360.

[25]Ibid., 363f.   [26]Ibid., 360-361.

never occurs in non-Jewish literature.[27]   Hence, the term "King of Israel" is appropriate when Jews are speaking. The difference in the titles in 15:2, 9, 12, 18, 26 and 15:32 suggests not that there are two different conceptions but that Mark is aware of appropriate terminology. Both terms describe Jesus as King. But the Jewish taunt has an additional component: the King is a religious as well as a political figure. He is the Messiah-king, the King promised in Scripture. Again, Mark's usage simply suggests that he is aware of the different connotations this "Kingship" has for the two parties involved in Jesus' death. The Romans could not be expected to appreciate the religious dimensions of the alleged royalty. Pilate is concerned about a political reality: Jesus is accused of being a pretender to kingship, which poses an obvious threat to the political order. For Jews, however, Jesus' alleged claim includes significant religious elements. What is important is that 15:32 is part of the theme that runs throughout the passion story.

    If this is correct, however, the use of the term "Christ" in the trial should be viewed as part of the same royal theme. The climax of the trial scene is the high priest's question and Jesus' response: "'Are you the Christ, the Son of the Blessed?' 'I am, and you will see...'" The use of the apparently synonymous term "Son of the Blessed" is certainly important, particularly in light of Mark's use of the term "Son of God" elsewhere in the Gospel.[28]   But the use of the title "Christ" in the mockery in 15:32 as a royal title, in an account of Jesus' passion that is dominated throughout by the royal motif, suggests that the accent must fall on the term "Christ" in the trial as well--on "Christ" in the royal sense, the Messiah-King. And it is because Jesus accepts the epithets "the Christ, the Son of the Blessed" that he is condemned by the Jewish high court. The legal problem poses certain difficulties, particularly since it does not appear that it was blasphemous in Jesus' day to claim to be the Messiah, and according to Mark he was condemned for blasphemy.[29]   But the proper approach to the interpretation of the Gospel is not first to determine how Jesus could have been condemned for blasphemy or precisely what in his statement or in

---

[27]Walter Gutbrod, art. Ἰσραήλ , TDNT III, 370.

[28]See below, excursus on Son of God, 108-114.

[29]See below on legal questions, 59-63.

the question of the high priest could have been construed as
blasphemy in the proper sense. The first task is to examine
the charge within the context of Mark's story to determine
first what it means for the author. And the presence of the
royal motif in chapter 15, and the use of "Christ" as a royal
title, suggest that for Mark, it is as Messiah-King that Jesus is
condemned by the Jewish court. If this is correct, the trial
initiates the royal theme: Jesus is tried by the Jewish court
as Messiah-King and found guilty; he is tried by Pilate as
King, mocked by the garrison as King, executed as King, and
mocked by Jewish religious leaders as King. The theme unifies
the passion story and establishes one link between the trial and
subsequent events.

There is another theme in Mark's Gospel, however, that
provides further clues about the precise relationship between
the trial and the rest of the passion story. It is the theme
of rejection/vindication, introduced in the first of the passion
predictions in 8:31 and further developed in the parable of the
wicked husbandmen in 12:1-11. To interpret the trial properly
it is important to view it in light of this theme, to look carefully for the clues the author has provided for his interpretation of the encounter between Jesus and the Sanhedrin. We shall
begin with the passion predictions.

There are three explicit predictions of the passion in
Mark. Whatever pre-Markan elements the predictions may contain,
the three statements function as foreshadowing in the present
story. They prepare the reader for what is to happen and they
provide an opportunity for the author to emphasize features of
the story he considers important. The first of the predictions
is 8:31, immediately after Peter's confession:

> And he began to teach them that the Son of man must suffer
> many things, and be rejected [ἀποδοκιμασθῆναι] by the elders
> and the chief priests and the scribes, and be killed, and
> after three days rise again.

The second is found in 9:31:

> for he was teaching his disciples, saying to them, "The
> Son of man will be delivered into the hands of men, and
> they will kill him; and when he is killed, after three days
> he will rise.

The last is in 10:33:

> Behold, we are going up to Jerusalem; and the Son of man
> will be delivered to the chief priests and the scribes, and
> they will condemn him to death [κατακρινοῦσιν αὐτὸν θανάτῳ],
> and deliver him to the Gentiles; and they will mock him, and

spit upon him, and scourge him, and kill him; and after
three days he will rise.

The last of the predictions is the most explicit. Here
the author seems concerned to spell out in detail what will
happen at the end of the story. There are two features in the
prediction of particular interest. First, Jesus will be tried
by the "chief priests and scribes" and condemned to death
(κατακρινοῦσιν αὐτὸν θανάτῳ). The terminology suggests a proper
legal verdict.[30] But the following statement is unexpected:
"and deliver him to the Gentiles." As we shall see, the actual
account of the trial is characterized by the same peculiarity.
Jesus is condemned by a Jewish court, but he is simply handed
over to the Romans (=Gentiles). There is no question in the
predictions who will actually execute Jesus. But the prediction
in 10:33 makes no effort to explain how the Jewish trial is related to Jesus' execution by the Romans, another peculiarity
present also in the account of the trial. The "delivering him
to the Gentiles" is not the result of a trial one might expect.
One would rather expect the execution of the sentence by the
court, as in the case of Stephen, or at least some explanation
why such a sentence was not carried out.

The first of the three predictions provides some possible
clues for understanding what the author is after. What is
particularly interesting about 8:31 is the amount of space devoted to a description of the role to be played by the Jewish
leaders in Jesus' demise. The only reference to the execution
by the Romans is the phrase "and be killed." The author seems
more concerned to emphasize the "rejection" of Jesus by the
Jewish religious leaders. The inordinate amount of space devoted to the role played by the Jewish leaders should be a signal
that this is a feature of the passion story of particular importance to the author. And a closer look at the term "reject"
provides further evidence that in the first of the three passion
predictions the author is especially concerned to point the
reader to the real significance of the "trial" recorded in 14:
55-65.

The term ἀποδοκιμάζειν is used only twice in Mark:
once in 8:31 and once in 12:11, where it is part of a quotation
of Ps 118:22. In the parable in chapter 12, Jesus tells a story

---

[30]See Bauer, A Greek-English Lexicon of the New Testament
on κατακρίνομαι.

of tenants who refuse to pay the rent due the owner of the vineyard and who eventually kill the son of the owner, foolishly
supposing that they will thus secure possession of the vineyard
for themselves. Whatever the original meaning of the parable,
Mark's interpretation is clear. The parable is concluded with
the quotation of Ps 118:22, and the following verse reads:

> And they tried to arrest him, but they feared the multi-
> tude, for they perceived that he had told the parable
> against them. (12:12)

The "they" in the verse can be no one but the religious
leaders (the scribes, high priests and elders) who are Jesus'
opponents throughout the passion story.[31] The Jewish religious
leaders are characterized as the builders of the Psalm who will
"reject" the stone (=Jesus). But God will make him "head of the
corner."

It has been recognized for some time that this verse from
Ps 118 was of great importance in traditional Christian apologetic use of Scripture.[32] The original use of the verse was
most probably connected with the resurrection, which was viewed
as God's vindication of the crucified Jesus. Acts 4:11 is perhaps a typical use of the verse: Jesus, rejected by "you
builders" (the Jewish leaders, "rulers of the people and elders"
in 4:8), has become the head of the corner (=raised from the
dead). This use of the verse and of the term "reject" fits Mk
8:31 perfectly. Jesus will be "rejected" by the Jewish leaders,
as prophesied in Scripture, but he will be vindicated by God--
"after three days he will rise." It is highly probable that
Mark has used the term "reject" in 8:31 with full awareness of
its scriptural connotations. Here he hints at what is made more
explicit in the parable in 12:1-11. In the first of the three
passion predictions, Mark thus seems concerned to present a
broad interpretation of the role of the Jewish leaders in
Jesus' end. He is suggesting for the reader the real significance of the trial: it represents the "rejection" of the "stone"
in accord with Scripture. This might also explain why Mark seems
unconcerned about making a clear transition from the Jewish
trial to the session before Pilate. This will have to be argued
in detail, but here we might at least suggest that the trial is
important for Mark as the scene of the scriptural "rejection" of

---

[31]Cf. note 23 above.

[32]Dodd, According to Scriptures, 35-36; Lindars, New
Testament Apologetic, 169-174.

Jesus.

In the trial, however, specific charges are raised against
Jesus, one of which provides the basis for his condemnation.
The first charge is in 14:57-58:

> And some stood up and bore false witness against him,
> saying, "We heard him say, 'I will destroy this temple
> that is made with hands, and in three days I will build
> another, not made with hands.'"

According to the text, however, this charge could not
provide the requisite evidence for condemnation because witnesses could not agree. The basis for the charge of blasphemy
is found in 14:61-62:

> Again the high priest asked him, "Are you the Christ,
> the Son of the Blessed." And Jesus said, "I am; and
> you will see...."

If the trial is the account of Jesus' rejection, the
specific charges may be quite important for the evangelist. In
light of the rejection/vindication theme, the specific charges,
at least the second, may provide not only the precise reason
for Jesus' rejection but also the basis for his vindication.
It is possible that the trial focuses on the aspects of Jesus'
betrayal, arrest, death and resurrection that the evangelist
considers most important. The presence of the rejection/vindi-
cation theme in 8:31 and 12:1-11 at least suggests that the
trial has an important function in the passion story and that an
interpreter must examine the charges at the trial carefully.

It is now possible to draw together the lines sketched
thus far and to indicate a direction of study. It has been
suggested that a study of the trial within the context of the
passion story should be approached as a literary problem in the
proper sense. An interpreter should first consider important
stylistic features of the author apparent in the rest of the
story. One such stylistic feature of Mark of great importance
for interpreting the passion story is the double-level narrative.
The suggestion has been made, by other students of the Gospel as
well, that Mark is telling a story the real point of which can
be found only at a deeper level, at a level of understanding
accessible only to the reader and not to the characters in the
story. It has further been suggested that the most important
application of this double-level of the story in the account
of the passion is Mark's use of irony. The events are described
to bring out the irony of the events--irony not for a character
in the story who knows what the other characters do not, but

irony for the Christian reader who knows what none of the characters in the story knows. The Jewish leaders, Pilate, the
Roman garrison, and the anonymous mockers all become unwitting
witnesses to a truth beyond their comprehension.

The irony and the double-level style may be important for
interpretation of the trial as well. Mark seems concerned to
emphasize the taunts made by on-lookers at the foot of Jesus'
cross. But the taunts in 15:20-32 repeat the two charges
raised at Jesus' trial in 14:58 and 14:61. If Mark intends the
reader to appreciate the ironic truth of the statements made by
the mockers, he must intend the charges at the trial to be viewed
in the same way. It is thus possible that the charges at Jesus'
trial point to something the author of the Gospel considers
to be true.

Literary study of the trial must also recognize themes
important to the author present in the narrative. One theme
that appears to dominate the passion story as a whole is the
royal-messianic motif. The theme is clearest in chapter 15,
where Jesus is tried, mocked and executed as "King of the Jews,"
and as "the Christ, the King of Israel." But the presence of
the term "Christ" in the mockery in 15:32 and in the question
of the high priest in 14:61 suggests that the royal theme is
present in the trial as well. And if this is correct, the function of the trial would seem to be to introduce the royal-messianic theme that runs through the rest of the story.

Further confirmation is found in another theme, the re-
jection/vindication motif introduced in 8:31 and developed in
12:1-11. The author of the Gospel seems particularly interested
in the role of the Jewish leaders in Jesus' passion, and he
characterizes the trial as the occasion for Jesus' rejection.
But by so doing he suggests that the basis for Jesus' rejection
at the trial also indicates the basis for his vindication at the
resurrection.

This provides at least some of the background for my
specific proposal. The purpose of this study is to show that
the function of the trial in Mark is to introduce the themes in
the passion story the author considers most important. The trial
provides the basis for Jesus' rejection and also, for the reader
who is able to understand the story at a deeper level, the basis
for his vindication at the resurrection. The author seems most
interested in Jesus as the Messiah-King. If it is as Messiah-

King that Jesus is tried, condemned, mocked and executed--i.e.,
"rejected"--then presumably it is as Messiah-King that he is
vindicated by God by his resurrection "after three days."

There are, however, two charges at the trial. And
despite the lack of obvious connection between 14:58 and its
context, despite the statements about "false testimony" and the
failure of witnesses to agree, there are indications that the
author intends this charge too to be viewed by the reader as
true in some sense, true at another level of understanding.
This charge is also repeated in the mockery in 15:29, and it is
treated in precisely the same manner as the second of the
charges. If Mark expects the reader to appreciate the ironic
truth of the mockery of Jesus as "the Christ, the King of
Israel," it is possible that he also intends the same ironic
truth to be recognized in the statement about the temple in
15:29. It also seems more than coincidental that one of the two
events to occur at the moment of Jesus' death, according to
Mark, is the tearing of the veil of the temple (15:38). From
chapter 11 to 15:38, Mark seems occupied with the temple. Jesus
cleanses the temple in 11:15-17; he tells a parable in 12:1-11
that uses imagery related to the temple in the targums; he predicts the destruction of the temple in 13:2; and he is accused
of having made a threat against the temple at his trial the
wording of which suggests great care and precision in the formulation and whose point seems less than appropriate in the context of the trial.

One of the real purposes of this study will be to argue
that the temple charge can be interpreted properly only on the
literary level. I hope to show that Mark intends the reader to
view the charge as true at a second level of the story--even if
Jesus never made such a statement. The charge reflects Mark's
view of the relationship between the Christian movement and the
temple establishment. The church is characterized as a
spiritual temple made without hands and is viewed as a replacement of the Jewish temple. I will also argue, however, that
the charge functions not only to point up some important result
of Jesus' death and resurrection, but that it has a place in
the trial as part of the messianic imagery. The temple charge
provides further testimony to Jesus as the Messiah and further
defines his Messiahship. He is not only the Messiah who must
suffer and die; he is also the Messiah who will build the escha-

tological temple "not made with hands."

CHAPTER 3

THE TRIAL NARRATIVE IN ITS IMMEDIATE CONTEXT

We will begin our examination of the trial itself with
some of the broader issues, gradually narrowing the focus to the
specific charges. A good place to begin is with the question
of the legality of the trial, since this has been an important
feature in the debate about Mark's account. When measured by
rabbinic legal standards, the trial as described by Mark is
highly irregular if not downright illegal. Using the list of
regulations set down in the Mishnah as a standard of comparison,
most scholars see at least four or five violations. The list
given by Lohse in his article in Kittel's Theological Dictionary
is representative:[1]

1) Sanhedrin 4:1 states that "in capital cases they hold
   the trial during the daytime and the verdict also must
   be reached during the daytime." According to Mark,
   the trial is conducted and the verdict pronounced at
   night.

2) Sanhedrin 4:1 also states: "Therefore trials may not be
   held on the eve of a Sabbath or on the eve of a Festival-
   day."[2] According to Mark, the trial was held on the eve
   of the Passover.

3) Sanhedrin 4:1 also states that "in capital cases a verdict of acquittal may be reached on the same day, but a
   verdict of conviction not until the following day."
   According to Mark, Jesus is convicted on the same day.

4) Sanhedrin 7:5: "'The blasphemer' is not culpable unless
   he pronounces the Name itself." Measured by this rule,
   nothing Jesus said at the trial could have been construed as blasphemy.

5) According to Sanhedrin 11:2, the regular meeting place
   of the high court was the "Chamber of Hewn Stone."
   According to Mark, the trial was held at the home of
   the high priest.

There have been numerous other suggestions about alleged
contradictions of Jewish law made by students of the trial, many
of which are either too technical or too minor to be considered.
But two additional suggestions made by Blinzler may be

---

[1] E. Lohse, συνέδριον, TDNT VII, 867-868.

[2] Cf. Mishnah, Betzah, 5:2.

mentioned:[3]

6) Sanhedrin 4:1 states that "capital cases must begin with reasons for acquittal and may not begin with reasons for conviction." According to Mark, the trial begins with (false) testimony against Jesus; there are no witnesses for the defence.

7) Sanhedrin 4:5 states that witnesses are to be solemnly warned and carefully examined regarding their testimony. Mark reports no such procedure, nor does he suggest that the false witnesses were in any way held accountable for their false testimony.

The principal difficulty with these alleged violations of Jewish law is that the source of the regulations is the Mishnah. This work, codified around the end of the second century, is the product of the rabbinic schools that assumed control of the Jewish legal system at Jabne after the destruction of the temple in A.D. 70. Its value as a source for Jewish legal practice prior to 70 is a matter of considerable debate. The Mishnah represents the legal views of Pharasaic Judaism. However popular and influential the Pharisees might have been within the Jerusalem establishment, the Sadducees represented an extremely important element and their opinions on legal matters were certainly reflected in the conduct of the high court.[4] Yet in the Mishnah the Sadducees "figure only as an insignificant, discredited, and heretical sect."[5] This is not the only difficulty posed by the Mishnaic legal code. It has ben argued, by H. Danby and others,[6] that many of the regulations represent little more than idealizations of the Rabbis that were never operative in a practicing court.

Josef Blinzler has been one of the most ardent proponents of this view. He argues that the Mishnaic rules cited as relevant to the interpretation of Jesus' trial by most scholars are almost without exception of dubious historical value.[7] The real problem according to Blinzler is the Pharisaic bias of the material. Their legal discussions clearly reveal an intense desire to avoid injustice; every precaution is taken to safe-

---

[3]Blinzler, The Trial of Jesus, 135.

[4]H. Danby, The Mishnah, xiv-xv.   [5]Ibid., xv, note 1.

[6]See especially H. Danby, "The Bearing of the Rabbinical Criminal Code on the Jewish Trial Narratives of the Gospels," JTS 21 (1919/20), 151-176.

[7]See especially The Trial of Jesus, excursis VI, 149-157.

guard the rights of the accused.[8] Sometimes the concern was
responsible for the formulation of a regulation that was
practically unenforceable. One of the most striking examples is
found in a gemara in the Talmud according to which the accused
must be set free if a unanimous verdict of guilty is returned
by the court--for this would imply that the court was prejudiced
against the accused![9]

What is striking, according to Blinzler, is that almost
every one of the alleged violations of proper legal procedure
has to do with one of the Mishnaic prescriptions formulated to
protect the rights of the accused. Since none of the prescriptions has scriptural basis and since each reflects a well-known
tendency among Pharisees, we may doubt that such rules were
actually in force in the Jerusalem high court prior to 70.[10]
The one applicable rule from the Mishnah with scriptural war-
rant--the demand that testimony be accepted only when substan-
tiated by two witnesses--was respected by the court, according
to Mark's account. Blinzler believes that the code operative
in Jesus' day was Sadducean, and that the trial as reported by
Mark "was completely in accordance with the criminal code then
in force."[11]

Lohse largely concurs with Blinzler, but he insists that
at one point there can be no question about a violation of
operative legal regulations. The ordinance forbidding court
sessions on the eve of a feast day (Sanhedrin 4:1) would have
been even more strictly observed by the Sadducees than by the
Pharisees.

There can be no doubt that in the days of Jesus judicial
proceedings were strictly forbidden on the Sabbaths,
on feast days, and on the related days of preparation.[12]

On the basis of this violation, Lohse believes that the
trial was a serious miscarriage of justice. Catchpole, on the
other hand, who devotes considerable space to the illegality
question, argues that not even this rule is attested in reliable
sources.[13] Furthermore, Catchpole believes that the legality
problems evaporate when one approaches study of the trial from
new source-critical perspectives. He believes that Luke turns
out to be the more reliable source for the real "trial," and

[8]Ibid., 153.   [9]Ibid., 136.   [10]Ibid., 157.

[11]Ibid.   [12]Lohse, TDNT 7, 869.

[13]Catchpole, The Trial of Jesus, 258.

thus "the illegality debate must be regarded as having burnt itself out."[14]

The legal questions regarding the actual "trial" of Jesus before the Jewish court, if there was such a trial, are probably incapable of solution. What is interesting is how little interest these scholars indicate in Mark's view of the proceedings. Before suggesting any final interpretation of Mark's view of the legality of the trial it is certainly important to raise the historical questions regarding the shape of pre-Mishnaic legal regulations, although the more accurate question would be what legal codes the evangelist would be likely to have known. But even before asking the historical question, we should examine the Gospel for clues the author provides regarding the propriety of the trial. Perhaps the most important clues are the comments he makes about the Jewish religious leaders who make up the high court. The following are the most important passages.

8:31 - Here Jesus predicts that he will be "rejected" by the elders, the chief priests and the scribes. The allusion to Ps 118:22 suggested above is important: the Jewish leaders are Jesus' enemies "according to Scripture."

10:33 - Jesus again predicts his suffering and notes specifically that he will "be delivered to the chief priests and the scribes, and they will condemn him to death, and deliver him to the Gentiles." The prediction, as do all three, ends with the promise of God's vindication "after three days."

11:18 - After Jesus "cleanses" the temple,[15] the chief priests and scribes seek a way to get rid of him, "for they feared him, because all the multitude was astonished at his teaching." The plot against Jesus intensifies throughout the remainder of the story until his opponents finally succeed.

12:1-12 - Jesus tells the parable of the wicked husbandmen and follows with a quotation of Ps 118:22. In v. 12, Mark reports that "they [the scribes, high priests and elders] tried to arrest him, but they feared the multitude, for they perceived that he had told the parable against them." In the parable Jesus' opponents are characterized as despicable and unscrupulous; they will murder God's own Son (12:6). But as promised in the Psalm, the work of these "builders" will be counteracted by God himself.

12:13 - "They" (the same opponents) send Pharisees and Herodians to trap Jesus in his speech, to find some excuse to have him arrested.

---

[14] Ibid., 260.

[15] See below,   on the cleansing of the temple.

14:1 - Mark calls attention again to the plot against Jesus and comments that the chief priests and scribes "were seeking how to arrest him by stealth and kill him."

14:10-11 - Judas goes to the chief priests to betray Jesus, and Mark comments that "when they heard it they were glad, and promised to give him money."

14:65 - Some of those in attendance at the trial, presumably members of the court, maltreat Jesus (perhaps in fulfillment of Isa 50:6).

15:10 - According to Mark, even Pilate knew that "it was out of envy that the chief priests had delivered him up."

15:11 - The chief priests stir up the crowd to demand the release not of Jesus but of Barabbas, a convicted revolutionary who was among those "who had committed murder in the insurrection."

15:31 - The chief priests and scribes mock Jesus as he hangs on the cross.

The information Mark provides about Jesus' opponents, the Jewish religious leaders, is hardly calculated to elicit respect or sympathy for them, and it certainly does not prepare the reader for a fair trial. Mark paints a picture of men totally committed to Jesus' destruction; their opposition is motivated by fear and jealousy, and they are ready to seize the first opportunity to destroy him--out of sight of the people. There is no significant change of characterization within the account of the trial itself.

Now the chief priests and the whole council sought testimony against Jesus to put him to death; but they found none. For many bore false witness against him, and their witness did not agree. (Mk 14:55-56)

The trial begins with the court committed to a guilty verdict. The court's only problem, according to Mark, is to find a charge that will stick--in this case, to secure the consistent testimony of two witnesses. The statement of the intent of the court is followed by mention of false witnesses. The reader can only infer that the witnesses are part of the plot to do away with Jesus; their function is to provide the excuse for condemning him. It is probably wrong to probe any deeper into the evangelist's mind at this point, to ask, for example, how in his eyes planted witnesses could have failed to agree. Once again it seems that Mark is less interested in providing a complete picture of the events themselves than with giving a characterization of their deeper significance. The opening remarks in his account of the trial tell us a great deal about his view of the real significance of the proceedings.

64

All of the information reviewed thus far suggests that the
evangelist intends the trial to be viewed as something less than
an example of justice. As we shall observe below, Mark's description of the response to blasphemy in 14:63 indicates his
knowledge of at least certain aspects of Jewish legal practice.
Viewed in this light, the numerous violations of Mishnaic regulations may be of some importance. It is probably impossible
to determine precisely what Mark knew about Jewish legal procedure and consequently what exact prescriptions he considers to
have been violated. But, as Bultmann has suggested, "we must
not . . . underrate the contradictions."[16] In light of Mark's
characterization of the Jewish religious leaders, an irregular
trial is not unexpected. The consistent violation of Mishnaic
rules fits the evangelist's concern too well to be entirely
coincidental. One might even suggest that the negative agreement between Mark and the Mishnah can be used as evidence that
at least some of the regulations in Sanhedrin 4:1 reflect
accepted legal practice at the time of the evangelist. Or the
agreements might at least suggest that Mark shares some of the
ideals of the Rabbis about fair trials. However the historical
question of pre-Mishnaic legal regulations is to be solved, it
is at least clear that for Mark, the trial was conducted by men
who were jealous, unscrupulous enemies of Jesus--and of God.
And it is certainly not Mark's view that the trial "was completely in accordance with the criminal code then in force."[17]
Blinzler can point to only one regulation that was observed,
according to Mark: the requirement that testimony be established by at least two witnesses. But as we shall observe, the
two statements about the failure of witnesses to agree (Mk 14:
56 and 59) are not intended to emphasize respect for the rules.
They have a very different function in the context.[18]

According to Mark, the trial is to be viewed as the outcome of the conspiracy against Jesus. But it is not clear precisely how the trial narrative itself is to be understood. From
10:33 it at least seems clear that the account in 14:55-64 is to
be viewed as a trial which results in a particular verdict.

[16]History of the Synoptic Tradition, 280. See also
Burkill, "The Trial of Jesus," 3.

[17]Blinzler, The Trial of Jesus, 157.

[18]See below, 118ff on the failure of the witnesses to
agree.

But there are inconsistencies in the account, the charges are somewhat peculiar, and the outcome of the trial is hardly what might have been expected.

1) In 14:56, Mark notes that the court was unsuccessful in securing testimony against Jesus because the witnesses were unable to agree. If the witnesses were planted by the court, which we may reasonably infer, it is difficult to understand how they could fail to agree.

2) Mark then reports the specific testimony of "some." Yet after giving a precise rendering of the charge, he reports that even then the witnesses were unable to agree (v. 59).

3) The high priest then moves to center stage and questions Jesus about the charges. After a strange silence by the accused, the high priest "again" asks Jesus if he is "the Christ, the Son of the Blessed"--as though the messianic issue were already before the court. After his silence, Jesus is strangely willing to answer a question which until this point in the story has been a closely guarded secret.

The events following the trial are equally strange:

1) Jesus is tried by a Jewish court and convicted of blasphemy according to Jewish law. It is not clear precisely how the charge relates to Jesus' statement, but it would seem that Jesus is convicted on the basis of his acceptance of the messianic designations ("the Christ, the Son of the Blessed").[19]

2) Immediately after the sentence is passed, Jesus is subjected to mockery. He is mocked, however, not as King, as one might expect, and as he is in 15:16-20. He is mocked as prophet, which seems to have little to do with the charge against him.

3) The scene immediately shifts to the courtyard, where the drama of Peter's denial is enacted. Nothing is said about Peter's escape or his repentance.

4) The scene abruptly shifts to the following morning and to a second meeting of the court. No mention is made of the nocturnal session. Nothing is said about the charge of blasphemy. No attempt is made to carry out the sentence of the court--which, as prescribed by law, was stoning. No attempt is made to have the sentence ratified by Pilate (which makes the question of the legal competency somewhat irrelevant in the case of Mark). Jesus is simply handed over to Pilate, presumably to be tried solely under his jurisdiction. No explanation for this strange procedure is offered, as in Jn 18:31.

5) Pilate questions and eventually executes Jesus as "King of the Jews," but the reader is never told how he received the information that Jesus had made such a claim.

As we observed in the first chapter, there have been several explanations offered for such features characteristic of Mark's narrative. One explanation for the lack of coherence is

----

[19] See below, 95-106 on the relationship of the charge to 14:61-62.

that Mark is using originally separate traditions in the composition of the trial narrative or that he has at least inserted
originally separate traditions into a previously exisitng
framework, and that he has not reworked his material sufficiently to eliminate the resulting inconsistencies. This is
the kind of explanation offered by many who have been trained in
form criticism.[20] An explanation for the failure of the author
to make a smooth transition from the Jewish to the Roman trial
or to indicate why Jesus was not stoned is that Mark knew something about Roman provincial law and the status of indigenous
courts within the system.[21] But neither proposal is a sufficient explanation. If Mark did know something about the Roman
legal system, he betrays no interest in the matter. He takes
pains to describe the confrontation with the Jewish authorities
as a trial with specific charges and issuing in a specific
verdict, but there is not even the minimal attempt to explain
the transfer of Jesus to Pilate of the sort found in the Fourth
Gospel (Jn 18:31). And even if Mark has inserted new material
into a story handed down to him, an interpreter must at least
ask if there are reasons the story reads as it does, if the
story in its present form reflects the intention of the
author.

A more adequate explanation for the peculiarities of the
trial account is that Mark is simply not interested in presenting
a complete, coherent account of the historical event. The lack
of detail suggests that the author's concern is to be located
at another level of the story. Jesus is tried and executed
under Roman law because, as Mark knew, this is what actually
happened.[22] If the verdict of the Jewish court is not the direct cause of Jesus' death, however, we must look elsewhere for
its function in the story.

According to 8:31, what is important about the Jewish
trial is that Jesus is "rejected" by the religious leaders of the
people. That rejection, viewed as the fulfillment of Scripture
(Ps 118:22), is of obvious importance to the author. It is
accorded the formal setting of a trial, at which specific charges

---

[20]See chapter 1, 20-29.

[21]See the work by Sherwin-White cited in Chapter 1, note
69.

[22]According to 10:33, it is the "Gentiles" who will put
him to death.

are made and as a result of which a specific verdict is reached.
The lack of causal relationship between the trial and the rest
of the passion story suggests that the historical events as
such are not the real focal point in the story. The author
seems more concerned to provide the reader with a more profound
understanding of this "rejection." Numerous commentators have
argued that the purpose of the trial is to emphasize the role
played by the Jewish leaders in Jesus' death.[23] The anti-Jewish
bias is certainly present, though it is interesting to note that
the trial has no causal relationship to the trial before Pilate.
In this regard, the chief priests' stirring up of the crowd in
15:11 is more obviously a cause of Jesus' death. The trial itself leads nowhere in the story. The charge of blasphemy does
not result in stoning; nothing is even said about making formal
charges to Pilate based on what was decided at the trial. But
the amount of space devoted to the trial before the Sanhedrin
suggests that what is happening here is highly significant.
One way to approach the problem of interpretation is to view
the trial as the scene of the "rejection" of Jesus and to explore the interior dimensions of the story for clues to the
author's point of view.

One clue to the deeper meaning of the scene can be seen
in Mark's bracketing of the account of the trial with the story
of Peter's denial. In 14:54, Mark takes pains to note that
while the trial is going on, Peter is standing just outside in
the courtyard. Immediately after the account of Jesus' mal-
treatment in 14:65, the scene shifts to the courtyard, where
Peter is apparently still waiting. The technique is rather
obvious. Mark wants to juxtapose the two scenes for the purpose
of comparison and contrast. The meaning of the trial is at
least to some degree to be seen in the contrast: When confronted
by his enemies, Jesus stands firm and makes a good confession
(or at least accepts a good confession), even though it means
death. Peter, on the other hand, collapses in the face of
pressure and denies Jesus. It is not accidental that while
Jesus is making his confession before the high priest, Peter
is denying him before a female servant of the high priest!

---

[23]Burkill, "The Trial of Jesus," 3; E. Lohse, History of
the Suffering and Death of Jesus Christ (tr. M. O. Dietrich;
Philadelphia: Fortress Press, 1967), 88; Klostermann, Mark,
155; Haenchen, Der Weg Jesu, 515; Lietzmann, "Der Prozess
Jezu," 321.

The contrasting scenes have obvious parenetic value. Taylor, for example, believes that the story of Peter's denial in this context is intended to "warn the primitive community of the perils of apostasy."[24] Dibelius takes more account of the contrast when he insists that Peter's denial is intended to provide a foil for Jesus' self-revelation.[25] He may also be right when he insists that the story of Peter's denial was important at all only because of a special Easter appearance granted to him:

> The Church's interest in Peter's fall could be explained if the event were felt in some way to be the pre-supposition of the Easter appearances. The oldest record of the Passion story may have borne this construction since it puts the promise of the appearances (Mk 14:28) alongside the prophecy of the denial (Mk 14:29-31).[26]

If, as seems likely, Mark was aware of Peter's importance in the early church and of traditions about a special appearance of the risen Lord to him (Mk 16:7), the account of Peter's denial may be another illustration that Jesus "came not to call the righteous, but sinners" (Mk 2:17).

But there is at least one important element in the contrast between the denial and the trial that has not yet been mentioned. One of the interesting details in Mark's account is the mention of the two cock crows (14:68[27] and 14:72). The narrative of the denial corresponds exactly to the prophecy of Jesus in 14:30 ("Truly, I say to you, this very night, before the cock crows twice, you will deny me three times."). Lohmeyer has suggested that the saying of Jesus in 14:30 dominates the account of the denial.[28] That is particularly interesting, however, in light of what immediately precedes. In 14:65, Jesus is mocked, and within the verse is included prophetic imagery. If Jesus is mocked as prophet at the conclusion of his trial, the contrast with 14:66-72 is striking: Jesus' prediction about Peter's denial in 14:30 is fulfilled to the letter. The contrast can hardly be accidental, which suggests that the prophetic motif may be of some importance for Mark. Our next question should

---

[24]Taylor, Mark, 572.

[25]Dibelius, From Tradition to Gospel, 214; cf. 193.

[26]Ibid., 215.

[27]For a discussion of the textual difficulties, see Taylor, Mark, 574.

[28]Lohmeyer, Mark, 333.

thus be what place this motif has in the account of the trial.

It is first necessary to examine the textual attestation of 14:65 with some care. The important variants and the manuscript evidence are given below.[29] Perhaps the most important variant is the reading "Prophesy to us, Christ, who is it that struck you?" (Προφήτευσον ἡμῖν Χριστὲ τίς ἐστιν ὁ παίσας σε;) The variant introduces the messianic theme and alters the focus of the mockery. Although the major uncials all read simply "Prophesy!", there is a surprisingly wide geographical distribution of manuscripts with the variant reading. The additional phrase is attested in three main streams of tradition:[30]

    a) Later Egyptian
    b) African (Augustine in "The Agreements of the
       Evangelists")
    c) Caesarean

The reading of the major uncials is probably to be preferred, but, as Streeter suggests, the wide distribution of manuscripts with the variant reading suggests that this passage invited assimilation. This is important for evaluating another peculiar feature in the verse: the phrase "cover his face" (περικαλύπτειν αὐτοῦ τὸ πρόσωπον). The reading is strangely absent from Matthew, which is difficult to explain since the phrase "who is it that struck you" (Matt 26:68) makes sense only if Jesus has been blindfolded. And in Mark, the point of the blindfolding is not clear if, as the best textual witnesses seem to suggest, Jesus is not asked to identify those who are mocking him.

Streeter believes that there has been assimilation to the text of Luke in both Matthew and Mark--in the case of Mark, even in the major Egyptian uncials. He insists that the reading "cover his face" was absent from the earliest text of the Gospel. This is supported not only by the absence of the phrase from Matthew but by the relationship between the statement about blindfolding and the question about the identity of the striker:

> These two stand or fall together. In Luke, they are both original; and from Luke the first has got into the Alexandrian (but not into the earliest Antiochene and Western)

---

[29]Most of the following discussion is taken from B. H. Streeter, <u>The Four Gospels</u> (London: Macmillan, 1964), 325-327. See Appendix, 75, for manuscript evidence.

[30]<u>Ibid.</u>, 326.

texts of Mark; the second has got into all the texts of Matthew.[31]

Streeter's arguments may not be absolutely convincing, but there does seem to be a clear difference between the scene in Mark and the scene in Luke. The prophetic gift in Luke seems to focus simply on the exercise of second sight. Catchpole has even suggested that the scene in Luke refers to a well-known test for the Messiah:

> In Lk the narrative shows the same test being applied to Jesus as was used in the case of Bar Kochba, bSanh 93b, whereby a messianic candidate was required to show his ability to work without the aid of sight or hearing and so to satisfy Isa 11:3.[32]

It is an interesting suggestion, but the text from the Talmud is not as clear as Catchpole seems to assume. According to the text, the Rabbis demanded that Bar Kochba (Bar Koziba) judge by smell:

> Bar Koziba reigned two and a half years and then said to the Rabbis "I am the Messiah." They answered, "Of Messiah it is written that he smells and judges: Let us see whether he [Bar Koziba] can do so." When they saw that he was unable to judge by the scent, the slew him.[33]

Read in light of the talmudic text, the mockery of Jesus in Lk 22:64 does not appear to be an obvious parallel. If Luke were describing a messianic test, it is surprising that the title "Christ," present in variants in Mark, is absent. But even if Catchpole were correct that Luke describes a well-known test for messianic claimants, the absence of such imagery from Mark is all the more striking. Jesus has just been found guilty of blasphemy, presumably for his willingness to accept the titles "the Christ, the Son of the Blessed." Yet he is mocked as prophet. Several scholars have proposed that the scene in 14:65 is a conscious allusion to Isa 50:6 (LXX).[34] Some have suggested that, as a reference to Isaiah, the scene is part of a consistent attempt to characterize Jesus as the suffering servant.[35]

---

[31]Ibid., 326-327.

[32]Catchpole, The Trial of Jesus, 175-176.

[33]Translation from The Babylonian Talmud (ed. I Epstein; London: Soncino Press, 1935).

[34]Lohmeyer, Mark, 330; Klostermann, Mark, 156-157; Bultmann, History, 281; Catchpole, The Trial of Jesus, 175-176; Winter, On The Trial of Jesus, 104-106.

[35]Lohmeyer, Mark, 330; Dibelius, From Tradition to Gospel, 187.

Not even Jeremias lists Isa 50 as[36] one of the servant passages,
however, and even if an allusion to Isa 50:6 is intended, the
focal point in the verse is still the verb "prophesy."

If Mark intends the reader to appreciate the contrast between the fulfillment of Jesus' prediction in 14:30 in Peter's
denial and the mockery in 14:65, and if the term "prophesy" does
not mean simply "exercise the gift of second sight" as in Luke,
we should next ask if there is something within the trial that
the author intends to be viewed as a prophecy. It seems quite
probable that the author has emphasized the prophetic motif for
a purpose, and the purpose seems to point back to the trial
itself.

Perhaps the most clearly prophetic statement in the trial
is Jesus' statement about the Son of Man in 14:62: "and you
will see the Son of man sitting at the right hand of Power, and
coming with the clouds of heaven." We will examine the saying
in detail in the next chapter, but even without careful study it
is possible to appreciate the prophetic character of the statement. At the climax of the trial, Jesus accepts the titles "the
Christ, the Son of the Blessed" and makes a rather spectacular
prediction. He is immediately condemned to death and mocked--as
a prophet. The author apparently wants to call the reader's
attention to the prediction. He does so by the use of the
prophetic motif and irony. Jesus makes a prediction (14:62)
that his opponents consider absurd. He is subsequently mocked
as prophet (14:65). But at that very moment, one of his predictions (14:30) is being fulfilled to the letter (14:66-72). The
reader is expected to appreciate the irony apparent at the
deeper level of the story, but he is also expected to make the
appropriate inference about Jesus' prophetic statement in 14:62:
despite appearances and despite the disbelief of Jesus' opponents,
his prophecy will be (has been?) fulfilled.[37]

This suggests that one important function of the mockery
in 14:65 and the report of Peter's denial is to focus attention
on the second of the charges at the trial and, in particular, on
Jesus' statement in 14:62. But it is also possible that the
first of the charges at the trial is to be viewed as prophetic.
Several commentators have suggested that the mockery of Jesus as

[36]Jeremias, παῖς θεοῦ, TDNT 5, 677-717.

[37]See below, 84-95 on 14:62.

72

a prophet does in fact point to the statement about the temple.[38]
The statement attributed to Jesus is not found in Mark's Gospel
outside the trial, and it is reported as false witness. But
the reference to the destruction of the temple "made with hands"
and to the building "in three days" of another temple "not made
with hands" certainly has all the characteristics of a carefully formulated prophetic statement. And if the propehtic
mockery in 14:65 does refer to the first of the two charges at
the trial, the use of irony would suggest that the author intends his "prophecy" to be viewed as true as well. To Jesus'
opponents, the idea that he will destroy the temple and build
another in three days is as absurd as the notion that he will
appear in spectacular fashion on the clouds of heaven. He is
condemned for his blasphemous claim,[39] but he is mocked as
prophet for his predictions. Yet at the very moment he is
being ridiculed as prophet, his prediction about Peter is being
fulfilled to the letter. The mockery in 14:65 would thus serve
to highlight both of the charges at the trial.

There is one further consideraton that makes a positive
view of the temple charge even more probable. It is the relationship between the trial and the rest of the passion story.
We have already observed that both of the charges in the trial
are repeated in the mockery at the foot of the cross (15:29-
32).[40] The two charges are treated in the same way, and at
least with the second of the taunts, the ironic significance is
clear. But the parallelism is repeated in 15:38-39. Mark reports two events which occur at the moment of Jesus' death: the
tearing of the temple veil (15:38) and the confession of the cen-
turian (15:39: "Truly, this man was a [the] son [Son] of God.")
The parallelism at the trial, at the mockery, and in the events
Mark reports at the moment of Jesus' death cannot be accidental.
And even without any careful examination of the meaning of the
tearing of the veil, it seems clear that the statement in the
trial has some prophetic significance, or, to put it another
way, the temple charge must be viewed as true in some sense.

---

[38]E. Best, The Temptation and the Passion (Cambridge:
Cambridge University Press, 1965), 97; Taylor, Mark, 570-571;
Klostermann, Mark, 156-157.

[39]See below, 95-104 on blasphemy.

[40]See chapter 2, 47-48, on mockery in 15:29-32.

Summary

A preliminary study of the trial within the context of
the passion story indicates first that Mark seems concerned to
portray Jesus' trial before the Sanhedrin as a miscarriage of
justice. But the lack of coherence and the omission of several
important details necessary to understand the historical con-
tinuity of the events also suggests that Mark is less interested
in the surface details of the story than with its deeper significance. The two-level narrative style is an important feature
of the trial narrative. The trial is, for Mark, the scene of
Jesus' "rejection" foretold in Scripture (Ps 118:22). The function of the trial is to specify the basis for Jesus' rejection
and, at a deeper level, to indicate the basis for his vindication by God (also foretold in Ps 118:22) at his resurrection
"after three days."

The interplay between the mockery in 14:65 and Peter's
denial (14:66-72) emphasizes Jesus' prophetic role and the irony
of the mockery: at the moment Jesus is being taunted by his
opponents, his prediction (14:30) is being fulfilled to the
letter. But the significance of the mockery of Jesus as prophet
cannot be found in 14:65 alone; the scene points back to the
account of the trial. According to Mark, Jesus makes prophetic
statements at the trial that his opponents view as absurd. The
most important of the statements is 14:62. But there are indications that 14:58, the temple charge, is to be understood in a
similar manner. The prophetic character of the charge, the
repetition of the two charges in the mockery at the foot of
the cross (15:29-32) and the report of the tearing of the veil
of the temple as one of the two climactic events to occur at the
moment of Jesus' death (15:58-59) may mean that Mark intends
both charges at the trial to be viewed as true in some sense.
Both are prophecies pointing to a fulfillment Mark's readers can
be expected to understand.

The function of the trial is to introduce the main themes
of the passion story. This is particularly true with regard to
the messianic theme, but it is possibly true with the temple
theme as well. The focal points in the account of the trial are
the two charges. The story is told to emphasize the irony of
the scene and the truth of the charges that only the Christian
reader can be expected to appreciate. If this is true, detailed
study of the two charges is necessary. The most important

question must certainly be why the temple charge is characterized as false testimony if Mark views the charge as true. The
temple charge will be examined in detail in Part II. First,
we shall look at the second of the charges, the obvious climax
of the trial.

Appendix

Mk 14:65	Matt 26:67-68	Lk 22:64
Καὶ ἤρξαντό τινες	Τότε ἐνέπτυσαν	καὶ περι-
ἐμπτύειν αὐτῷ [καὶ	εἰς τὸ πρόσωπον	καλύψαντες
περικαλύπτειν αὐτοῦ	αὐτοῦ καὶ	αὐτὸν
τὸ πρόσωπον] καὶ	ἐκολάφισαν αὐτόν,	ἐπηρώτων
κολαφίζειν αὐτὸν	οἱ δὲ ἐράπισαν	
καὶ λέγειν αὐτῷ,	λέγοντες	λέγοντες
Προφήτευσον [ἡμῖν,	Προφήτευσον ἡμῖν,	Προφήτευσον,
Χριστέ, τίς ἐστιν	Χριστέ, τίς ἐστιν	τίς ἐστιν
ὁ παίσας σε;]	ὁ παίσας σε;	ὁ παίσας σε;

καὶ περικαλύπτειν κτλ: omit in Dafsy[S]

ἡμῖν, Χριστέ, τίς κτλ: W X (Δ ὁ πέμψας σε) Θ 33, 579, 700
    cop[sa] & bo syr[h] arm eth geo Diatessaron (Augustine)

CHAPTER 4

THE DECISIVE CHARGE: 14:61-62

Dibelius has termed 14:61-62 the first high point in
Mark's passion story.[1]   The verses may with equal justification
be viewed as one of the climaxes of the whole Gospel.   Throughout the story, Jesus' identity has been a closely guarded secret.
But here, for the first and only time in the story, Jesus strips
away the veil and openly reveals himself: he is "the Christ, the
Son of the Blessed," the "Son of Man" who will be seated at God's
right hand and will return with the clouds of heaven.   But even
his climactic revelation is characterized by the ambiguity that
runs through the story.   Jesus' opponents understand but they do
not understand.   They understand the claim that has been made,
but they do not hail Jesus as Messiah but rather condemn him to
death.   If the reading 'Ιησοῦ Χριστοῦ υἱοῦ θεοῦ in 1:1 is the
preferable reading,[2] the repetition of the two titles in 14:61
is all the more striking.

Verses so important within the structure of the Gospel
must be examined with some care.   This is particularly necessary
in the case of 14:61-62 because the verses pose several problems.
Within these two verses, three key christological titles are
used.   The precise relationship among the titles is still a
matter of dispute.   Further, there is some question about the
reading in 14:62a, whether "I am" or "You have said that I am"
has the best support in the manuscripts and in the parallel
verses in Matthew and Luke.   Finally, it is not clear how the
high priest's question and Jesus' response are related to the
charge of blasphemy in 14:63, i.e. what occasions the precise
legal charge.   Each of these problems will be examined in detail
in this chapter.

The first aspect of the verses to be examined is the expression "the Son of the Blessed [One]" (ὁ υἱος τοῦ εὐλογητοῦ).

---

[1]M. Dibelius, _From Tradition to Gospel_, 183.

[2]For a discussion of the evidence, see Taylor, _Mark_, 152.
The reading υἱοῦ θεοῦ has good textual support (B D L W etc),
and the importance of the title throughout the Gospel provides
strong internal evidence for the reading.

The expression presents two problems. First, the term "the Blessed One" as a circumlocution for the name of God is almost completely unattested in Jewish literature. Second, the title "Son of the Blessed" (Son of God) in the verse seems to be synonymous with "the Christ." But the title "Son of God" is rarely used as a messianic designation in extant Jewish literature, which has led several scholars to assert that the whole expression "the Christ, the Son of the Blessed" is thoroughly unjewish, Christianized terminology.[3] Our concern here will not be to determine the meaning of the verses within the context of the historical trial, assuming there was such a trial and such a question was asked. It is to determine what the verses mean in the present context. While it would be difficult to argue that the expression "the Christ, the Son of the Blessed" is purely Jewish terminology unaffected by Christian usage, it is at least important to examine with some care the possible connotations of "Son of God" in pre-Christian Jewish circles. The precise meaning of the term and its relationship to "the Christ" must be determined within the context of Mark, but it is important to know what possible range of meanings the term had. Such knowledge will have an important bearing on the decision whether the force of the high priest's question is messianic in the proper sense, Son of God being understood as a synonym for Messiah, or is more "Christian," Messiah being defined by Son of God and the emphasis being on the Christian notion of Jesus' divine Sonship.[4]

The expression "Son of the Blessed" is unique in the New Testament and in all extant Jewish literature. Even the use of "the Blessed One" as a paraphrase for the name of God is rarely encountered. Billerbeck lists only a few examples,[5] but even these few are not unquestionable parallels. Dalman argues that they are,[6] but the expression that appears in the Mishnah and the two Talmuds is translated by Danby, "Bless ye the Lord who is

---

[3]W. Wrede, Das Messiasgeheimnis in den Evangelien, 75; H. Lietzmann, "Der Prozess Jesu," 316; E. Haenchen, Der Weg Jesu, 514.
[4]J. Schreiber ("Die Christologie des Markusevangeliums," 164) argues that divine Sonship is the real issue at the trial.

[5]Bill II, 51. The passages are: Enoch 77:1; Mishnah Berakoth 7:3; jBerakoth 7:11c; bBerakoth 50a. The same expression occurs in the rabbinic texts: ברכו את י"י המבורך.

[6]G. Dalman, The Words of Jesus (tr. D. M. Kay; Edinburgh: T. and T. Clark, 1909), 200.

to be blessed."[7] The participle in this phrase does not function as a substitute for God's name in any case, but as an
adjective: it defines God as the one who is to be (or is)
blessed. It appears that the only use of the participle as a
paraphrase for the divine name is to be found in Enoch.

On the other hand, the Jewish character of the expression
is obvious. It reflects the well-known tendency to avoid direct
reference to the name of God, a tendency present also in the use
of τῆς δυνάμεως in the response of Jesus. Further, the use of
the participle εὐλογητός must be related to the liturgical use of
the term common in Jewish and Christian literature.[8] It must
also be related to the standard expression in rabbinic literature, "the Holy One, Blessed be He."[9] It is difficult to know
the precise character of this relationship, however, and to
determine the implications for interpreting the expression in
Mark. Although the Jewish character of the expression seems unquestionable, the absence of the expression "the Blessed One"
from almost all extant Jewish and Christian literature as a
paraphrase for the divine name, and the complete absence of the
expression "the Son of the Blessed" in the literature suggest
that the best explanation for the phrase in Mark is that it is
a pseudo-Jewish expression created by the author as appropriate
in the mouth of the high priest.[10]

The more difficult and important question has to do with
the relationship of "Son of the Blessed" to "the Christ." In
Mark, the terms seem to be synonymous. But there are many
scholars who have insisted that "Son of God" was never a designation for the Messiah in Jewish circles.[11] There are others

[7]H. Danby, Mishnah Berakoth 7:3. In the Soncino edition
of the Talmud, the term is translated "who is blessed."

[8]H. Beyer, εὐλογητός, TDNT 2, 759-65.

[9]It is interesting to note, however, that in a recent
monograph by S. Esh on the origin of the rabbinic expression
(הקב"ה "Der Heilige - sei er gepriesen: "Zur Geschichte einer
nach-biblisch-hebräischen Gottesbezeichung [Leiden: Brill,
1957]), the term "the Blessed One" is not even discussed.

[10]F. Hahn (The Titles of Jesus in Christology [tr. H.
Knight and G. Ogg; New York: World, 1969], 285) argues that the
usage indicates that the verse stems from early Palestinian
tradition. This seems unwarranted. It need only suggest that
the author is capable of imitating Jewish style.

[11]Haenchen, Der Weg Jesu, 512; Lietzmann, "Der Prozess
Jesu," 316; Schweizer, Mark, 324; Lohse, History, 83;

who argue from the usage in Mark that the title must have been
used of the Messiah prior to Christianity, although the evidence
to which they appeal is scanty.[12] The problem is a difficult
one, both because the evidence is scarce and because the sources
we have are obviously tendentious. The evidence is examined in
some detail in the excursus on Son of God appended to this
chapter. As suggested in the excursus, the use of the title in
the midrash on II Sam 7 in 4QFlorilegium probably tips the bal-
ance in favor of those who argue that the title could be used in
pre-Christian Jewish circles as a designation for the royal
Messiah. The obvious tendencies in the targums and in rabbinic
literature are not difficult to explain on the basis of anti-
Christian polemics or the tendency to avoid any violation of the
oneness of God by attributing divine qualities to any human figure.[13] The mere possibility that the title "Son of God" could be
used by Mark in the scriptural sense as a royal designation, however, does not prove that he has done so. This can only be
determined by a careful study of the Gospel itself.

We will approach the use of the title in 14:61 from two
perspectives: from its use within the Gospel as a whole and from
its use within the context of the passion story. Within the
Gospel, the title is of obvious significance. Norman Perrin is
representative of many scholars when he argues that the title
is the most important in Mark.[14] He cites two occurrences of
the title as particularly important within the structure of the
Gospel: the use of the title in 1:1 in the superscription of
the Gospel,[15] and in the "climactic christological statement of
the Centurion at Calvary."[16] It is important to determine, however, what connotations the title has in Mark. The use of the
title by the Roman Centurion, for example, tells us little about

Lightfoot, History and Interpretation, 142.

[12]Blinzler, The Trial of Jesus, 102; Benoit, The Passion
and Resurrection of Jesus Christ, 105-106; Taylor, Mark, 567
(though not certain); Hahn, Titles, 279-288; Catchpole, The
Trial of Jesus, 200 (just coming into use as a messianic
designation at Qumran).

[13]See excursus on Son of God, 108-114.

[14]N. Perrin, "Creative Use of Son of Man Traditions in
Mark," USQR (1968), 358.

[15]Perrin offers no arguments for accepting υἱοῦ θεοῦ.

[16]Ibid., 358.

what the title means. Perrin argues that the content of the
title is provided in statements about the Son of Man by the
author of Mark's Gospel.[17] But before accepting his arguments,
we should examine the use of the expression within the Gospel to
determine if the title has an important meaning of its own.

The title is intended first of all to define Jesus by his
unique relationship to God. The term "Son" appears twice in the
Gospel at key points in the story, at Jesus' baptism (1:11) and
at his transfiguration (9:7). In both passages, the term is
used by God himself. Mark is not as clear as Luke or John
about the precise character of the relationship, but the importance of this unique sonship is unquestionable.

It is also possible that the title Son of God is used in
the sense of "divine man." It is used twice in the context of
exorcisms ((3:11 and 5:7). The first occurrence is perhaps the
less decisive for interpretation, since the term is used within
a general summary statement and must be interpreted in light
of the author's use of "Son of God" in the rest of the Gospel.
Furthermore, the real focus in the verse (3:11) is the supernatural knowledge of the demons and not necessarily the relationship between "Son of God" and an exorcism. In 5:7, on the
other hand, the singular "Son of the Most High" may indicate
such connotations. It is part of the recognition motif familiar
to exorcisms,[18] and is strikingly similar to 1:24, where the
term ὁ ἅγιος τοῦ θεοῦ is used. Although, as Schweizer has
pointed out in his article in Kittel, Son of God is rarely used
as a designation for "divine man,"[19] the use of the term in the
apocryphal Joseph and Asenath as a designation for Joseph provides some evidence for such a usage in Mark.[20] This suggests
that the term may be used in Mark to mean "divine man."

But the use of the title in the rest of the Gospel suggests that the most important connotations are royal. The one
occurrence of the title Perrin fails to mention as decisive in
the Gospel is the occurrence in 14:61. We have already noted
the importance of the verse within the structure of the Gospel.
What is striking about the use of "the Christ" and "the Son of
the Blessed [God]" in 14:61 is the parallel to 1:1. Perrin
assumes that in 1:1, the reading "Christ, the Son of God" is to

---

[17]Ibid.   [18]Bultmann, History, 210.

[19]E. Schweizer, υἱός, TDNT 8, 376-377.

[20]This was suggested to me by Prof. Dahl.

be preferred. He fails to note the presence of the title
"Christ" in the verse, however. But in both of these key passages, Son of God is used with Christ. Nor is this usage
unique. There are two important Old Testament passages in which
God, as speaking subject, calls the king "Son." These two passages, of obvious christological importance for the early church,
are Psalm 2:7 and II Sam 7:14. The oracle in II Sam 7 was interpreted prior to Christianity as messianic, as referring to the
Messiah-King who was to come at the end of days.[21] The importance
of these oracles for the development of early Christology cannot
be overestimated. The use of "Son" in the account of Jesus'
baptism and of his transfiguration probably reflects an awareness of the "scriptural" (i.e. royal) connotations of the title.

Examination of the title within the passion story, however,
provides the decisive evidence. The relationship of the trial
to the subsequent account of the passion story indicates the force
of the expression "the Christ, the Son of the Blessed." The expression is rendered by Mark as "the King of the Jews" and "the
Christ, the King of Israel" in chapter 15. The parallelism of
the titles in 14:61 suggests that they point to the same figure.
If that figure is clearly depicted with royal imagery in what
follows, we can only assume that "Son of God" is being used by
Mark as a royal title. It may well be that the use of "Son of
God" with "the Christ" suggests that for Christians, Jesus is
something more than the messianic king promised in Scripture.
The title may well have other overtones that the Christian reader
is expected to catch. In other words, the verse may be viewed
as a Christian confession. But there is no justification for
arguing on the basis of 14:61 that the issue at Jesus' trial is
"divine Sonship."[22] The title "Son of the Blessed" in 14:61 is
clearly a part of the royal ideology. Jesus, according to Mark,
is asked by the high priest if he is the Messiah-King promised
in Scripture.

If the royal connotations of the title "Son of God" are
present in 1:1 and 14:61, however, we must examine the use of
the title in the Centurion's confession a bit more closely. The
phrase υἱὸς θεοῦ used in 15:39 is ambiguous. It may mean simply

_____

[21]See excursus on Son of God, 110-111, and the interpretation of 4QFlor,

[22]Schreiber, "Die Christologie des Markusevangeliums,"
164.

"a righteous man." Luke, in fact, renders the confession
ὁ ἄνθρωπος οὗτος δίκαιος ἦν (Lk 23:47). The title in Mk 15:39
is translated "a son of God" in the RSV. On the other hand, the
anarthrous use of both υἱός and θεός is attested in 1:1,[23] where
the title clearly implies the fullest christological sense.
Whether the grammatical peculiarities favor the full "the Son
of God" or "a son of God," the confession is clearly of fundamental significance in Mark. It is one of the two results of
Jesus' death Mark reports. The reader is certainly expected to
view the use of the title as a proper confession. If Mark intended the expression to be understood in the sense of "a son of
God" as well, the usage would best be viewed as a further expression of the messianic secret: the Centurion is impressed in
some strange way by the helpless man who has just died, but his
simple expression of amazement--unknown to him but obvious to
the Christian reader--becomes a true confession. Contrary to
all appearances and unknown to the bystanders, Jesus is the Son
of God.

The interesting question, however, is what the title
implies in 15:39. Perrin has pointed out the relationship between 15:39 and 1:1, but as we have already observed, there is
also a clear relationship between 1:1 and 14:61, if we may
assume that the reading υἱοῦ θεοῦ in 1:1 is the correct one.
And even if the title "Son of God" did not appear in the original
superscription of the Gospel, the messianic sense of the title is
clearly present in 14:61. The royal theme runs consistently
through the passion story. The title "the Son of the Blessed"
is used in 14:61 with full awareness of its messianic connotations. Can we assume that when, according to Mark, the Centurion
witnesses the death of the "King of the Jews," who has been
mocked by soldiers as "King of the Jews" and by his Jewish enemies as "the Christ, the King of Israel," his use of the title
υἱὸς θεοῦ is unrelated to the use in 14:61? At least from the
perspective of the author it seems highly probable that the relationship is intended, that the confession of the Centurion belongs with the royal motif as well. It would be most reasonable
to assume that if this is the case, the Centurion makes his
statement without understanding what he is saying. But the relationship of his confession to the trial and crucifixion
accounts in the present context is difficult to ignore.

---

[23]See above, note 2.

The next problem that requires some comment is the textual attestation for the reading Ἐγώ εἰμι in 14:62. The manuscript evidence for the variant Σὺ εἶπας ὅτι ἐγώ εἰμι is not unusually strong. The reading is supported in Θ, 13, 472, 543, 565, 700, 1071, geo, arm, Or.[24] What lends more weight to the variant, however, is the use of Συ εἶπας ὅτι in Mt 26:64 and Ὑμεῖς λέγετε in Lk 22:70. The readings in Matthew and Luke are easier to explain if the Markan text read Συ εἶπας ὅτι. A decision between the two readings is perhaps unnecessary, although most commentators assume that the Ἐγώ εἰμι has the greater claim to authenticity.[25] What can be demonstrated in Mark is that even if the reading Σὺ εἶπας ὅτι ἐγώ εἰμι is adopted, the author intends no reservation on Jesus' part regarding the appropriatness of the titles "the Christ, the Son of the Blessed." The confession of the Centurion indicates the appropriateness of the title "Son of God," and the mockery in 15:32 ("Let the Christ, the King of Israel, come down from the cross....") indicates that in the eyes of Jesus' opponents, he has accepted the messianic designations as an appropriate characterization of himself.

There is an interesting possibility for interpretation if the reading Εὺ εἶπας ὅτι be chosen, however. We have already noted the author's concern to point up the irony of Jesus' trial, mockery and death. Particularly in chapter 15, Jesus' opponents are made unwittingly confessors to his true identity. This is also the case at the trial. The real confession at the trial is made by the high priest. The important titles appear on his lips. The reading would simply make the irony more apparent, "You have said that I am." It is the high priest himself who testifies to the truth, quite against his intentions. And if, as we shall argue in the following chapters, Mark intends the first charge against Jesus to be viewed as true in some sense, the irony is consistent. Both at the trial and in the mockery in chapter 15, it is Jesus' opponents who consistently appear as witnesses to the truth about Jesus at a level of reality beyond their comprehension and contrary to their intentions. The Σὺ εἶπας ὅτι would not be intended to qualify the titles in the

---

[24] See the discussion of the evidence in Taylor, Mark, 568, and Streeter, The Four Gospels, 321-322.

[25] Taylor, Mark, 568; Lohmeyer, Mark, 328 (with some uncertainty); Klostermann, Mark, 157.

question of the high priest but to heighten the ironic character of the proceedings. Whichever reading is chosen, however, the positive attitude toward the titles in the question of the high priest is apparent.

This raises a further problem with regard to the Son of Man saying in 14:62:

and you will see the Son of man sitting at the right hand of power and coming with the clouds of heaven.

The first problem posed by the statement is its function. We have argued that the author has a positive attitude toward the titles "the Christ, the Son of the Blessed," and that this confession is viewed as primary by the author. There are several recent scholars, however, who have argued that it is the Son of Man saying that is primary in the account of the trial and that the saying is intended by the author as a qualification of the messianic designations. The following are the more important proposals:

1. E. Lohse[26] believes that Jesus' reply to the question of the high priest does constitute an acceptance of the titles, but that the Son of Man saying is intended to add important information to the "confession."

2. J. Schreiber[27] argues that the purpose of 14:61-62 is to explain the proper relationship among the three christological titles. Schreiber ignores the messianic overtones and focuses on the "Sonship" of Jesus. He believes that the purpose of the Son of Man saying is to indicate in what sense "Sonship" is an appropriate category to describe Jesus. Jesus' response, he argues, "den Titel [Son of God] im Sinne der hellenistischen Erhöhungs-christologie bejaht."

3. F. Hahn[28] offers the following interpretation:

But the answer [14:62] cannot be otherwise understood than as an "interpretation" of the Messiah question in terms of the eschatological expectation of the Son of man, conse-quently as an acceptance, in reference exclusively to the eschatological work of Jesus, of the dignity of the Messiah, the terrestrial setting being thereby replaced by the trans-cendent conception of apocalyptic. Jesus thus professes messiahship and divine sonship in that he speaks of his eschatological office, and of his appointment to the dignity and power of the one who, appearing in splendour, brings

---

[26]Lohse, _History_, 85.

[27]Schreiber, "Die Christologie des Markusevangeliums," 164.

[28]Hahan, _Titles_, 285.

salvation.

4. John Donahue[29] also views the Son of Man saying as intended to qualify the messianic designations. One quotation will make his position clear:

> He [Mark] has brought together all the major titles used of
> Jesus in his gospel in a context which shows he is about to
> give a definite meaning to them. The secret so long held
> throughout the gospel is about to be revealed, and the Son
> of Man title in 14:62 serves as it does in other parts of
> the gospel to give content and meaning to the other titles,
> all of which appear here.[30]

The views have been considered in some detail here because they seem to be gaining adherents. The scholars cited
approach the verse in Mark from different perspectives. Hahn
considers the whole question as part of his study of the history
of christological traditions. Schreiber is a redaction critic
who accepts the standard German view of Son of Man as a well-de-
fined mythical entity prior to Christianity. Donahue is also a
redaction critic, but he is a student of Norman Perrin, one of
the most vocal opponents of the traditional view of the Son of
Man. Perrin has done a great deal of work on Son of Man traditions,[31] and he insists that the figure in Christian literature
is not due to borrowing of a full-blown mythical conception from
Jewish Apocalyptic, but that the figure enters Christian tradition as a result of the study of Scripture. What is interesting
about this group of scholars is that they all share the same
view of the function of the Son of Man saying in Mk 14:62, although they study the verse from different perspectives: the
verse is intended to qualify the titles in 14:61 in some way,
whether to supplement, replace, modify or define. The question
of function, however, is a literary question that must be
studied from the literary perspective. Any interpretation of the
Son of Man saying, from whatever perspective, must be able to explain the function of the saying within the present context in
the Gospel of Mark.

Norman Perrin has made some specific proposals about the

---

[29]Donahue, Are You the Christ?, 95.

[30]Ibid., 548.

[31]In addition to his article cited above, note 15: "Mk
14:62: The End Product of a Christian Pesher Tradition?"; What
is Redaction Criticism?, 40-57.

[32]Perrin, "Creative Use of Son of Man Traditions in Mark,"
358.

function of Son of Man sayings in Mark. Although his interest
in the Son of Man material extends beyond the Gospel of Mark,
much of his attention has been focused on Mark's use of such
traditions. We have already noted one of his conclusions: Son
of Man material in Mark is used to provide content for the title
Son of God.[32] One of the most important occurrences of the Son
of Man is in 8:31. But Perrin also believes that this verse
betrays a technique important in the Gospel as a whole:

> It was the purpose of the evangelist to teach the Christians
> of his day a true Christology in place of the false Christo-
> logy that he felt they were in danger of accepting. The
> method he chooses is that of a most carefully constructed
> narrative in which the false Christology is put on the lips
> of the disciples and the true Christology on the lips of
> Jesus.[33]

Perrin himself has not devoted much attention to the use
of Son of Man in 14:62 as reflective of the concerns of Mark.
In his article on the verse,[34] he argues that the use of the
term here is traditional. It is thus not as clear an indication
of the author's creative work with Son of Man as 2:10-10:45.[35]
From Perrin's view of Mark's christological corrective and his
view of the author's technique of presenting proper Christology,
focused particularly on 8:29-31 and Mark's use of Son of Man, it
is not difficult to understand how one of his students could
extend the pattern to 14:61-62. As we noted above, Fr. Donahue
argues that the Son of Man saying in 14:62 provides a kind of
christological corrective for the title used in the high
priest's question.[36] To determine how appropriate a view of
Mark's use of Son of Man this is, however, we must examine with
some care the relevant occurrences of the title in the Gospel.
There are in fact three instances in the Gospel where the terms
"Christ" and "Son of Man" are paired: 8:29-31, 13:21-27, and
14:61-62. It would be interesting to determine if there is any
common pattern of relationship discernable in these three uses
of Son of Man traditions.

---

[32]Perrin, "Creative Use of Son of Man Traditions in
Mark," 358.

[33]Ibid., 357. See also What is Redaction Criticism?, 56.

[34]See note 33.

[35]See "Creative Use," 360-364. He does, however, include
14:61 as one of the places where the "correct" christological
statement occurs using "Son of Man" (Ibid., 358).

[36]Donahue, Are You the Christ?, 177-180.

88

The use of Son of Man in 8:31 is primary for those who argue that the use of the title in 14:62 signals some dissatisfaction with the titles used by the high priest. In 8:29-31, the titles Christ and Son of Man are juxtaposed, and the Son of Man saying of Jesus is clearly intended as a qualification of Peter's confession. The passage is central for Perrin.[37] It is the origin of the notion that Mark places false Christology on the lips of the disciples and the true Christology on Jesus' lips, and it provides support for Perrin's insistence that Mark presents true Christology by using the term Son of Man.[38] The verses are obviously of great importance within the structure of the Gospel. Here for the first time Jesus predicts his suffering. But this is also the first time in the story that the title "Messiah" is used of Jesus (with the possible exception of 1:34). There is something deficient in Peter's confession, but the term "Christ" is not purely negative. It does appear in the superscription of the Gospel. And Perrin himself suggests that the term does reflect "the fundamental confession of early Christianity."[39] It is important that we understand what it is about Peter's confession that, according to Mark, is deficient, that we understand how the confession of Jesus as Christ and the Son of Man saying are related.

Again we may begin with Perrin's suggestions. Following T. Weeden,[40] Perrin argues that Peter's confession inaugurates an important new stage in the development of Mark's story. Until now, the disciples' response to Jesus has been characterized by a lack of understanding.[41] Now the lack of understanding changes to misconception:

Whereas before they had not been able to recognize Jesus as the Messiah, now they recognize him as Messiah but misunderstand the nature of that messiahship.[42]

But according to Perrin, Peter's confession, followed by his refusal to accept suffering as part of Jesus' ministry, suggests that Peter views Jesus as "divine man."

---

[37]What is Redaction Criticism?, 40-57.

[38]"Creative Use," 358.

[39]What is Redaction Criticism?, 41.

[40]T. Weeden, "The Heresy that Necessitated Mark's Gospel," 146.

[41]What is Redaction Criticism?, 54.   [42]Ibid., 54-55.

Peter confesses Jesus as a "divine man." In fact, if 1:
1-8:29 were the only extant section of the Gospel, one
would be forced to believe that from the Markan perspective
the only authentic understanding of Jesus was as a "divine
man-Messiah."[43]

The function of the Son of Man saying, according to Perrin,
is to correct this false Christology. The complex process by
which the title Son of Man has become attached to predictions of
suffering is discussed by Perrin in his articles.[44] What is
important here is his conclusion:

> The purpose of the schematization of the disciples' mis-
> understanding of Jesus in Mark's Gospel is to press for an
> acceptance of a suffering servant Christology in the church
> for which Mark is writing.[45]

There are a number of questions that need to be asked.
The first has to do with Perrin's suggestion about a "divine-man
Messiah." He suggests that Peter's confession reflects the impression (false) created by the miracle stories in the early
chapters of the Gospel.[46] Some time ago Albert Schweitzer argued that Jesus' miracles would have convinced no one that he
was the expected Messiah. The more appropriate response is
suggested by Mark himself in 6:14-15 and 8:28: Jesus is John the
Baptist (returned from the dead), Elijah, or one of the
prophets.[47] If the miracle stories are intended to describe
Jesus as the "divine man," it is far easier to understand the
characterization of him as a prophet, perhaps modeled after
Elijah or even Moses.[48] What is striking about Peter's confession is that the title "Christ" appears at all. According to
Mark, it has occurred only to the disciples that Jesus is the
Messiah. By viewing Peter's confession as a culmination of the
"divine man" motif present in the miracle stories, Perrin fails
to observe the contrast in 8:28-29 between the views of out-
siders and the view of Jesus' disciples as expressed by Peter.
It is the prophetic figures in 8:28 that seem to reflect the
view of Jesus as divine man, as wonder worker. The clear contrast between Peter's confession and the views of others suggests that there is also a contrast present between the

[43]Ibid., 55.   [44]"Creative Use," 361-362.

[45]What is Redaction Criticism?, 56.   [46]Ibid., 55.

[47]On this, see P. Achtemeier, "The Origin and Function
of the Pre-Markan Miracle Catanae," JBL 91 (1972), 198-221, esp.
202-205 and the literature cited.

[48]Ibid., esp. 202-205.

prophetic and the messianic imagery. There is a sense in which Peter's confession represents a more profound estimate of Jesus.

But there is also a sense in which Peter's confession is inappropriate. He understands but he does not understand. His refusal to accept Jesus' sufferings indicates that he has not yet understood what Jesus' ministry is all about, what Jesus has come to do. His misunderstanding does not necessarily mean that his confession is false, however. Perrin's contrast between false and true is oversimplified. Jesus' qualification of Peter's confession in his saying about suffering and his characterization of Peter as Satan does not necessarily suggest that the title Christ is false. It may simply imply that Peter does not yet understand the nature of Jesus' Messiahship. It is not necessary to create a new category of "divine man-Messhiah" to describe the contrast between Peter's conception of Messiahship and Jesus'. The tension can be explained simply by appeal to the contrast between popular messianic expectations and the image of Jesus as the crucified Messiah. Peter's confession does not itself indicate that the title "Christ" is decisive for Mark. But the presence of the term in 1:1 and in the passion story would suggest that the problem in 8:29-31 is not the messianic imagery as such but differing messianic conceptions. It is not necessary to contrast the image of the Messiah with that of the suffering servant, as Perrin does.[49] Apart from important objections that have been raised regarding the image of the suffering servant in the Gospels,[50] there is nothing in the passion prediction that demands the introduction of the image of the servant. The qualification of Peter's confession by appeal to the sufferings to come may simply point up the contrast between the Messiah of popular expectation and the suffering Messiah, Jesus.

This raises the further question about the function of Son of Man in 8:31. There is little question that the Son of Man saying is intended as a qualification or as a redefinition of the title "Christ" as used in Peter's confession. But the point of the first of the passion predictions would be just as clear if nothing more were known about the title "Son of Man" than that it was an enigmatic self-designation of Jesus. The content of the saying, not the title, is decisive. Jesus is the

---

[49] What is Redaction Criticism?, 56.

[50] See esp. M. Hooker, Jesus and the Servant (London: S.P.C.K., 1959).

one who will be rejected and will die--and who will rise after
three days. Whether it is important to the author that Jesus
will suffer and die as Messiah or Son of Man will become clear
only as the story develops. On the basis of our study of 8:29-
31, we cannot infer that there is any contrast between a Son of
Man conception and a messianic conception, nor between a suffering servant conception and a messianic conception. Peter's
inability to accept Jesus' suffering indicates that his confession was inadequate. How Mark views the title "Christ" can be
determined only from the rest of the Gospel.

There is another use of Son of Man that provides some
interesting possibilities of comparison with the verse 14:62.
The passage is 13:26. To appreciate its relevance, it is necessary to quote the preceding verse as well:

> And then if any one says to you, "Look, here is the Christ!"
> or "Look, there he is!" do not believe it. False Christs
> and false prophets will arise and show signs and wonders
> [σημεῖα καὶ τέρατα], to lead astray [πρὸς τὸ ἀποπλανᾶν], if
> possible, the elect. But take heed; I have told you all
> things beforehand.
> But in those days, after that tribulation, the sun will
> be darkened, and the moon will not give its light, and the
> stars will be falling from heaven, and the powers in the
> heavens will be shaken. And then they will see the Son of
> man coming in clouds with great power and glory. And then
> he will send out the angels, and gather his elect from the
> four winds, from the ends of the earth to the ends of
> heaven. (13:21-27)

The function of chapter 13 in Mark is to serve as an exhortation to watchfulness. The disciples (and the readers of
the Gospel) are warned of the difficult times ahead. In this
section they are warned about the "false Christs" and "false
prophets" who will arise. The false prophet imagery is familiar
from other sources, both from Jewish tradition and from the
Fourth Gospel.[51] Both features characteristic of the tradition
are present.[52] What is unusual is the addition of "false
Christs." The imagery does not fit well with the imagery of the
false prophet, and it has even been suggested that the statements about Christs have been added by Christians to a Jewish
exemplar. We may simply note that the specific mention of false
Christs is appropriate in chapter 13 in its present setting.
The chapter is followed by the account of the death of the true

---

[51]Wayne A. Meeks, The Prophet-King, 47-57.

[52]The passage uses [ἀπο]πλανᾶν and σημεῖα καὶ τέρατα
from Deut 13:2-6; see Meeks, Prophet-King, 48-50.

"Christ, the Son of the Blessed," "The King of the Jews," "the Christ, the King of Israel." What is particularly interesting is that in this chapter, there is a juxtaposition of the two titles "Christ" and "Son of Man."

Christians are warned to beware of false Christs (and false prophets). They are given encouragement by the prediction that after the tribulation, the Son of Man will return with power and will gather together all his elect. Those who have remained watchful will be rewarded and their faith will be vindicated. It is clear from the emphasis in the passage that the title "Christ" is primary. The contrast is not between the Son of Man who will return in the clouds and false Christs, but between false Christs and the true Christ. The Son of Man saying does not provide new information about Jesus' identity; its function is to point the reader to the final, public vindication of Jesus and of the faith of those who confess him to be the true Christ. The emphasis in the saying is on "they will see." The Son of Man saying points to the final vindication of the "gospel of Jesus Christ, the Son of God."

We may now focus our attention on the use of Son of Man in 14:62. Norman Perrin has written an important article on this verse,[53] in which he argues that the verse represents the end product of a long exegetical tradition. It is unnecessary to treat his arguments in detail here. What is important is his insistence that 14:62 is inherited by Mark from tradition and that he has done little to alter this traditional usage.[54] The verse is thus not of great importance for understanding the creative work of the evangelist. Perrin also views the passage in chapter 13 as traditional. The "apocalyptic Son of Man" traditions are derived from the exegetical tradition represented in 14:62, according to Perrin, but such developments occurred prior to the writing of Mark's Gospel and Mark does little to alter this tradition as well.[55] Perrin approaches the use of Son of Man in Mark from the study of the history of tradition, but this is not the only way the problem may be viewed. However little Mark may have altered the Son of Man traditions in 13:26 and 14:62, we must still ask what place they have in the present context of his story. And the presence of the Son of Man saying

---

[53] "Mk 14:62: The End Product of a Christian Pesher Tradition?"

[54] Ibid., 155; "Creative Use," 359.   [55] "Creative Use," 359.

in 14:62 cannot be unimportant for understanding Mark's concerns.

The relationship between the messianic titles in 14:61 and the use of the titles in chapter 15 suggests that the Son of Man saying is not intended as a serious qualification of the titles. The relationship between 14:61-62 is unlike that between 8:29 and 31. Jesus' Messiahship expressed in 14:61 is not being re-defined by a prediction of suffering. Here the titles "the Christ, the Son of the Blessed" introduce the basis for Jesus' condemnation, mockery, and death. It is possible that the Son of Man saying is intended to fill out the confession of the high priest, as Lohse suggests.[56] But the use of Son of Man in 13:26 provides a more likely view of the function of 14:62. The verse is not intended to provide more information about Jesus without which the confesssion of the high priest would be false. Its purpose is to point the reader to the vindication of Jesus that is to come.

As we have already observed, the theme of rejection/vin-dication dominates the account of the trial.[57] The royal motif that runs through the passion story, a theme introduced by the question of the high priest, suggests that it is as Messiah-King that Jesus is rejected--and that it is as Messiah-King he will be vindicated. The predictions of the passion in 8:31, 9:31 and 10:33, as well as the quotation of Ps 118:22 in 12:11 seem to view the resurrection as Jesus' vindication. Chapter 13 points to a final vindication at the close of the age, when the Son of Man returns. The verse at the trial would function equally well as a reference to the resurrection, the parousia, or both. The point of the saying is that "you will see!" It is directed to those who refuse to accept Christian claims about Jesus, or perhaps more accurately to Christians who make such claims in the face of opposition. As Lohmeyer has correctly seen, by the identification of Jesus as the returning Son of Man

> wird dann der Widerspruch aufgehoben, der zwischen der Erscheinung des Gefangenen und Seiner Aussage besteht.[58]

The saying is not intended to replace, redefine, or quali-fy the titles "the Christ, the Son of the Blessed." It is in-tended to point to the vindication of Jesus the reader knows has already taken place or is soon to occur. The prophetic character

---

[56]Lohse, History, 85.   [57]See chapter 2, 53-55.

[58]Lohmeyer, Mark, 329.

of the statement is confirmed by the mockery of Jesus as prophet in 14:65.[59]

Some comment should be made on the peculiar imagery in 14:62. The difficulty is that the verse seems to contain two distinct images, two separate scriptural allusions that do not fit together coherently. Imagery is combined that is separated elsewhere in the New Testament, most notably the picture of enthronement from Ps 110:1 and the picture of the return of the Son of Man from Dan 7:13 (e.g. Mk 13:26). V. Taylor represents a tradition in British scholarship when he suggests that the image of the Son of Man on the clouds from Dan 7 was not intended to imply a coming _from_ God to earth but a coming _to_ God from earth.[60] But even if the original image in Daniel 7 was intended to describe a coming to God, and even if in early Christian use of this verse the concern was to describe Jesus' coming to the Father (= resurrection), it is most unlikely that in its present context the reference to Dan 7:13 adds nothing to the imagery from Ps 110.[61] The image of Jesus on the clouds seems clearly to refer to an event subsequent to his enthronement/resurrection.

Norman Perrin and Barnabas Lindars have approached the verse from a different perspective, locating the traditions contained in 14:62 in early Christian apologetic use of the Old Testament.[62] Perrin in particular has attempted to write a history of the development of the verse in early Christian apologetic tradition. The strength of his argument is that he can account for the presence of every word in the verse; its weakness is that the development of the tradition is rather complex. It is not absolutely clear that it is necessary to assume that the word ὄψεσθε comes from Zech 12:10 and that the verse in 14:62 is thus bound up with traditions like those in Rev 1:7 and Matt 24:30. What is important is that the traditions to which Lindars and Perrin point all focus on Jesus'

---

[59] See chapter 3, 71-72 on the mockery of Jesus as prophet.

[60] Taylor, 569. T. F. Glasson, _The Second Advent_ (London, 1945); J. A. T. Robinson, _Jesus and His Coming_ (Nashville: Abingdon, 1958).

[61] Contrary to Taylor, _Mark_, 569. Lindars, _New Testament Apologetic_, 48-49.

[62] Perrin, "Mk 14:62: The End Product..."; B. Lindars, _New Testament Apologetic_, esp. 48-49.

death and resurrection. By appealing to Ps 110:1 and Dan 7:13, Christian exegetes were concerned to demonstrate that Jesus' death and resurrection took place "according to Scripture," that is, according to the will of God.

Whatever the precise history of the verse, it seems most probable that in the present context it is intended to describe two separate scenes: the first, Jesus' enthronement at God's right hand, as a traditional representation of the resurrection. This would fit well with the references to the resurrection in the three passion predictions and in 12:11. The second scene, Jesus' return with the clouds, would represent the view of Jesus' return present in Mk 13:26. Jesus' resurrection would represent for Mark and his readers the provisional vindication of Jesus, whereas Jesus' return with the clouds would represent a final, public vindication expected in the near future. But whatever the precise meaning of the verse, its function is clear. Using scriptural imagery, it points the reader to the vindication of Jesus as "the Christ, the Son of the Blessed." It is not· accidental that this promise is made with scriptural imagery. It again reflects Mark's interest in the internal dimension of his narrative. It is only at this level of the story, at which the events are viewed as occurring in accordance with God's will, that the events can properly be "understood."

The final aspect of the verses that requires some comment is the relationship between the statements in 14:61-62 and the charge of blasphemy in 14:63-64.[63] According to Mark, immediately after Jesus responds to the high priest's question, there is a dramatic reaction among members of the court:

> And the high priest tore his mantle, and said, "Why do we still need witnesses? You have heard his blasphemy. What is your decision?" And they all condemned him as deserving death [κατέκριναν αὐτὸν ἔνοχον εἶναι θανάτου]. (Mk 14:63-64)

The first question is how the κατέκριναν αὐτὸν ἔνοχον εἶναι θανάτου should be interpreted. A few scholars have argued that the phrase does not imply that an actual legal verdict has been passed by the court. E. Bickermann, for example, has argued that the term "blasphemy" in 14:64 means simply outrage or gross impropriety, and that κατέκριναν αὐτὸν ἔνοχον εἶναι θανάτου means something like "pronounced hims worthy of death,"

---

[63]For a discussion of views expressed on this subject by commentators, see esp. Catchpole, The Trial of Jesus, 221-260.

representing nothing more than a preliminary charge.[64] Such a grand-jury like hearing would be appropriate from the perspective of Roman law.[65] Others have argued that the scene describes simply a grand-jury investigation at which the court agrees that Jesus should be tried for a capital offence but without passing a verdict at all.[66] It is an understatement to suggest that the problem is complex. It is difficult to determine to what extent Judea was a typical Roman province and to what extent indigenous Jewish courts were permitted to manage their own affairs. That means it is difficult to determine to what extent Jesus' so-called trial would have been determined by Jewish law. As Catchpole notes, in Jewish law there never seems to have been any provision for grand jury-like procedures.[67] The issue of the competency of the Sanhedrin has not yet been settled and perhaps cannot be. There is thus little likelihood of settling the interpretation of the phrase κατέκριναν αὐτὸν ἔνοχον εἶναι θανάτου on the historical level.

Within the context of the Gospel, however, the meaning of the phrase is much easier to determine. As we have observed, Mark provides interpretations of the trial in the passion predictions. In 10:33, the text reads:

And the Son of man will be delivered to the chief priests and the scribes, and they will condemn him to death [κατακρίνουσιν αὐτὸν θανάτῳ].

Here there can be little question that the author views the outcome of the trial as anything less than a legal verdict of the court that Jesus is guilty of a capital offence. At least for Mark, it appears that the outcome of the trial is an official condemnation by the Jewish high court.[68] If this is the case, however, it is necessary to determine if the charge,

---

[64] E. Bickermann, "Utilitas crucis. Observations sur les recits du proces de Jesus dans les Evangiles canoniques," RHR 112 (1935), 182-183.

[65] See Sherwin-White, Roman Society and Roman Law in the New Testament.

[66] Most notably R. W. Husband, C. G. Montefiori, J. Klausner, and others. Their views are all discussed by Catchpole, Trial, 254-60.

[67] Ibid., 255.

[68] Taylor, Mark, and Klostermann, Mark, on 10:33 and 14: 64; Winter, On the Trial of Jesus, 25-26; Bauer on κατακρίνομαι; see Blass-Debr 92,2, on the unusual use of the dative. Cf. Mt 20:18 for the more usual construction.

according to Mark, is blasphemy in the proper legal sense.

The decisive feature in the story is the tearing of the high priest's robe. We have already considered briefly the problem of the relationship between the mishnaic code and legal procedure in the first century.[69] However the question is to be answered in detail, the reference to the tearing of the robes in Mark must be related to the mention of this practice in Mishnah Sanhedrin 7:5. When, in the course of a trial of a man for blasphemy, the blasphemy is finally uttered,

> the judges stand up on their feet and rend their garments, and they may not mend them again.

It is true, as Catchpole observes,[70] that there are other occasions at which the tearing of one's robe is appropriate. There is a list of such occasions in Billerbeck.[71] What is obvious, however, is that the list mentions no other situation at which the tearing of a robe is appropriate in a legal context. The other instances are on such occasions as the news of the death of a father or mother. The reference in the Mishnah and the other rabbinic evidence makes it difficult to view the tearing of the robe in Mk 14:63 as anything but an appropriate response to blasphemy. The term must mean more in Mark than gross impropriety; it must represent a legal concept.

This makes the interpretation of the trial more difficult, for when viewed in light of the mishnaic definition of blasphemy, there is nothing in Jesus' response that could occasion such a charge. According to Mishnah Sanhedrin 7:5

> "The blasphemer" is not cuplable unless he pronounces the Name itself.

If this second-century conception of blasphemy is an appropriate reflection of early first-century legal standards, it is impossible that Jesus could legally have been condemned for this offence. In fact, his response to the question of the high priest contains clear indications of respectful avoidance of the name of God ("The right hand of power"). Most scholars insist, therefore, that the legal definition of blasphemy must have been considerably broader in the first century. The difficulty with such proposals is the lack of source material for reconstructing Jewish legal practice prior to A.D. 70. A summary of evidence

---

[69]See above, chapter 2, 59-62.

[70]Catchpole, Trial, 259.   [71]Bill I, 1007.

98

is provided by Catchpole.[72] Billerbeck also provides a list of
passages,[73] but the discussions still focus on the name of God.
The concern is to determine if blasphemy is to be restricted to
use of the ineffable Name, or if it is to be extended to other
names of God. R. Meier seems to have been an advocate of a
broader application, but his opinion was not that of the
majority.[74] Even if the broader application is accepted, however, Jesus' statement in no way constitutes misuse of the name
of God. The evidence cited by Billerbeck provides no decisive
support for those who want to argue that the concept meant
"violation of God's majesty" or "usurping the prerogatives of
God." Nevertheless, there seems to be general agreement among
most students of Jewish legal traditions that the definition of
blasphemy in the Mishnah is narrower than would have been the
case early in the first century:

> The formal exposition of the concept by later Rabbinic
> law, which finds fulfillment of the substance of
> blasphemy in such things as the clear enunciation of the
> name of God (Sanh 7:5), is not yet present in the time of
> Jesus.[75]

Even if the broadest definition of blasphemy be accepted,
however, the problem is far from solved. It is still unclear
precisely what in the question of the high priest or Jesus'
response would constitute a blasphemous statement or claim.
There have been a number of proposals, most of which have been
conveniently listed by Catchpole.[76] The following are some of
the more important:

1) Jesus' reply in 14:62 is such an unlikely candidate for
   the charge of blasphemy that one must assume the temple
   charge to have provided the real basis for the condemnation. The difficulties in the present text are to be
   explained by the editorial activity of Mark.[77] As we

---

[72]Catchpole, Trial, 259. The texts he discusses are
Tosephta Sanhedrin 1:2 and bSanhedrin 38b and 56 a.

[73]Bill I, 1007.   [74]Ibid., 1013-4.

[75]H. Beyer, βλασφημία, TDNT 1, 622. Beyer cites Dalman,
Words of Jesus, 258.

[76]Catchpole, Trial, 126-148 (with special attention to
Jewish scholars).

[77]Wellhausen, Kilpatrick. See chapter 1, 8-11 and
13-15.

have already noted, however, this proposal does not explain the present text. There can be no doubt that for Mark, the charge of blasphemy is related to Jesus' statement.

2) Jesus is accused of blasphemy because his reply, 'Εγώ εἰμι, represents a self-application of the ineffable Name.[78] The proposal must assume that the reading 'Εγώ εἰμι has more claim to authenticity than Σὺ εἶπας ὅτι ἐγώ εἰμι.[79] The usage would be quite unparalleled in Mark, where Jesus is never identified with God. Stauffer's arguments must depend upon an interpretation of the usage in John being applied to the phrase in Mark.[80] It is also difficult to argue that Matthew and Luke have understood the term in Mark as the ineffable Name. In neither Matthew nor Luke is the charge of blasphemy in any way related to the use of the expression ἐγώ εἰμι. As O. Linton has pointed out, if the blasphemy were related to the ἐγώ εἰμι, the high priest would have responded immediately. In the present setting, the response follows the statement about the Son of Man.[81] The suggestions offered by Borgen[82] and Catchpole[83] for understanding the function of the expression in Mark are far more plausible than those of Stauffer. By the use of the expression 'Εγώ εἰμι, Jesus accepts the designations in the question of the high priest (if we assume that 'Εγώ εἰμι is the preferred reading).

3) It is Jesus' claim to be the Messiah that is blasphemous. With the exception of J. Blinzler,[84] most scholars seem agreed that legally such a claim could not possibly have been viewed as blasphemous, however pretentious it might

---

[78]This view has been most vigorously defended by E. Stauffer, Jesus and His Story (London: SCM, 1960), 121-128.

[79]See above 84.

[80]E. Stauffer, Jesus and His Story, 124-125.

[81]O. Linton, "The Trial of Jesus and the Interpretation of Psalm 110:1," NTS 7 (1961), 259.

[82]P. Borgen, Bread from Heaven (Leiden: Bril, 1965), 73.

[83]Catchpole, Trial, 135.

[84]Blinzler, The Trial of Jesus, 105-112.

seem.[85]

4) It is Jesus' claim to be Son of God that is blasphemous. The difficulty with this view, according to many scholars, is that the title in Mark seems to be synonymous with "Christ" and thus could not possibly have been used by the high priest at Jesus' trial.[86] There is little evidence that the title was used in pre-Christian Jewish circles as a messianic designation, which must mean that it reflects Christian conceptions. If the term is to be accepted as historical, the most natural reading suggests that it is in apposition to "the Christ" and hardly represents a separate category on which a charge could be based.

Catchpole is convinced that it is this title that elicits the charge of blasphemy. His arguments are based on analysis of Jesus' sayings that he considers "ipsissima verba,"[87] and on a source-critical view of Luke's version of the trial as independent of Mark and as historically more reliable. In Luke 22:70, the question about Jesus' claim to be the Son of God is posed as a separate question. For Catchpole, this is of great significance:

Although the equivalence of messiah and Son of God in pre-Christian Judaism has been disputed, it yet seems probable that the equation of the two was being established in Qumran at the time. Lk 22:67-70 belongs to circles where divine Sonship is a repugnant concept sealing the doom of the claimant. By contrast with this passage Mk 14:61 emerges as secondary theologically and influenced kerygmatically in a way which Lk is not.[88]

Catchpole's opinion is cited because it is representative and because it is one of the most recent to appear. His suggestions are far from absolutely convincing on the historical level. His conclusions are based upon debatable approaches to life of Jesus research, debatable source-critical views, and a highly hypothetical reconstruction of Jewish legal procedure. Furthermore, there are probably few scholars who would agree that the relationship

---

[85]Wellhausen, Mark, 124; Taylor, Mark, 569-570; Bill I, 1017; Catchpole, Trial, 132; Schweizer, Mark, 325; Klostermann, Mark, 154.

[86]Schweizer, Mark, 325; Haenchen, Der Weg Jesu, 154; Lohse, History, 84.

[87]Catchpole, Trial, 143-148.   [88]Ibid., 200.

of the use of Son of God imagery to Jesus' possible use
of Father/Son terminology is as simple as Catchpole seems
to assume.[89] And even if his views of the historical
trial are accepted, they do not explain the text of Mark,
especially the reference to blasphemy. In Luke, the term
is never mentioned. Even Catchpole insists that Mark is
"influenced kerygmatically," and that he equates the
titles "Christ" and "Son of the Blessed."[90] One must
still ask,. therefore, to what the charge of blasphemy is
related in the Markan version of the trial.

5) The charge of blasphemy is related to Jesus' self-exalta-
tion as Son of Man.[91] Once again the evidence is scarce.
There is some evidence, cited by Billerbeck and discussed
by Catchpole,[92] that the notion of a heavenly enthronement of someone other than God himself was considered
suspect. The most famous text is found in the Babylonian
Talmud: The question is how Dan 7:9 is to be interpreted:

How explain: "'till thrones were placed"?--One throne was
for himself (the Ancient of Days) and one for David. Even
as it has been taught: One was for himself and one for
David: this is R. Akiba's view. R. Jose protested to him:
Akiba, how long will you profane the Shechinah? Rather,
one throne for justice and the other for mercy?[93]

As Catchpole's discussion suggests, the interpretation of
the passage and inferences made regarding first century legal
practice must remain highly hypothetical. Even the text from
the Talmud does not use the term "blasphemy" to characterize the
opinion of Akiba, although the notion of "profaning the Shekinah"
approaches such a characterization. And perhaps the decisive
argument against a view of the Son of Man saying as motivation
for the charge of blasphemy on the historical level is the insistence of most scholars that the whole of 14:62 represents the
result of a long period of careful study of Scripture by
Christians.[94]

It seems most unlikely that the relationship between

---

[89]Ibid., 143-148. See excursus on Son of God.

[90]Catchpole, Trial, 200.   [91]Especially Bill I, 1017-8.

[92]Ibid., Catchpole, Trial, 140-141.

[93]bSanhedrin 38b; Catchpole, Trial, 140-141.

[94]Contrary to Catchpole, Trial, 136-140; Perrin and
Lindars are but two of the most recent scholars to advocate such
views.

14:61-62 and the charge of blasphemy will be settled on the historical level. Again, however, we must attempt to determine what the charge means within the Gospel of Mark, to determine if the author provides any clues to his view of the verdict and its relationship to the crucial verses 14:61-62. Such a study must involve both an examination of Mark's use of the term "blasphemy" in the rest of the Gospel as well as a careful reading of the trial scene. We have already determined that in Mark's mind, the court passes a verdict, and that, in light of the tearing of the robes, this verdict can only be based on conviction of Jesus for blasphemy. We must now attempt to determine what "blasphemy" means in Mark.

It is immediately clear that "blasphemy" is a rather broad term in Mark. The most important occurrences of the term are in 2:7, 3:28, and 15:29. The term appears in a list of vices in 7:22 and most probably means little more than "slander" or "defamation." Of these occurrences the one in 2:7 is clearly the most significant:

> And when Jesus saw their faith, he said to the paralytic, "My son, your sins are forgiven." Now some of the scribes were sitting there, questioning in their hearts, "Why does this man speak thus? It is blasphemy! Who can forgive sins but God alone?"

The verse supports those who insist that, at least for Mark, the term blasphemy is broader than as defined in the Mishnah. Here Beyer seems to be correct:

> In the New Testament the concept of blasphemy is controlled throughout by the thought of violation of the power and majesty of God.[95]

In claiming the right to forgive sins, Jesus infringes on the prerogatives of God. Beyer probably goes too far when he interprets the verse in Mark by appeal to Jn 10:33-36,[96] but at least for both evangelists the term blasphemy implies more than misuse of the ineffable Name. The use of the term in 2:7 is important in Mark because it is the only occasion in the Gospel outside 14:62 at which Jesus is accused of blasphemy. And the story in which the term appears initiates a controversy section in Mark that ends with the first indication of a plot against Jesus (3:6). The use of the term here suggests that Jesus' claims represent an infringement on the prerogatives of God.

The next occurrence is in 3:28:

---

[95]Beyer, TDNT 1, 622.   [96]Ibid., 623.

"Truly, I say to you, all sins will be forgiven the sons of
men, and whatever blasphemies they utter; but whoever
blasphemes against the Holy Spirit never has forgiveness,
but is guilty of an eternal sin"--for they had said "He has
an unclean spirit."

The passage suggests that one's attitude toward Jesus may
also constitute blasphemy. In Mark, Jesus' opponents "blaspheme
the Holy Spirit" when they insist that Jesus is inspired not by
the Spirit of God but by Satan. Because of Jesus' relationship
to God through the Spirit, such remarks directed at Jesus constitute blasphemy. The use of the term in 15:29 confirms this
usage:

And those who passed by derided [ἐβλασφήμουν!] him wagging
their heads, and saying....

It is most probable that the verse contains an allusion
to Ps 22:7. In the LXX (Ps 21:8), the phrase reads πάντες οἱ
θεωροῦντές με ἐξεμυκτήρισάν με, ἐλάλησαν ἐν χείλεσιν, ἐκίνησαν
κεθαλήν ("All who see me mock at me, they make mouths at me,
they wag their heads."). It is interesting to note, however,
that the verb Mark chooses to describe the mockery is not
ἐκμυκτηρίζειν from the LXX, but βλασφημεῖν. Luke (23:35) does
use the verb ἐξεμυκτήριζον, though it is not certain that it is
intended as a conscious allusion to the Psalm. The verb
βλασφημεῖν can mean simply "slander," so that it is not out of
place in Mark's account of the mockery.[97] But the choice of
the slightly unusual verb in place of the scriptural
ἐκμυκτηρίζειν may suggest that the evangelist wishes the term to
be understood to mean more than "slander" or "deride." The term
may well represent an ironic signal to the reader that more is
occurring than first meets the eye. The passers-by mock the
pathetic figure on the cross, taunting him with the claims made
at the trial, a trial in which he was found guilty of blasphemy.
But in reality, they are the blasphemers. They are the ones who
violate the Spirit and majesty of God by rejecting and ridiculing
his Son.

If these interpretations of "blasphemy" in Mark are
correct, we may infer that the term in the trial may mean something like violation of the majesty of God or infringement on
God's prerogatives. But we may also infer that the charge is of
some importance to the author, that he intends the reader to

[97]The meaning "deride," used in the RSV, is not listed
in Bauer. According to Bauer, the meaning is more "abusive
speech" than simply "mockery."

appreciate the irony implied by the use of the terms in 14:64
and 15:29 when the story is understood at a deeper level. It is
still necessary to determine, however, how the evangelist understands the relationship between 14:61-62 and the charge.

There are some strong arguments that can be advanced for
the view that the Son of Man statement should be considered the
basis for the charge of blasphemy. As O. Linton has noted, the
response of the high priest follows the Son of Man saying, not
'Εγώ είμι.[98] And there is an interesting comparison to be made
between Mk 14:62ff and Acts 7:55-58. Stephen is not taken by
the mob until he makes his statement about Jesus' standing at
the right hand of God:

> and he said, "Behold, I see the heavens opened, and the
> Son of man standing at the right hand of God." But they
> cried out with a loud voice and stopped their ears and
> rushed together upon him. Then they cast him out of the
> city and stoned him.

Luke does not say that Stephen is accused of blasphemy;
in fact, he is not really granted a trial. But the reference
to the stopping of ears and the stoning make blasphemy a probable charge. The parallel between Luke and Mark would suggest
that for both, it is the Christian confession that Jesus is
seated at God's right hand that is blasphemous to Jews. Linton
insists that this is the case. He argues that Christians have
interpreted Psalm 110:1 literally,

> Then it [sitting at God's right hand] is a privilege for
> only one person, then it is a session intruding into God's
> exclusiveness, a "blasphemy"--not a "blasphemy" in the
> technical sense, but in the sense of intruding on God's
> special privileges, as an attack on the confession of the
> one God, besides whom there is none else.[99]

There is some further support for this view within Mark's
account itself. As we have noted, the mockery of Jesus as
prophet immediately after his condemnation calls into relief
the "prediction" in 14:62. This may be further evidence that
the evangelist views the Son of Man saying as the immediate
cause of the blasphemy.

There are also indications, however, that it is the
messianic confession that Mark considers the basis for the charge
of blasphemy, even though this has the least claim to historical

---

[98]Linton, "The Trial of Jesus and the Interpretation
of Psalm 110:1," 259.

[99]Ibid., 261.

probability. From the remainder of the passion story it is
clear that for Mark, the titles "the Christ, the Son of the
Blessed" are decisive. Jesus is tried, rejected, mocked and
executed as "the King of the Jews," "the Christ, the King of
Israel." Further, the Son of Man saying seems to function not
as an independent source of information about Jesus or as a
separate claim, but as a promise that Jesus will be vindicated
as "the Christ, the Son of the Blessed." And if the centrality
of the messianic imagery in the passion story indicates that
this is where the evangelist intends to place the emphasis in
14:61-62, it is reasonable to infer that the charge is to be
related to the messianic claim.

It is equally possible to explain how Mark could characterize the messianic confession as blasphemous by appeal to
Jewish/Christian conflicts at the time of the evangelist. If
as Linton suggests, the Christian application of Ps 110:1 to
Jesus might sound blasphemous to Jews, it is also possible that
the claim that Jesus is the Christ, the Son of the Blessed
might be viewed as blasphemous. Numerous scholars have suggested that the conflict between Jesus and his Jewish opponents
at the trial tells us more about the evangelist's situation than
it does about the historical trial.[100] Burkill's remarks are
typical:

> They [Christians] interpreted the situation anachronis-
> tically; they assumed that what applied to themselves in
> their relationships to the Jewish authorities applied to
> Jesus in a similar relationship.[101]

> The Jews condemned Christianity because of its affirmation
> of the Messiaship of Jesus and, reasoning by analogy, cer-
> tain sections of the apostolic church came to suppose that
> the sanhedrin condemned Jesus to death simply because he
> made claim to messianic dignity.[102]

It is still perhaps difficult to determine why in Mark's
eyes the claim that Jesus is the Christ, the Son of God should
be viewed as blasphemous in Jewish eyes. Here the reference to
blsaphemy in 2:7 is important. Christian claims made about
Jesus the Messiah, for instance that forgiveness is offered in
his name, strike Jews as infringement on the prerogatives of
God, thus blasphemous. Perhaps by emphasizing the helplessness

---

[100]The list of those supporting such a view would include
Bultmann, Burkill, Bertram, Lightfoot, Winter, Lietzmann, and
others.

[101]Burkill, "Trial of Jesus," 9-10.   [102]Ibid., 2.

of Jesus and the contrast between the messianic claims and his
powerlessness in his account of the passion, Mark is consciously
reflecting something of the "offence" of the Christian confession. Perhaps it would be considered blasphemous to claim
that one so helpless, so powerless, could be God's Messiah.
For Paul, the suggestion that one who had died accursed by
the Law (Gal 3:11, with reference to Deut 27:26) was God's
Messiah was certainly an offence. There are probably numerous
such ways in which the confession that Jesus the Crucified
One is the Christ, the Son of God could be viewed as blasphemous to Jews--blasphemous in the broad sense. All that is
necessary here is to note that Mark seems to be aware of the
differences between the Christian confession of Jesus as
Christ, Son of God, and Jewish messianic expectations,[103]
differences that would make the Christian confession of Jesus
sound blasphemous to Jews.

Viewing the relationship between the charge and 14:61-62
in light of the historical situation of the evangelist, it is
possible to view either the messianic titles in 14:61 or the
Son of Man saying in 14:62 as the direct occasion for the charge
of blasphemy. There is evidence in Mark to support either view,
though the evidence seems to favor the messianic claim. But
regardless of which option is preferred, the function of the
charge in the present context is apparent. The charge of
blasphemy may first serve to highlight the injustice of the
trial. It is conceivable that Mark knows the legal character
of the charge and has purposely juxtaposed it with a proper
paraphrasis for the name of God in Jesus' reply. But even if
this is the case, the charge and the dramatic tearing of the
robe further highlight 14:61-62 as the climax of the trial and
as a decisive moment in the Gospel. The charge of blasphemy,
further, provides an ironic contrast to the "blasphemy" of
Jesus on the cross by his Jewish opponents in 15:29. Finally,
the charge motivates the handing of Jesus over to Pilate in
15:2. He could hardly have been bound over to Pilate had not
the trial ended with a guilty verdict.

Summary

Study of the trial in Mark suggests that the author is
interested in the story at a sub-surface level. The trial is

---

[103]This is especially clear in 8:29-31 and 15:31-32.

the setting for Jesus' "rejection" by the Jewish leaders,
prophesied in Scripture. The focus of the account is the two
charges, which provide the basis for Jesus' rejection as well
as for his vindication by God. The high point of the trial
is reached with the question of the high priest and Jesus'
response. The claim to be "the Christ, the Son of the
Blessed" not only motivates the decisive rejection by the court,
but it also introduces the royal theme that runs throughout the
passion story. It is as Messiah-King that Jesus is tried,
mocked and executed. Son of God, whatever other connotations
the term might have, is used with awareness of its scriptural
roots in royal ideology. The Son of Man saying is intended
not to supplant the titles in 14:61 but to point the reader to
the vindication of Jesus as Christ, Son of God--whether at his
resurrection, parousia, or both.

EXCURSUS: SON OF GOD

One important question that requires some comment is the
meaning and use of the title Son of God in pre-Markan Christianity and in pre-Christian Judaism. Interpretation of the title
in Mark will not be settled by such an investigation of the history of christological traditions, but it is necessary to reconstruct some picture of the options available to the author in
his use of the title.   Such study is particularly relevant
to the interpretation of the use of the title in 14:61. The
problem is not whether the question of the high priest should be
viewed as essentially Jewish or as essentially Christian. We
have already dealt with that problem above, suggesting that Mark
intends the question of the high priest to be understood by the
Christian reader as a true confession.[1] The real problem is
how the title in this statement is to be understood, what
associations the author intends. Here it is necessary to know
something about pre-Markan usage. If the title had no messianic
associations in pre-Markan Christianity or in pre-Christian
Judaism, the use of the title would suggest a de-emphasis of
the messianic theme and perhaps even a complete redefinition
of "the Christ."[2]

One important consideration for study of early Christian
usage of the title Son of God is the meaning of the term in
pre-Christian Judaism. There are several scholars, as we have
previously noted, who insist that the title was not used as a
messianic designation in pre-Christian Jewish circles.[3] There
is not only the argument from silence, the lack of such usage in
extant literature, but positive indications in rabbinic and
targumic traditions that the title was expressly avoided as a
designation for the Messiah. Probably the most striking evidence is to be found in the targums, where efforts are made to
circumvent the clear meaning of the scriptural passage:

	MT	Tg
II Sam. 7:14	אני אהיה לו לאב	[4] אנא אהוי ליה כאב
	והוא יהיה לי לבן	והוא יהי קדמי לבר

---

[1]See above, 82-83.

[2]One advocate of such a view is J. Schreiber, "Die
Christologie des Markusevangeliums," 164. See above, 78.

[3]See above, chapter 4, note 11.

I Chron 17:13   אנא אחבב יתיה כאבא לבריה   אני אהיה לו לאב[5]
                         והוא יהי קדמי כברא לאבא   והוא יהיה לי לבן

The passages are self-explanatory. The tendency to avoid
the suggestion that the Son of David will be called "Son" by
God, present in the targum to Samuel, is even more developed in
the targum to Chronicles. It is interesting to note, however,
that in neither targum is there an attempt to historicize the
verses, to insist that the promise made about a Son of David
refers to Solomon. There is little evidence to suggest that the
targumists understood the text to be anything but a prophecy of
the future Messiah.[6]

It is unnecessary to review all of the arguments that
have been advanced by those who insist that Son of God could not
have been used as a messianic title in pre-Christian Judaism.
The views have been widely held for some time and are bound up
with the view that there was a clear distinction in Jewish
circles between an earthly, political eschatological figure
(the Messiah), and a supernatural figure (the Son of Man).[7]
More recently, however, Nils A. Dahl has insisted that in light
of the Qumran literature such clear distinctions are probably a
great over-simplification,[8] that messianic expectations and
use of traditional messianic texts were far more subject to
historical and sociological influences and that the expectations
were far more fluid than has previously been assumed. It is
certainly true that there are tendencies in rabbinic Judaism to
guard against any suggestion that the Messiah is a divine being.
Such tendencies may reflect anti-Christian polemics, but also a
more general tendency to avoid the divinizing of any human

---

[4]The text is taken from A. Sperber, The Bible in Aramaic
II: The Former Prophets according to Targum Jonathan (Leiden:
Brill, 1959).

[5]The text is from Sperber, The Bible in Aramaic IVa: The
Hagiographa (Leiden: Brill, 1968).

[6]S. Aalen, "'Reign' and 'House' in the Kingdom of God in
the Gospels," NTS 8 (1963), 235. This is made even more certain
in light of 4QFlor.

[7]See esp. S. Mowinckel, He That Cometh (tr. G. W.
Anderson; Nashville: Abingdon, 1954).

[8]Nils A. Dahl, "Eschatology and History in the Light of
the Dead Sea Scrolls," The Future of Our Religious Past (ed.
J. M. Robinson; New York: Harper and Row, 1971), 9-28.

figure.[9] Such tendencies may also reflect the disastrous
effects of messianic enthusiasm in the two revolts against
Rome.

The real question is to what extent these tendencies
represent Jewish views both during and prior to the Christian
era. It is at this point the evidence from the Qumran literature is decisive. The literature is decisive even if there has
been little direct contact between Christians and the community
that produced the Qumran scrolls.[10] What is important about the
literature in this context is that it has been unaffected by the
cataclysmic events beginning in A.D. 66 and has been uncensored
by members of "normative" Jewish circles. With regard to the
use of "Son of God," the corpus provides one piece of evidence
that may well be decisive in the debate about pre-Christian use
of the term. The text from cave 4 reads:[11]

ורה]גיד לכה יהוה כיא בית יבנה לכה
והקימותי את זרעכה אחריכה
והכימותי את כסא ממלכתו [לעו]לם
אני אהיה לוא לאב והוא יהיה לי לבן
הואה צמח דויד העורמד עם דורש התורה
[...] בצי [ון בא]חרית הימים

"["And Yahweh] tells you that he will build a house for you,
and I shall set up your seed after you, and I shall
establish his royal throne [foreve]r. I shall be to him
as a father, and he will be to me as a son." He is the
"Shoot of David" who will arise with the Interpreter of the
Law [...] in Zi[on in the l]ast days."

The text is decisive evidence that Nathan's oracle was
viewed as a promise of the coming Davidic Messiah in pre-Christian Jewish circles. The "Son" promised in the text is identified with the "Branch of David," a designation for the Davidic
Messiah used elsewhere in the scrolls.[12] The English translation

---

[9]On such concerns present in Moses traditions, see
Wayne A. Meeks, The Prophet-King, 140-142, and 207, note 5;
J. Goldin, "The First Chapter of the Abot de Rabbi Nathan,"
Mordecai M. Kaplan: Jubilee Volume on the Occasion of His
Seventieth Birthday (New York: The Jewish Theological Seminary
of America, 1953), 279-280.

[10]See Dahl, "Eschatology and History," 12-13, for a
negative view of the possibility of positive contacts between
Christians and the Qumran sectarians.

[11]4QFlor. The text and translation are taken from J.
Allegro, Discoveries in the Judean Desert V: Qumran Cave IV
(Oxford: Clarendon Press, 1968), 53-54.

[12]See below, 172-73.

of the text is perhaps deceptive. The force of the Hebrew is
certainly more aptly rendered, "I will be his father and he
will be my son."[13] The language was understood as suggesting
too real a view of sonship by the targumists and was conse-
quently modified. No such attempt is made by the interpreter
from Qumran. The clear implication is that the "Branch of
David" who will stand at the end of days will be called "Son"
by God himself. This is particularly noteworthy in light of the
tendency in the Qumran literature to subordinate the royal
Messiah to the eschatological high priest.[14]

It is true, as Lohse observes,[15] that the use of "Son"
for the Messiah occurs even here only in a quotation of Scripture. But that in no way detracts from the clearly messianic
character of the oracle and of the title. It does suggest that
there is still no evidence that the evolution of the title "Son
of God" as a messianic designation from the use of the term
"Son" in messianic oracles like Ps 2:7 and II Sam 7:14 occurred
outside Christian circles. The issue might be settled by an
unpublished fragment presently in the possession of J. T.
Milik.[16] In the fragment, an otherwise unidentified figure is
designated both "Son of God" and "Son of the Most High." Milik
does not believe that the figure so identified is the Davidic
Messiah, but J. Strugnell does. No final decision will be
possible until the text is published, and even then any final
identification might be impossible. Until such an identification, the question of the use of the title "Son of God" of the
royal Messiah in pre-Christian circles will have to remain
open.[17]

At least, however, there is clear evidence from Qumran
that oracles like II Sam 7 and perhaps Ps 2:7[18] were interpreted

---

[13]RSV and the reading used in Yadin, "A Midrash on 2 Sam
vii and Ps i-ii (4Q Florilegium)," IEJ 9 (1959), 97.

[14]See below, 178-79. [15]Lohse, υἱός, TDNT 8, 362.

[16]The following information was provided in a personal
letter from Prof. J. Fitzmeyer.

[17]Hahn (Titles, 282-284) argues that the title was so
used, that even "Son of the Blessed" was current in pre-
Christian Judaism.

[18]The eschatological midrash clearly included portions
of Ps 1-2 (cf. DJD V, 53), but unfortunately the text breaks
off prior to 2:7.

eschatologically as prophecies of the Davidic Messiah and that,
according to such prophecies, the Messiah was called "Son" by
God himself. Professor Dahl has argued that these oracles have
been extremely important for the development of New Testament
Christology.[19] There are a number of passages in the New
Testament where such influence is apparent. Of particular note
are Acts 13:33, where Ps 2:7 is quoted in the context of Jesus'
resurrection, and Rom 1:3, where a reference to the verse is
not explicit but highly probable.[20] II Sam 7:14 is quoted in
Heb 1:5 in conjunction with Ps 2:7, and the verse is probably
behind the statement in Lk 1:32-33. It is also probable that
the oracles, particularly Ps 2:7, have been involved in the
development of the accounts of Jesus' baptism. Jeremias has
argued that the earliest version of the baptismal text probably
was based on Isa 4:1 alone and that the title υἱός μου stood
for the עבדי in the text of Isa 42:1 (which is rendered παῖς
μου in the version of the passage in Matt 12:18).[21] According
to Jeremias, the point of the early versions of Jesus' baptism
is that he has been annointed with the Spirit, as prophesied in
Isaiah.[22] He even conjectures that the development of the
messianic use of "Son of God" depends upon the earlier designation of Jesus as παῖς θεοῦ.[23]

Whatever the view of the history of the baptismal text,
however, it seems improbable that the use of Son of God in
Christian tradition has developed from an original παῖς θεοῦ.
Hahn argues that the baptismal texts reflect later christological developments.[24] The most probable view of the traditions
contained in the NT is that according to the earliest view, the

---

[19]"Eschatology and History," 16. The following views are
heavily dependent on printed but unpublished lectures on New
Testament Christology delivered by Professor Dahl at the Yale
Divinity School in 1968-69.

[20]On Paul's speech in Acts 13, see esp. E. Lövestam,
Son and Savior (Tr. M. Petry; Lund: Gleerup, 1961).

[21]J. Jeremias, παῖς, TDNT 5, 701-702.

[22]Ibid., 701--despite its absence from the text of Mark.

[23]Ibid., 702, note 354. This is clearly a conjecture.

[24]Hahn, Titles, 280.

title Son of God and the corresponding royal office were thought
to have been conferred on Jesus at his resurrection (Rom 1:4;
Acts 13:33); the conferral of office can then be traced back to
his baptism (Mk 1:11) and to his birth (Lk 1:32-35). There
appears to have been no exclusive concern to tie the conferral
of the title to one particular moment, as is clear from the
varied usage in Luke (birth, baptism, and resurrection) and in
Rom 1:2-4 (where the notion of conferral of the status "Son of
God" at the resurrection can be combined with the notion of the
pre-existence of the "Son").[25] The baptismal texts do not provide the starting point for the christological development of
the title "Son of God,"[26] and the use of "Son" in Mark 1:11 must
certainly be related to the usage in 14:61 (and 1:1, if the
longer reading is accepted).

There is a distinct use of father/son imagery in the New
Testament, however, that appears to be unrelated to "Son of God,"
both in early usage and in origin. The peculiar usage is
clearest in Mk 13:32 and Mt 11:27 (par Lk 10:22); it is characterized by the absolute use of "the Son" in sayings traditions.
This particular usage is not reminiscent of Old Testament
language and is probably derived from Jesus' own usage.[27] Both
Dahl and Hahn agree, however, that this usage does not explain
"Son of God" traditions, but is rather a source for later
christological developments.[28] They both agree that the title
"Son of God" enters Christian tradition as a messianic designation. According to Hahn, the title was first employed to
describe Jesus as the coming Messiah, that is, with reference
to his eschatological activity:

In the Palestinian primitive church, the idea of the
Messiah was related most of all to the future work of
Jesus.[29]

Dahl has presented an alternative view of the origin of

---

[25]See esp. Dahl, "Lectures on New Testament Christology,"
18-19.

[26]Hahn, Titles, 280.

[27]See B. M. F. van Iersel, Der Sohn in den synoptischen
Jesusworten (Nov TSup III; Leiden: Brill, 1961); J. Jeremias,
ABBA: Studien zur neutestamentlichen Theologie und Zeit-
getchichte (Göttingen: Vandenhoeck and Ruprecht, 1966).

[28]Dahl, "Lectures," 17: Hahn, Titles, 280.

[29]Hahn, Titles, 284. See the reference above, chapter
4, note 30, to Hahn's interpretation of Mk 14:61 (Titles, 285).

the messianic imagery in his article "The Crucified Messiah," already cited,[30] and believes that the title Son of God was first used with reference to Jesus enthronement/vindication at his resurrection (esp Rom 1:4 and possibly Acts 13:13).

It is unnecessary to examine the use of the title in Christian tradition in further detail. By the time of Mark, the title had come to have numerous associations. These seem to represent a development of a traditional, messianic use of the term, however. The title "Son of God," even if its evolution from the use of "my Son" as a designation of the king occurred only within Christian circles, seems to be related to the usage in messianic oracles like II Sam 7:14 and Ps 2:7. What is important for interpreting Mark is that his use of the title as a messianic designation would not have been at all unprecedented. There is evidence both in pre-Markan Christianity as well as in pre-Christian Judaism that the title was used with clear awareness of its scriptural (=royal) origin. This is not to say that the title was used by Mark only as a synonym for "the Christ." Interpretation of the title in Mark must be based on a careful examination of the whole Gospel. What is indicated, however, is that among the evangelist's options for employment of the title "Son of God" was an established messianic use of the title.

---

[30]See chapter 2, note 22.

EXCURSUS: MESSIAH

Some brief comment on the title ὁ χριστός is necessary.
Our principal concern is with the meaning of the term in Mark,
but some consideration of the background of the title is useful.
One of the matters that requires some comment is the absolute
use of the title, present in 8:29, 12:35, 14:61 and 15:32. Although such usage is typical of the rabbinic and targumic
traditions,[1] the absolute use of the term is virtually unattested in pre-Christian Judaism.[2] The biblical (Old Testament)
usage exhibits the term משיח (χριστός in the LXX) with a
genitive. The following examples are typical:

"the anointed of Jahweh" (משיח יהוה ; χριστὸς κυρίου);
I Sam 24:7, 26:9, etc.

"his anointed" (משיחו; χριστὸς αὐτοῦ):
I Sam 2:10, 12:3, 16:6, etc.; Ps 2:2, 18:50, etc.

"my anointed" (משיחי ; χριστός μου):
I Chron 16:22 (pl), Ps 105:15, etc.

The usage in pseudepigraphical literature follows the
biblical pattern:

Ps Sol 17:32   "and their king, the anointed of the Lord"
       18:5   "His anointed"
       18:7   "The Lord's anointed"
Enoch 48:10   "The Lord of Spirits and His Anointed"

Among New Testament authors, only Luke and the Seer of
Revelation follow the biblical pattern, using "anointed" with
a genitive:

Lk   2:26   "The Lord's Christ" (τὸν χριστὸν κυρίου)
      9:20   "the Christ of God" (τὸν χριστὸν τοῦ θεοῦ)
Acts 3:18   "his Christ" (τὸν χριστὸν αὐτοῦ)
Rev 11:15   "of his Christ" (τοῦ χριστοῦ αὐτοῦ)
     12:10   "of his Christ" (τοῦ χριστοῦ αὐτοῦ)

Although there is no definite proof of the use of the
absolute "the Anointed One" in pre-Christian Jewish literature,
we may infer that such a usage was current at the time of Jesus,
at least in some Jewish circles, from the combined testimony of
the New Testament, the targumic and the rabbinic literature.[3]
It is not clear, however, whether the form "the anointed one"

---

[1]The usual expression is   המשיח (משיחא) or   מלך המשיח
(מלכא משיחא)

[2]The source for much of the following discussion is the
printed but unpublished lectures on New Testament Christology
by Prof. Nils A. Dahl, cited above, 112, note 19.

[3]Dahl, "Lectures," 64.

is an abbreviation for "the Lord's anointed," "the anointed
king," "the anointed of Israel," "the anointed of righteousness,"
or the like.[4] Based on evidence from Qumran, van der Woude has
argued that the absolute form can no longer be viewed as an unambiguous designation of the messianic king, the royal "anointed
one."[5] Dahl has pointed out, however, that in almost every
case, the use of the term מ(ה)שיח is best translated "the
anointed of...," thus providing no real parallel to the New
Testament usage.[6] One possible exception is IQSa 2:11f, but
here the text is uncertain as well as the translation.[7] According to Dahl, there is little substantial evidence that "the
Messiah" was used to refer to anyone but the royal Messiah.[8]

The use of the term in Mark provides fewer difficulties.
In 8:29, 12:35, 14:61, and 15:32, the title is used with the
clear implication that it refers to a well-known figure in
Jewish eschatology. The use in 12:35 and 15:32 indicates that
the Messiah is a royal figure, the Messiah ben David. Further,
the charge at the trial and the mockery of Jesus as "the Christ,
the King of Israel" in 15:32 suggests that Jesus does not fit
the usual image of the Messiah. This contrast is implied in
8:29-33 as well. Peter confesses that Jesus is the Christ, but
he is immediately rebuked for his refusal to accept suffering
as part of Jesus' messianic ministry. The passage reflects two
contrasting views of Messiahship: the popular view, according
to which the Messiah was to appear as a conquering ruler, and
the Christian view of the suffering Messiah. The use of the
title in the passion story and in the account of Peter's confession seem to presuppose a contrast between general messianic
expectations and the confession of the crucified Jesus as
Messiah.

---

[4]The terms משיח אהרן וישראל and משיח הצדק are all
found in the literature of the Qumran community.

[5]A. S. van der Woude, Die messianischen Vorstellungen
der Gemeinde von Qumran (Assen: van Gorcum, 1957), 245.

[6]Dahl, "Lectures," 64.

[7]Van der Woude, Die messianischen Vorstellungen, 92-104;
O. Michel and O. Betz, "Von Gott Gezeugt," Judentum, Urchristen
tum, Kirche (BZNTW 26; Berlin: Töpelmann, 1960), 1-23; M.
Smith, "God's Begetting the Messiah in IQSa," NTS 5 (1959), 218-
24.

[8]Dahl, "Lectures," 64.

CHAPTER 5

THE TEMPLE CHARGE (14:58)

Thus far in our study of the trial we have observed that the entire account is characterized by a two-level narrative and by irony. Mark is concerned to bring out the real meaning of the story, but at a level to which only the reader has access. The meaning of the trial in Mark is first of all bound up with its relation to the theme of rejection/vindication, a theme introduced in 8:31 and further developed in 12:1-11. The theme, as we have noted, is related to the apologetic use of Ps 118 in early Christianity. In Mark, the trial provides the setting for Jesus' "rejection" by the Jewish religious leaders. But just as the verse from the Psalm promises vindication, so at a deeper level of the story the trial provides the basis for Jesus' vindication by God as well. The focus of the rejection/vindication theme at the trial is clearly the two charges, particularly the second.

We have observed also that the trial serves to introduce the theme that dominates the passion story: the theme of Jesus' Messiahship. Here the relationships between the trial and the rest of the passion story are clear. Jesus is tried and condemned by the Jewish court as "the Christ, the Son of the Blessed"; he is tried by Pilate, mocked by the guards, and executed as "King of the Jews"; and he is mocked on the cross as "the Christ, the King of Israel." And at the moment of his death, a lone Roman Centurion confesses, perhaps unknowingly, that Jesus is the "Son of God." The question of the high priest and Jesus' response in 14:61-62 are the decisive verses in the trial and indeed represent a climax in the Gospel as a whole. Jesus openly acknowledges his identity, and this self-revelation not only provides the basis for his condemnation by the Jewish court, but also for his trial and execution at the hands of Pilate.

As we noted at the conclusion of chapter 2, however, there are two charges at the trial. In 14:58, certain false witnesses bring forward a specific charge:

"We heard him say, 'I will destroy this temple that is made with hands and in three days I will build another, not made with hands.'"

117

The charge is made by false witnesses. The charge is followed in 14:59 by the statement that even in this case, witnesses were not able to agree. Thus the charge cannot be used as evidence and the trial must continue. The first impression is that the author intends the reader to view this charge as false. But a closer reading of the passion story as a whole suggests that this first impression is not entirely correct. The first charge at the trial is carefully formulated. It contains strange terms like "made with hands" and "not made with hands" that contribute little to the actual charge but suggest something mysterious about the statement. The mention of "three days" looks suspiciously like a reference to the resurrection. Further, in chapter 15, in the account of the mockery to which Jesus is subjected as he hangs on the cross, the temple charge is treated in the same manner as the messianic charge (15:29-32). If, as we argued in the case of the mockery in 15:31-2, the purpose of the taunt is to highlight the charge made at the trial for the purpose of irony, it is possible that the same function is intended in the repetition of the temple charge in 15:29. Again, it is perhaps important that one of the two climactic events reported at the moment of Jesus' death is the tearing of the temple veil (15:38). And finally, Mark's preoccupation with the temple in the last chapters should make one suspicious that the temple charge in 14:58 is included not simply because the evengelist has inherited something from tradition or because there is a charge he wishes to discredit.

If the author intends the charge to be true in some sense, to be viewed by the Christian reader as prophetic, there are two initial problems that must be solved: the mention of the failure of the witnesses to agree in 14:59 and the characterization of the charge as false testimony (14:57). We shall deal first with the statement about the failure of the witnesses to agree.

The explanation of the statement in 14:59 cannot be provided on the historical level. The reader is given the impression in 14:55-7 that the court, committed in advance to a guilty verdict, has planted witnesses to provide an excuse for doing away with Jesus. "Some" of these false witnesses make a very precise charge. But then we learn that even in this case they were unable to agree. It is not at all clear how planted witnesses could have failed to agree on such a precise charge, particularly when the charge (or some version of it) seems to be public knowledge (15:29). There is absolutely no indication that the author is concerned about the historical problem, and any explanation of the text on this level must rest on pure speculation.[1]

Rather than turning to source reconstruction as the best method of explaining the difficulty,[2] we should first determine if this peculiar feature has some literary function in the story. It is first of all possible that the verse serves some purpose at another dimension of the story. As part of the "internal" events, it is possible to assign to the strange verse (14:59) an important function in the account. As we have noted, the climax of the story is the interchanage between Jesus and the high priest in 14:61-62. The statement in 14:59, together with Jesus' silence in 14:60, makes it possible for the trial to move on to the decisive charge:

> An accusation is brought foreward and supported but it is not effective because a second reason must be mentioned. Thus we have in front of us not a unified narrative, but an interfusion of motives. It is hard to say what was in the earliest report...but it is easy to say what motive the evangelist Mark wished to bring out. It is the motive which is decisive in the narrative: the confession of Jesus as the Messiah.[3]

It is necessary to examine the function of the verse with greater care, however. It may well be, as form critics have argued, that the difficulties in vv 55-60 may be accounted for on one level by appeal to the history of the trial tradition.[4] But the decision regarding the precise function of the verse in its present context can be made only on the basis of an examination of the present text of Mark. The verse does serve to move the story on to the climax. But it is also possible that the verse (14:59) is intended to permit the author to introduce an

---

[1]See the proposals by Kilpatrick in chapter 1, 9-10.

[2]Compare with the approach of Bultmann, Linnemann and Donahue described in chapter 1, 22-35.

[3]Dibelius, From Tradition to Gospel, 192, cf. 213; see also Lohmeyer, Mark, 330; Bertram, Leidensgeschichte, 58; Klostermann, Mark, 155.

[4]See chapter 1, 22-35. I agree with Bultmann and Donahue that the temple charge is secondary in Mark; it seems highly probable that Mark has inserted the charge into the account of the trial. I disagree, however, that this observation explains the function of the charge in Mark, which is the real concern of this study.

additional charge into an account of the trial in which Jesus is condemned as Messiah. There is nothing in the mention of the failure of the witnesses to agree that in itself reveals the evangelist's view of the temple charge. The failure of the witnesses to agree leaves the truth of the charge open to question. By itself, v. 59 simply indicates that the temple charge is not decisive at the trial. The evangelist's view of the charge can only be determined by looking elsewhere in the account. We may view 14:59 as part of an attempt by the author to discredit the charge only if it can be demonstrated elsewhere in the Gospel that Mark views the charge as false. If there is evidence that Mark views the charge as true in some sense, however, v. 59 may be assigned the very positive function of permitting the introduction of the temple charge into a trial whose essential purpose is to narrate how Jesus was condemned for claiming to be the Messiah. In this case, 14:59 would call special attention to the temple charge. And in fact, what is striking about the charge in Mark is not that it is indecisive with respect to the outcome of the trial, but that it receives as much attention as it does.

The far more difficult problem is the characterization of the charge as false testimony. Twice in the space of two verses (14:56-57) the author mentions that those testifying against Jesus were ἐψευδομαρτύρουν, and the specific charge in v. 58 is simply a specific account of the false testimony of "some." The immediate impression is that the testimony itself is false in the eyes of the author. This is the view of a sizeable group of commentators.[5] What is interesting is that there is also a group of scholars who insist that the "falseness" cannot refer to the charge itself but must refer to something else like the motive of Jesus' accusers.[6] The division of opinion suggests that the first impression is not necessarily the best. But the repetition of ψευδομαρτυρεῖν cannot be without importance. What is necessary at this point in our study is to suggest other options for interpreting the mention of false witnesses, understanding that final interpretation of the temple

---

[5]Taylor, Mark, 566; Schweizer, Mark, 324; Linnemann, Studien, 131.

[6]Bertram, Leidensgeschichte, 57, note 7; Lohmeyer, Mark, 331; Burkill, "Trial," 6. Donahue (Are You the Christ?, 72-3) agrees that the charge must be true in some sense, but he bases his interpretation on a study of Mark's compositional techniques.

charge itself must await careful study of the context as well.

Most of the attempts to explain the relationship between the false testimony and the specific charge in 14:58 begin with source analysis. The attempt is made to reconstruct
the history of the verses, indicating where sources are being
used and at what points the activity of the editor is apparent.
Most recent commentators, including Schweizer, Linnemann,
Donahue and Schreiber go a bit farther than Bultmann in his
remarks on the passage in History of the Synoptic Tradition.[7]
They are not satisfied simply to isolate independent traditions
but are concerned to ask what Mark intended by combining traditions in precisely this way. But there seems to be among these
interpreters the confidence that separating tradition from redaction is the proper way to approach the problem. A survey of
the various reconstructions of the sources indicates the highly
hypothetical nature of such work, however. The rules employed
by these redaction critics are hardly ironclad principles.
And it is interesting to observe that using the same approach
to the material, these scholars arrive at different conclusions
about the solution to the particular problem of the temple
charge. Linnemann[8] and Schweizer[9] argue that the evangelist's
composition of the three verse complex indicates his view that
the temple charge is false. Donahue[10] and Schreiber,[11] on the
other hand, argue that Mark's work on the text indicates he
views the charge as true.

Others have insisted that the mention of false witness
should be viewed as a conscious scriptural allusion (usually to
Psalm 27:12). The difficulties involved in determining the
presence of indirect allusions to the Old Testament cannot be
discussed in detail here. The issue is still hotly disputed.[12]
But even if the presence of false witnesses is to be understood

---

[7]Bultmann, History, 270-271. See the discussion in chapter 1,

[8]Linnemann, Studien, 131. [9]Schweizer, Mark, 324.

[10]Donahue, Are You the Christ?, 73ff.

[11]Schreiber, Theologie des Vertrauens, 47, note 106.

[12]See the works of C. Maurer cited in chapter 2, note 18;
the work by M. Hooker, cited in chapter 4, note 53; and A. Suhl,
Die Funktion der alttestamentlichen Zitate und Anspielungen
im Markusevangelium (Gütersloh: Gütersloher Verlagshaus,
1965).

as a scriptural allusion[13] it does not solve the problem of the relation of the false testimony to the temple charge. Scholars who agree on the scriptural allusion still disagree about the truth of the charge in 14:58. Donahue[14] and Lohmeyer[15] argue that the charge is true, Lohse[16] and Linnemann[17] that it is false.

This lack of agreement suggests that the interpretation of the temple charge will only be settled by other arguments. One important task, to be undertaken later, is to examine the temple charge in light of Mark's other statements about the temple in the last chapters in the Gospel. But there are further observations to be made with regard to the mention of false testimony within the narrower confines of the trial and passion story that are best made first.

It is not impossible, as several scholars have suggested, that the force of the statements about false witnesses in vv 56-57 has to do as much with the intent of the witnesses as with the truth or falsity of the testimony.[18] There is some support for such a view in the apparent attempt of the author to characterize the proceedings as unjust.[19] Nevertheless, it is difficult to escape the impression that the "falseness" of the testimony has something to do with the charge itself. In Mark's account of Jesus' ministry, Jesus has never said such a thing as the witnesses report. His only prediction regarding the temple is reported in 13:2, and the obvious differences in the wording make it difficult to assume that in Mark's eyes, the charge is simply a restatement of Jesus' prediction. What is particularly striking in Mark, however, is that there is also a difference in wording between the charge at the trial (14:58) and the repetition of the charge in the mockery (15:29). The repetition

[13]Lohse, History, 83; Linnemann, Studien, 131; Donahue, Are You the Christ?, 74-77; Lohmeyer, Mark, 330-331 (although he believes the allusions are made to servant passages in Deutero-Isaiah).

[14]Donahue, Are You the Christ?, 72ff.

[15]Lohmeyer, Mark, 326-327, 330; cf. his work Lord of the Temple (tr. S. Todd; Richmond: John Knox, 1962), esp. 51-55.

[16]Lohse, History, 83.   [17]Linnemann, Studien, 119.

[18]Bertram, Leidensgeschichte, 57, note 7; Burkill, "Trial," 6-7.

[19]See above, chapter 3, 62-64.

itself indicates that the charge is important for Mark, but the difference in the wording may be equally as important for understanding what the author has in mind. It may also be important for determining what the false testimony means in the trial narrative.

The difference in wording may well reflect Mark's editorial activity in reworking traditional material.[20] It also signals his willingness to move to the real point of the narrative without filling out the portrait of the event on the external level. The version of the statement in the mockery (15:29) probably indicates how the charge has been understood by Jesus' opponents, according to Mark. There seem to be two components in the statement: a threat against the temple (which would make the statement an appropriate charge),[21] and an impossible boast. The focus in the mockery is on the latter. To the on-lookers, the idea that Jesus would destroy the temple and in three days build it again appeared absurd. He could not even help himself! Both components seem to be present in the charge at the trial as well.[22] As numerous commentators have noted, the use of "made with hands/not made with hands" and the distinction between two temples fits poorly in the account of the trial.[23] The version in 15:29 would fit far better in the context of the trial as well. But that raises the question what purpose the distinction between two temples and the use of the "made with hands" terminology have in the version of the statement at the trial. If the additions make little sense as part of the charge, if in fact they detract from the apparent force of the charge,[24] it is possible that the author is providing important clues for the reader as to its meaning in spite of the

---

[20]Lohmeyer, _Mark_, 326-327.

[21]The interpretation of the temple saying as a threat against the temple is particularly clear in Acts 6:14, where the statement is made simply that Jesus will destroy the temple, coupled with the treat to "change the customs which Moses delivered to us."

[22]For the suggestion that the charge implies that Jesus is a magician, see Linnemann, _Studien_, 132, and W. Grundmann, _Das Evangelium nach Markus_ (THNT 2; 3rd ed.; Berlin: Evangelische Verlagsanstalt, 1965), 301.

[23]P. Vielhauer, _Oikodome: Das Bild vom Bau in der christlichen Literatur vom Neuen Testament bis Clemens Alexandrinus_ (Karlsruhe, 1940), 63.

[24]_Ibid._

impact the details have at one level of the story.

If this is true, the features would have to be viewed as
"unhistorical" additions to the charge, features unimportant for
the participants in the drama for whom the statement represents
simply a threat against the temple and/or an impossible boast,
perhaps implying that Jesus is a magician. The clues would be
intended for the reader, pointers to the deeper level of meaning
at which the truth of the charge could be appreciated. It would
be as inappropriate in this case to ask how the false witnesses
could have understood so little of what they were saying as to
ask how those around Jesus could have failed to hear the confes-
sions of Jesus as the "Son of God" by demoniacs (esp. 3:11 and
5:7). As Burkill has suggested, the failure of the witnesses to
grasp the truth of what they are saying is a consistent feature
of the passion story and an appropriate expression of the
messianic secret in the Gospel as a whole.[25]

If Mark is willing to sacrifice coherence at one level
to portray what is "really" happening, however, the differences
between the charge and its repetition might indicate how the
statement could be both true and false. The version in 15:29
might indicate that the statement has been interpreted by Jesus'
opponents as implying that Jesus is a magician, that he has made
an impossible threat against the temple. The version of the
charge in 14:58, however, might be intended to indicate the
sense in which the charge is true. It is even possible that,
for Mark, the statement could be true if Jesus never said such
a thing. As we shall observe, the statement allegedly made by
Jesus about the temple was apparently a sore point for early
Christians.[26] The version of the charge in 15:29 is closer to
the versions in the other Gospels. Perhaps Mark is suggesting
that Jesus never made such a statement and that it is therefore
false. But the differences in the version in the trial suggest
that something positive is being done with the charge as well.
Jesus' opponents are being made unwitting confessors to a truth
beyond their level of understanding. They can be both "false
witnesses" and prophets. It is possible that the mockery of
Jesus as prophet in 14:65 is intended to point up not only
Jesus' prophecy in 14:62 but also the "prophecy" in 14:58.[27]

_____

[25]Burkill, "Trial," 11.   [26]See below, 207-208.

[27]Klostermann, Mark, 157.

Although absolute clarity is probably unattainable, a close study of the statement about the failure of the witnesses to agree (14:59) and the mention of false witnesses (14:56-57) demonstrates that the features of the story can be understood as an integral part of the story whether the temple charge is true or false. The decision about the truth of the charge, however, can be made only by looking at other evidence. In what follows, we will consider carefully the temple theme in the last chapters of Mark in an attempt to interpret the temple charge in its present context. We shall also examine the particular features of the charge in 14:58, especially the features that distinguish 14:58 from 15:29. Of particular concern will be the terms "made with hands/not made with hands," the distinction between two temples in the first and second half of the statement, and the reference to "three days." After determining the truth or falsity of the charge, we will examine its meaning by a careful study of the background of the imagery in the verse.

CHAPTER 6

THE TEMPLE THEME IN MARK

Perhaps the most important observation that can be made about the temple charge in 14:58 is that it is only one of a series of statements about the temple beginning with chapter 11. Any interpretation of the charge at the trial must consider the verse within its context, and it appears that the verse is part of a theme. From the moment Jesus enters Jerusalem, the story focuses on Jesus and the temple. It is important that we examine these references to the temple in some detail.[1]

We may first observe that there is a difference in terminology between chapters 11-14:49 and 14:58-15:38. The term used in the earlier chapters is ἱερόν, while the term used in 14:58, 15:29 and 15:38 is ναός. Of the two terms, ναός is the more unusual. It is used infrequently in the Gospels. The term appears in the versions of the temple charge in Matthew and John. In Mark, it occurs only within the passion story. This suggests that the three statements about the temple in 14:58, 15:29 and 15:38 are related in a special way.

J. Schreiber has argued that the absence of ναός in most of Mark indicates that the term derives from tradition, while Mark himself prefers the term ἱερόν.[2] For the redaction critic, this would seem to suggest that the creative activity of the author should be located in the ἱερόν passages. This is not the case in Schreiber's study, however, since he argues that the placement of the temple saying in the trial and in the account of the crucifixion, as well as the mention of the tearing of the temple veil, are all the work of Mark.[3] Even his suggestion about the two terms ἱερόν and ναός turns out to be of little

---

[1]At this point Fr. Donahue and I follow a similar approach (see Are You the Christ?, 113-135), though we come to somewhat different conclusions.

[2]Schreiber, "Der Kreuzigungsbericht des Markus-evangeliums," 205, note 1; followed by Donahue, Are You the Christ?, 104-105.

[3]Ibid., 61 and 103; Theologie des Vertrauens, 47, note 106.

use, however. The choice of the terms is dictated by the
meaning of the terms in Mark, and there appears to be a clear
distinction between the terms.[4] The differences are clear when
the context of each statement is examined:

> 11:11, 15, 16--Jesus visits the temple (ἱερόν), where he
> casts out merchants. The action obviously takes place
> in the temple courts. The term chosen to describe the
> temple site is ἱερόν.
>
> 11:27, 12:35, 14:49--In each of these verses, reference
> is made to Jesus' teaching in the temple. Again the
> term chosen is ἱερόν. The setting for the teaching
> would certainly be the temple courts. Mark's usage is
> thus far consistent.
>
> 13:2--Jesus predicts the destruction of the temple
> buildings (plural!) after leaving the ἱερόν. The pre-
> diction refers to the coming destruction of the whole
> temple area, which would make the term ἱερόν appro-
> priate.

On the other hand, the ναός in 15:38 clearly refers to
the temple building housing the holy of holies. At the moment
of Jesus' death, the veil of the ναός is torn. The term used
here is not ἱερόν because for Mark, ἱερόν is used to refer to
the whole temple complex, not to the sanctuary proper. The
usage is consistent and need reflect nothing about Mark's
traditions. Nor does Mark "prefer" the term ἱερόν. It is used
more frequently because in most instances Mark is speaking
about the temple complex.

Even such a cursory examination of terminology provides
some important suggestions for interpretation. The use of ναός
in the temple charge at Jesus' trial rules out any clear identity
between the prediction in 13:2 (which refers to buildings) and
the charge at the trial.[5] The charge represents something more
than a mere restatement of Jesus' earlier prediction. The
charge in 14:58, the mockery in 15:29, and the report of the
tearing of the veil in 15:38 all focus on the ναός, the particular building. The replacement of the ναὸς ὁ χειροποίητος by
ἄλλος ἀχειροποίητος is of special importance to the author.

If the three verses in the passion story are related in
a special way, it also seems clear that the statements are
not unrelated to the other references to the temple in the last

---

[4] Contrary to O. Michel (ναός, TDNT 4, 882), who insists
that there is no difference in "either meaning or range" between
these terms in the New Testament.

[5] Against Wellhausen, Mark, 123, and Donahue, Are You
the Christ?, 72; thus Linnemann, Studien, 118.

chapters:

11:16-17--Jesus "cleanses" the temple and makes statements about its misuse by the Jewish religious leaders.

12:1-12--Jesus tells the parable of the wicked husbandmen, which ends with a promise that the "tenants" will be replaced by "others." The "tenants," identified with the "builders" of Ps 118:22, are the religious leaders who know that "he had told the parable against them" (12:12).

12:32-34--In response to a question asked by a scribe, Jesus recites the first part of the Shema and provides a summary of the commandments (28-31). The commands, according to the scribe, are "more important than all whole burnt offerings and sacrifices"--to which Jesus replies, "You are not far from the kingdom of God."

13:1-2--Jesus predicts the destruction of the entire temple complex.

14:58--Jesus is charged with having made a statement according to which he would destroy "this temple made with hands" and in three days build "another not made with hands."

15:29--The charge is repeated in a taunt by passers-by as Jesus hangs on the cross.

15:38--At the moment of Jesus' death, the temple curtain is torn from top to bottom.

Although the charge at the trial is not a repetition of the prediction in 13:2, the statements about the temple are certainly related.[6] And if there is no obvious link between the cleansing in 11:16-17 and the charge at the trial, there are indications that at a deeper level these two passages are related as well. We can begin a close examination of the temple theme with the short account of the cleansing in 11:16-17.

It is astonishing that so little is made of the cleansing by Mark. The short account has figured prominently in the reconstructions of the ministry of Jesus by numerous scholars, S. G. F. Brandon being one of the more recent.[7] Brandon insists that this must have been an extremely important event in Jesus' ministry. He could not have succeeded in driving out the merchants by himself, but must have had the support of the crowds.[8] The failure of the temple police to intervene suggests that the mob was too large to control.[9] In fact, Brandon views this event as the real basis for Jesus' arrest and eventual execution.[10]

[6]Thus Donahue, Are You the Christ?, 128-138; Schreiber, Theologie des Vertrauens, 41; Burkill, "Trial," 6-8.

[7]S. G. F. Brandon, Jesus and the Zealots (Manchester: Scribner's, 1967).

[8]Ibid., 332-333.   [9]Ibid., 334.   [10]Ibid., 334-336.

It was an attack on the temple establishment and, in the eyes of the Romans, a revolt. The silence about the event and the absence of any mention of it in the trial reflects the editorial activity of Mark, who was concerned to remove any suggestion that Christianity was in any sense a revolutionary movement.[11]

Others insist that the event could not have occurred as Mark describes it. Had Jesus driven all of the merchants out of the temple courts, the Roman legion stationed in the fortress Antonia would surely have intervened.[12] Or perhaps the act was not as serious as many have assumed and that the Romans would simply not have construed Jesus' actions as revolutionary.[13] What is astonishing is how little interest the author reveals in such concerns. The story seems clearly to have a didactic function in the Gospel.[14] Since it is the first of a series of comments on the temple, it is important to determine how the story functions in its setting, what the author intends the reader to understand. There are four features of the account that we will examine: the placement of the scene between two parts of the cursing of the fig tree, the allusion to Isa 56:7 in v. 17, the allusion to Jer 7:11 in the same verse, and the phrase "house of prayer" in v. 17.

The framing of one account with another is a familiar Markan literary device; we have already observed the device in the account of Peter's denial and Jesus' trial. Its function as an interpretive device here is clear. The story of the cursed fig tree, whatever its original meaning in Christian tradition, provides an insight into the meaning of the cleansing of the temple. The story is narrated not simply to display Jesus' miraculous power nor simply to introduce the saying on prayer, even if this is the function of the pericope with respect to form.[15] The use of the imperfect ἤκουον in v. 14 helps extend the action into the account which follows, to be picked up again in v. 21 ("And Peter remembered and said to him..."). Mark intends the reader to keep the story of the fig tree in mind while reading the story of the cleansing.

---

[11]Ibid., 221-282.   [12]Lohmeyer, Mark, 237.

[13]Taylor, Mark, 463.

[14]Lohmeyer, Mark, 237; Bultmann, History, 36.

[15]Bultmann, History, 218; Taylor, Mark, 458.

The interpretation is rather obvious. The cleansing of the temple must in some sense imply the rejection of the official representatives of Israel, the leaders of the temple establishment. Some care is necessary at this point. It is perhaps inaccurate to suggest that the events point to the rejection of Israel. Jesus' opponents in the last chapters of the Gospel are clearly the leaders of the temple establishment, the scribes, the high priests, and the elders. The question will be considered later.[16] At this point it is at least possible to say that the cleansing, interpreted by the cursing of the fig tree, points to the rejection of a particular group within Israel. Those in charge of the temple have borne no fruit; they have perverted God's intentions and will thus be rejected. This interpretation is confirmed by the account of the cleansing itself as well as by the parable of the wicked husbandmen (12:1-12).

The two scriptural allusions in v. 17 are decisive for interpreting the event in Mark. The references comprise half the extant account. The first is introduced as a direct quotation from Isa 56:7:

"Is it not written, 'My house shall be called a house of prayer for all nations?'"

Our concern here is to determine what the quote means for Mark, not what it might have meant as spoken by Jesus. Two features that seem particularly appropriate in Mark are the reference to the "house of prayer" and the reference to "all nations" (πᾶσιν τοῖς ἔθνεσιν). We shall examine the term "house of prayer" separately. The absence of the phrase τοῖς ἔθνεσιν in Matthew and Luke does not necessarily indicate anything about Mark's emphasis, but in fact, there does seem to be some concern for Gentiles present in the Gospel. In 13:10, in the farewell discourse of Jesus, it is said that "the gospel must first be preached to all nations (εἰς πάντα τὰ ἔθνη)." And perhaps it is not accidental that the first to make a true confession after Jesus' death is a Gentile, the Roman Centurion. If this does represent an important emphasis in Mark, the quotation from Isaiah is well chosen. The verse is part of a promise to the "eunuch" and to the "foreigner" (ἀλλογενής) who have kept justice, done righteousness (v. 1) and kept the Sabbath (v. 2), that they will have a share in the

---

[16]See below, 212-13.

promises soon to be fulfilled for God's people. They too will
have a place on God's "holy mountain" (v. 7); their sacrifices
too will be accepted (v. 7). The verse quoted in Mark is the
concluding promise, explaining God's final purpose: "For my
house shall be called a house of prayer for all peoples
(πᾶσῖν τοῖς ἔθνεσιν)" (Isa 56:7 LXX).

It is more difficult to determine if the next scriptural
reference in 11:17 is intended as a direct quotation or as an
allusion. It is at least clear that the statement "But you have
made it a den of robbers (σπήλαιον λῃστῶν)" comes from Jer 7:11.
What is striking about the terms σπήλαιον λῃστῶν from Jeremiah
(LXX) is how inappropriate they are in the present context.
The term λῃστής is not aptly chosen to describe the merchants
and money changers, for it does not mean "hishonest man" or
"thief." The term λῃστής means "robber, highway man, bandit,"
or even "revolutionary, insurrectionist."[17] If, as most commentators seem to assume, the terms are intended as a characterization of the dishonest merchants who "fleeced" festival
pilgrims,[18] the quotation is simply inappropriate. The statement in Jn 2:16 is far more sensible: "you shall not make my
father's house a house of trade."[19] If Lindars is correct when
he argues that this verse is an allusion to Zech 14:21, we would
have to agree that John has hit upon an excellent verse. It
both fits the situation and it is derived from a text which is
speaking about the future temple.

But that simply makes the reference to Jer 7:11 in Mark
more peculiar. And when we observe the way Mark uses the term
λῃστής elsewhere in the Gospel, the situation is complicated
even further. In 14:48, in the context of Jesus' arrest, Jesus
asks:

Have you come out as against a robber (ὡς ἐπὶ λῃστήν)
with swords and clubs, to capture me?

The image here is hardly of a dishonest merchant. And in
15:27, the term is used to describe the two men who were crucified with Jesus. In the context of chapter 15, the term can
only mean "revolutionary," "insurrectionist." The term λῃστής
is thus hardly appropriate as a characterization for the

---

[17]Bauer, λῃστής.   [18]For example, Taylor, _Mark_, 463.

[19]As Lindars (_New Testament Apologetic_, 108, note 3)
suggests, the quote in John is an allusion to Zech 14:21 that
probably represents a translation from the Hebrew.

dishonest merchants in the temple or even for the Jewish religious leaders. The verse from Jeremiah has not been chosen because the image of the temple as a σπήλαιον ληστῶν is particularly appropriate to the historical situation of the
cleansing.

We must therefore determine if the verse from Jeremiah
points in a different direction, if it provides clues to the
interpretation of the cleansing at another level of the story.
Perhaps one clue is provided by the context of the verse in
Jeremiah. The verse is part of an oracle directed against the
House of Judah, particularly against those who have come to regard the presence of the temple as proof of God's continued
blessing. Jeremiah tells them:

> Do not trust in these deceptive words: "This is the
> temple of the Lord, the temple of the Lord, the temple of
> the Lord." (v.4) ...Behold, you trust in deceptive words
> to no avail. Will you steal, murder, commit adultery,
> swear falsely, burn incense to Ba'al, and go after other
> gods that you have not known, and then come and stand be-
> fore me in this house, which is called by my name, and say
> "We are delivered!" - only to go on doing all these abomin-
> ations? Has this house, which is called by my name, become
> a den of robbers [σπήλαιον ληστῶν] in your eyes? (vv 8-11)
> ...therefore I will do to the house which is called by my
> name, and in which you trust, and to the place which I gave
> to you and your fathers, as I did to Shilo. And I will
> cast you out of my sight, as I cast out all your kinsmen,
> all the offspring of Ephraim. (v. 14)

It is not necessarily the case that a verse from the Old
Testament quoted in the New Testament should be understood
within its original context. Atomistic exegesis, quoting a
verse without regard for its context, is a practice familiar to
Christian and Jewish exegetes. But in this case, the setting
of the verse in Jeremiah cannot be accidental. If the phrase
"den of robbers" is inappropriate for the historical cleansing,
the verse itself is most appropriate in Mark. It is part of an
oracle prophesying the destruction of the temple! The rejection
of those who have misused their rights as God's chosen is in
Jeremiah predicted in terms of the destruction of the temple.
This verse is not only historically appropriate in Mark; it
also fits perfectly into the context of the last chapters of his
Gospel. The verse is thus quite important in the interpretation
of 14:58--at a deeper dimension of the story. The cleansing is
important not as an isolated event, but as part of a theme that
concludes with the tearing of the veil in 15:38. In the reference to Jeremiah, Mark characterizes the cleansing as a

134

prophetic anticipation of what is to come. Because they have
misused the temple and their privileges, the leaders of the
people (11:18--the chief priests and the scribes) and their
temple will be destroyed. The statement about a replacement
of "this temple made with hands" in 14:58 may indicate what
Mark believes to be the successor to the temple establishment.

The last aspect of the verse in Mark (11:17) that deserves
some comment is the reference to the "house of prayer" in the
quotation of the verse from Isaiah. The phrase is attested
elsewhere in Jewish literature as a name for the temple.[20] The
term need not imply an opposition to the sacrificial cult. It
certainly does not in the text of Isaiah. There are indications
in Mark, however, that the author does oppose the sacrificial
cult. The most important piece of evidence is the statement
by the scribe in 12:33 that the twin commandment "is much more
than all whole burnt offerings and sacrifices."[21] The precise
controversies considered in chapter 12 seem to have been carefully chosen and probably deserve equally careful study. What
is important in the context of our study is the observation that
some opposition between "house of prayer" and sacrificial cult
is not inconceivable in Mark. And it is at least clear that
the temple is not the "the house of prayer for all nations"
God intended, but instead a "den of robbers."[22] The present
order will be cursed like the fig tree; the vineyard will be
given to others (12:9). The temple will be destroyed (13:1-2;
cf. 14:58 and 15:29), to be replaced by a new reality (a
"temple not made with hands," 14:58).

We are perhaps anticipating the results of the study of
the verse in the trial, but such details within the chapters
preceding the trial certainly provide important clues to the
meaning of 14:58. There is a further indication in Mark that
the saying about the "house of prayer" may be important for
understanding 14:58. There is a discussion of prayer immediately following the conclusion to the cursing of the fig tree

[20]Cf. Isa 60:7 (LXX); Bill I, 852-3 for references.

[21]Lohmeyer, Lord of the Temple, 47.

[22]In private conversation, Geza Vermes made the interesting suggestion that if Mark were writing post-70, the reference
to the temple as a σπήλαιον λῃστῶν would be striking in light
of Josephus' account of the last stage of the siege of Jerusalem,
during which the revolutionaries (λῃσταί) used the temple as
a stronghold (see esp. the account in Jos JW 6: 130-210).

that suggests the term "house of prayer" may be more than simply a scriptural quotation for Mark.

In 11:20-25, the story of the cursing of the fig tree is resumed. But Peter's notice of the withered tree is immediately followed by a small group of sayings by Jesus on faith and prayer. Form critics have long observed that the transition is artificial.[23] Furthermore, the verses are an intrusion. In 11:27, the issue of Jesus' authority is discussed, which would be most appropriate immediately after the cleansing. Bultmann has even suggested that v. 25 is not original in Mark.[24] Matthew includes the saying about casting "this mountain" into the sea in the same context (21:18-23), but he also has a parallel version of the saying in 17:20. Luke's version of the saying (17: 6) is different from Matthew's and is apparently from Q ("if you had faith as a grain of mustard seed" Matt 17:20/Lk 17:6), without clear influence from Mark. The saying about forgiveness (Mk 11:25) is found in Matthew, but in the context of the Sermon on the Mount (6:14-15); another version of the saying is found in Matt 18:35. All this seems to indicate that in Mark, several independent logia have been combined and appended to the story of the cursing of the fig tree. The most striking additions have to do with prayer and forgiveness (11:24-25).[25]

The presence of the sayings should be viewed as something more than an accident of tradition whose history has been completed prior to the writing of Mark's Gospel. The juxtaposition of the saying on prayer with a story whose point seems to be that the temple establishment will be rejected because it has not made the temple into a "house of prayer for all nations" may be quite important for the author. The saying on prayer is clearly intended for Mark's church. Perhaps Mark wishes to characterize the community of the faithful as a community typified by prayer and forgiveness.[26] The contrast between the praying community and the "house of prayer" that has become a "den of robbers" already suggests that the distinction between a "temple made with hands" and a "temple not made with hands" in

---

[23] Bultmann, _History_, 25 and 218.   [24] _Ibid._, 25.

[25] See the essay by K. Stendahl, "Prayer and Forgiveness," SEA 22/23 (1957-58), 75-86.

[26] The suggestion that the saying on prayer and the "house of prayer" might be related in Mark was made to me by Prof. Dahl.

136

4:58 may reflect the author's view of the Christian community
as a replacement of the rejected temple establishment.

It is not obvious that the parable of the wicked husbandmen in 12:1-11 belongs with the statements about the temple.
It is at least clear, as we have noted, that the tenants referred to in the parable are, in Mark, the leaders of the
temple establishment, Jesus' opponents throughout the last section of the Gospel. The parable promises that their rejection
of the Son will result in the vineyard being taken from them and
given to "others," as well as their destruction (12:9). The
quotation of the verse from Psalm 118 in 12:10-11 relates the
rejection on the part of the tenants to the theme of the vindication of the "stone," a reference to Jesus' resurrection. If
the temple theme in Mark is bound up with the idea of the rejection of the religious leaders, as it clearly seems to be,
the parable belongs to the same constellation of ideas. But
there is even another possibility for linking the parable with
the temple theme. The parable in Mark begins with allusions
to Isa 5:1-7, features not found in the version of the parable
in Luke (20:9-18) or in the Gospel of Thomas (65). This has
led Jeremias to believe that the additions are part of the
process of allegorization observable in the transmission of the
parable.[27] The reference to the famous Song of the Vineyard in
Isaiah is quite intelligible within the context of the Gospel.
The symbol of the vineyard, with the mention of the hedge, the
wine press and the tower, would represent Israel, as it clearly
does in Isaiah. What is fascinating about the details, however,
is the interpretation they receive in the targum to Isaiah.
The translation of 5:1a-2 reads:[28]

תושבחת רחמי לכרמיה עמי הביבי ישראל
יהבית להון אחסנא בטור רם בארע שמינא
ולקדישהנון ויקרתינון וקיימחינון כמיצר גפן בחירא
ובנית מקדשי ביניהון
ואף מדבחי יהבית לכפרא על חטאיהון

"The song of my beloved regarding his vineyard," (that is
my people, my favorite, Israel.) "I gave them an inheritance

[27]J. Jeremias, The Parables of Jesus (tr. S. H. Hooke;
New York: Scribner's, 1963), 70.

[28]The text is taken from A. Sperber, The Bible in Aramaic
III: The Latter Prophets according to Targum Jonathan (Leiden:
Brill, 1962). In translating this text I had the assistance
of Professors Henry Fischel and Kalman Bland of Indiana
University.

on a high mountain in a rich land. And I sanctified them
and honored them and upheld them like a planting of choice
vines. And I built my sanctuary among them, and my altar
also I gave them for atonement for their sins...."

We shall examine the Isaiah Targum in detail below.[29]
There is no need to consider at this point all of the problems
involved in dating targumic traditions. What is striking is
simply the interpretation of the Song of the Vineyard in Isa
5:1ff by the targumist as a reference to the destruction of
Jerusalem and the temple (see esp. 5:5). The Watchtower in the
Hebrew is interpreted by the targumist as a reference to the
temple--which is subsequently destroyed because of the sins of
the people. As we shall see, this is a predominant theme
throughout the Isaiah Targum. The verse certainly presupposes
the destruction of the temple in A.D. 70 and subsequent reflection on that event. But what is interesting is that the parable
of the wicked husbandmen in Mark is related to Isa 5:1ff by the
use of terms from the verse in the Septuagint. It is perhaps
more than pure coincidence that Mark uses such imagery in the
context of a parable about the rejection of the Jewish religious
leaders. If Mark knew about such targumic traditions or if the
imagery in Isa 5:1ff had been traditionally applied to Jerusalem
and the temple, the imagery in Mk 12:1 would suggest that the
parable should be related to the temple theme present from
chapter 11 on. It is at least possible that the author has provided another clue regarding what is to happen, another suggestion that the rejection of the leaders and the destruction of
the temple belong together (11:17, 13:1-2, 14:58).

The final verse important for the interpretation of 14:58
is 15:38, the mention of the tearing of the veil of the temple.
We have already noted the special relationship that exists among
14:58, 15:29 and 15:38. The peculiar use of ναός seems to suggest a particularization of the concern for the temple. The
statement in 15:38 that at the moment of Jesus' death, the
temple καταπέτασμα was torn from top to bottom represents a
culmination of the temple theme in some sense and a decisive
climax to 14:58 and 15:29. The restatement of the charge from
the trial in the mockery clearly heightens the importance of
the tearing of the veil. As Burkill has noted:

---

[29]See the discussion of the Isaiah Targum in chapter
9 below.

138

> And now in a supernatural fashion the temple itself sets
> the scoffers at naught by bearing witness to the doom to
> which it is condemned.[30]

The problems involved in the interpretation of the
tearing of the veil will be considered in a separate excursus.[31]
The context would seem to support the interpretation of the
verse as a portent of the impending destruction of the temple.
If that is the case, the verse represents the culmination of
the references to rejection and destruction begun in 11:17.
The presence of the verse immediately following Jesus' death
suggests that with Jesus' death, the temple establishment comes
to an end--or at least a decisive sign is given that its doom
is sealed. The relationship between Jesus' death and the destruction then becomes highly significant for the author.[32] One
of the two results of Jesus' death is the end of the temple
order. But that also represents partial fulfillment of the
"prophecy" made at the trial, which in turn suggests that Mark
must view the charge in 14:58 as true in some sense. And if,
with Jesus' death, the negative half of the prediction is fulfilled, we must ask if there is in Mark's mind a corresponding
fulfillment of the prediction of a new "temple not made with
hands" after three days.

The last chapters in Mark provide convincing evidence
that the charge at Jesus' trial in 14:58 is more than a statement Mark wishes to discredit. In 11:17, the theme of the rejection of the Jewish religious leaders is linked with the
impending destruction of the temple by the reference to Jer
7:11. In 12:1-12, Jesus tells a parable according to which the
Jewish religious leaders, the tenants, will be destroyed and
their "vineyard" given to others. The reference to Ps 118:22
that concludes the parable links this rejection with the coming
rejection of Jesus by these "builders," as well as with his
vindication at the resurrection. In 12:32-34, negative statements are made about sacrifice. In 13:1-2, Jesus explicitly
predicts the destruction of the temple complex. And in 15:38,
at the moment of Jesus' death, the temple veil is torn from top
to bottom. There can be little doubt that Mark intends the
charge at the trial to be viewed as true in some sense. It at

---

[30]Burkill, "St. Mark's Philosophy of the Passion," 267.

[31]See the excursus on the temple veil, 140-42.

[32]Burkill, "Philosophy," 267.

least points to the destruction of the temple, interpreted as the sign of the rejection of the very leaders who, ironically, reject Jesus.

There are also hints that the positive statement in 14: 58 about the building of a temple not made with hands in three days refers in some way to the Christian community, viewed as a replacement of the temple establishment. The saying about prayer in 11:24-25, immediately after the statement about the "house of prayer for all nations," as well as the mention of the giving of the vineyard to others in 12:9 points in this direction. Now what is needed is a careful study of the verse, focusing on the reference to three days, the distinction between two temples, and the "made with hands/not made with hands" terminology.

EXCURSUS: TEMPLE VEIL

A few comments on the image of the temple veil in Mark are in order. The interpretation of the tearing of the veil in 15:38 has been disputed for some time. Which καταπέτασμα is meant in the verse? According both to the Old Testament and to post-biblical sources, the term καταπέτασμα could be used for either of two veils: the veil separating the sanctuary from the forecourt or the veil concealing the holy of holies.[1] According to Jos Ant 8:75, the outer curtains were hung over the doors by Herod, presumably to act as a kind of replacement for the doors when they were opened during the day. The question is, therefore, which of these two veils is meant in Mk 15:38.

Some interpreters have argued that the reference must be to the inner veil separating the holy of holies from the rest of the sanctuary.[2] The inner veil has particular cultic significance, and there is a well-developed Christian tradition about this inner veil in Hebrews (6:19 and 9:3; cf. 10:20). The meaning of the tearing of this inner veil at the moment of Jesus' death would not be difficult to determine. The image could mean that in Jesus' death, access to the holy of holies, i.e. to God's presence, has been opened. The imagery might well be associated with traditions about the cosmic veil.[3] If Mark views Christianity as the replacement of the temple institution, such a meaning would fit well within his account of the passion story.

Other interpreters have argued that the veil referred to in Mk 15:38 is the outer veil.[4] What makes this suggestion particularly attractive is the existence of Jewish traditions about miraculous portents signaling the impending doom of the temple.[5]

The account of such an event is recorded in Jos JW

---

[1] The references are found in C. Schneider, καταπέτασμα TDNT 3, 629, and Bill I. 1045.

[2] Schneider, TDNT 3, 629; Bill I, 1045; Taylor, Mark, 596; Haenchen, Der Weg Jesu, 534; Burkill, "Trial," 7.

[3] Taylor, Mark, 596.

[4] Lohmeyer, Mark, 347; idem., Lord of the Temple, 52; Klostermann, Mark, 167; Burkill, "Philosophy," 267.

[5] Jos JW 6:290ff; bYoma 39b; jYoma 43c; Tacitus, Hist, V, 13.

6:293-296:

> moreover, the eastern gate of the inner court – it was of brass and very massive, and, when closed towards evening, could scarcely be moved by twenty men; fastened with iron-bound bars, it had bolts which were sunk to a great depth into a threshold consisting of a solid block of stone – this gate was observed at the sixth hour of the night to have opened of its own accord. The watchman of the temple ran and reported the matter to the captain, and he came up and with difficulty succeeded in shutting it. This again to the uninitiated seemed the best of omens, as they supposed that God had opened to them the gate of blessing; but the learned understood that the security of the temple was dissolving of its own accord and that the opening of the gate meant a present to the enemy, interpreting the portent in their own minds as indicative of coming desolation.[6]

These events, according to Josephus, occurred at the time of Passover in the year A.D. 66. A similar story is reported in the Talmud (bYoma 39b):[7]

> Our Rabbis taught: During the last forty years before the destruction of the Temple the lot ["For the Lord"] did not come up in the right hand; nor did the crimson-coloured strap become white; nor did the western-most light shine; and the doors of the Hekal would open by themselves, until R. Johanan b. Zakkai rebuked them, saying: Hekal, Hekal, why wilt thou be the alarmer thyself? I know about thee that thou wilt be destroyed, for Zechariah ben Ido has already prophesied concerning thee: "Open thy doors, O Lebanon, that the fire may devour thy cedars." (Zech 11:1)

No clear relationship exists among the various accounts, but there are some interesting similarities. According to Josephus, the portent occurs at the time of Passover. According to the Talmud, the miraculous opening the doors occurs during the 40 years prior to the destruction of the temple. The similarities to the setting of the passion story and the date of Jesus' death are striking. If the reference to the tearing of the veil in Mk 15:38 refers to the tearing of the outer veil, and if this is in some way related to the traditions about the portents of the coming destruction of the temple, the reference would fit particularly well into Mark's account of the passion. It would represent the mysterious culmination of the statements about the destruction of the temple (11:17, 12:9 [?], 13:1-2, 14:58, 15:29). And occurring at the moment of Jesus' death, it would represent a rather precise fulfillment of the prediction

---

[6] Josephus (LCL 210; trans. H. St. J. Thackeray; Cambridge: Harvard University Press, 1928), III, 461-463.

[7] The translation is taken from the Soncino Edition of the Babylonian Talmud.

in 14:58 that Jesus would destroy the temple. The result of Jesus' death is the end of the Jewish temple, foreshadowed in the tearing of the veil.[8]

Final decision about the precise interpretation is perhaps impossible. From our study of Mark, however, the second of the two possibilities seems to fit best with the statements made about the temple leading up to the dramatic tearing of the veil.

CHAPTER 7

INTERPRETIVE DETAILS IN 14:58

In 14:58, Jesus is charged with having threatened to
destroy the temple made with hands and in three days build
another not made with hands. We have already noted that one of
the differences between the charge at the trial and the version
of the charge in the mockery in 15:29 is the distinction between
two temples. In 15:29, Jesus is described as the destroyer and
builder of the same temple. In 14:58, he is characterized as
the destroyer of one temple and the builder of another (ἄλλον)
of a different order. From study of the surrounding chapters
we have determined that the verse should be viewed as a prophecy
of some sort. The mention in the verse of a different temple
which Jesus is to build "in three days" confirms what has already been suggested: the verse points not only to the destruction of the old temple, but to the replacement of the old
temple with a "temple not made with hands." The most obvious
possibility is that the "temple not made with hands" refers to
the Christian community. It is also significant, as we shall
observe, that Jesus is characterized as the builder of the new
temple.[1]

The only "fulfillment" of the prophecy in 14:58 referred
to in the Gospel is the destruction of the temple (15:38), and
the tearing of the veil is only a portent of what is to come.
But the same lack of clear fulfillment characterizes the second
of the charges at the trial and the "prophecy" associated with
it. The only vindication of Jesus reported in the Gospel is
the confession of a lone Centurion in 15:39 that may well be intended by the author, on the surface level of the story, to be
an expression of amazement and conviction that Jesus was a good
man ("a son of God"). Even the empty tomb fails to convince the
women, who are too afraid to say anything. In the case of the
second of the charges, however, the author clearly points the
reader to the vindication of Jesus at the resurrection (predicted in 8:31, 9:31, and 10:33). In context, the reference to

---

[1]See below, chapter 9.

144

"three days" in the temple charge can hardly be understood as
anything but a reference to the resurrection. The difference in
form between διὰ τριῶν ἡμερῶν in 14:58 and the μετὰ τρεῖς
ἡμέραις in the three passion predictions may indicate diverse
origins within tradition,[2] but the difference cannot be an indication that a reference to the resurrection is not intended
in 14:58. Many scholars have suggested that διὰ τριῶν ἡμερῶν
means "in a short time,"[3] although no one has presented any convincing evidence to substantiate the claim. If that is the
case, however, the use of διὰ τριῶν ἡμερῶν in 14:58 would fit
well with Mark's use of irony. Jesus' opponents take the reference to "three days" to mean "in a short time." The Christian
reader understands that the reference is to the resurrection,
at which time Jesus will be vindicated as the Christ, the Son of
the Blessed and the "temple not made with hands" will be built.
The secret of Jesus' identity as builder of the temple and as
the Christ, Son of God is preserved on the surface level of
the story. Both claims sound absurd to Jesus' opponents. But
the Christian reader is directed to the level of the story at
which the truth of the claims can be known.

The third feature of 14:58 that requires special comment
at this stage of our study is the use of the terms χειροποίητος/
ἀχειροποίητος. From our study thus far, it seems probable that
the "temple made with hands" refers to the Jerusalem temple,
while the "temple not made with hands" refers to the Christian
community. Since the two terms are absent from the version of
the charge in 15:29, their presence in 14:58 is all the more
important for understanding what Mark intends the reader to
understand. Apparently the two terms are important clues. If
the charge is to be viewed as a prophecy, and if the two temples
can be identified as suggested, it should be possible to indicate why Mark has used the two terms χειροποίητος/ἀχειροποίητος
and what function they have in the verse.

The suggestion that "temple not made with hands" refers

_____

[2]8:31, 9:31, 10:34: μετὰ τρεῖς ἡμέρας 14:58 διὰ τριῶν
ἡμερῶν 15:29 ἐν τρισὶν ἡμέραις. For the meaning of διά in 14:58,
see Blass-Debrunner, par 223 ("within three days").

[3]Taylor, Mark, 556; Klostermann, Mark, 155; Cathcpole,
Trial, 130. The only substantial evidence that "three days"
means "a short time" is the use of the term in Hos 6:2 ("After
two days he will revive us; on the third day he will raise us
up"), but here the Greek is τῇ τρίτῃ ἡμέρᾳ, found in Matthew
and Luke but not in Mark.

to the Christian community is not new. The following is a
representative selection of students of Mark who have made this
identification:

E. Lohmeyer suggests that the saying in 14:58 points
forward to the "eschatologische Gottesgemeinde."[4]

O. Michel: "Mark distinguished between the temple made
with hands and the wonderful new structure of the eschatological community, which is not made with hands."[5]

V. Taylor points out that the term "made with hands" is
usually employed to translate "idol" in the LXX and in the
papyri. The second half of the saying, he argues, points to a
"new spiritual system or community. The saying promises the
destruction of the old building but also the erection of a new
religious order."[6]

E. Klostermann: The saying means "in kürzester Frist
wird die Christengemeinde an Stelle des Tempels treten."[7]

P. Benoit: The statement must reflect a "common belief."
In Mark it must refer to the replacement of the temple institution with a new religion, "a Temple 'not made by human hands,'
that is to say a new worship and a new age of religion."[8]

E. Schweizer: The "temple not made with hands" refers
to the Christian community, a concept familiar from Matt 16:18,
I Cor 3:17, II Cor 6:16, Eph 2:22, and perhaps Rev 3:12.[9]

J. Schreiber: "Die Gegner müssen mit ihren falschen
Anklagen (14:57f) und ihrem Spott (15:29) das von Jesus
prophezeite (13:1-3) Gericht über den alten Tempel (15:38)
und die Gründung des neuen, nicht mit Händen gebauten Tempels
(14:58), d. h. die Gründung der christlichen Gemeinde (15:39-
41), vorhersagen."[10]

If this interpretation of the phrase in Mark is widespread, it is also imprecise and unsupported with relevant
evidence in most commentaries. Recently strong counterarguments
have been offered by Eta Linnemann. Her own proposal is not as
important as her criticisms of previous attempts to explain the

---

[4]Lohmeyer, _Mark_, 566.   [5]O. Michel, TDNT 4, 883.

[6]Taylor, _Mark_, 566.   [7]Klostermann, _Mark_, 155.

[8]Benoit, _The Passion and Resurrection of Jesus Christ_,
101.

[9]Schweizer, _Mark_, 329.

[10]Schreiber, _Theologie des Vertrauens_, 41

phrase in Mark. Her criticisms are incisive and point up the lack of careful argumentation by many commentators. They thus deserve careful attention:

1. There is no justification to be found in the precise wording of the charge in 14:58 for linking the charge with Jesus' prediction in 13:2.[11] The possibility thus remains that Mark views the charge as false testimony.[12]

2. A more primitive version of the charge is found in Mk 15:29, in which the terms χειροποίητος and ἀχειροποίητος are missing and in which there is an identity between the temple to be destroyed and the one to be (re) built. She argues that the charge in Mk 14:58 should be interpreted via 15:29, and that the additions (χειροποίητος/ ἀχειροποίητος) do not alter the original sense. According to her view, the saying must be interpreted in light of the realistic expectations for the replacement of the temple as found in Jewish apocalyptic (Enoch 90: 28-29).[13]

3. There is no justification for viewing the expression "temple not made with hands" as a reference to the Christian community. Her first objection is that the term ἀχειροποίητος does not mean "spiritual."

   Die Wortebedeutung erlaubt es nicht, ἀχειροποίητος mit "geistlich" gleichzusetzen, weil jeder Bezug zum Pneuma fehlt.[14]

   There is no evidence in the rest of the N.T. that the term can be used as a synonym for "spiritual," and certainly not that it means spiritual when combined with "temple."

4. Finally, she finds no evidence that the image of the temple has been applied to a community with any consistency. The image is not sufficiently attested to provide a basis for the argument that the saying points forward to the Christian community.

   Kurzum, die Bezeichnung der Gemeinde als Tempel Gottes kommt gelegentlich vor (I Cor 3:16, II Cor 6:16, Eph 2: 21f), ist aber keineswegs eine geprägte ekklesiologische Grundanschauung, wofür sie in der Auslegung gehalten wird. Die geringe Verbreitung dieser Anschauung erlaubt es nicht, sie für Mk 14:58 vorauszusetzen und unter dem

---

[11]Linnemann, _Studien_, 118.

[12]_Ibid._, 119.   [13]_Ibid._, 122.   [14]_Ibid._

Tempel der nicht mit Händen gemacht ist, die Gemeinde zu verstehen, zumal das Tempelwort und sein Kontext dafür keinen Anhalt bieten.[15]

We have already considered Ms Linnemann's views above.[16] It has been argued that in Mark there is some relationship between 13:1-2 and the charge in 14:58, although at a deeper level of the story and not a relationship of identity. We have further argued that for Mark's view of the charge, the terms χειροποίητος/ἀχειροποίητος and the addition of ἄλλον are fundamental. In this respect Ms Linnemann's approach is the reverse of the one we are following. What the verse may have meant in a pre-Markan form cannot be decisive for interpreting Mark. An interpreter must first be concerned with the verse in its present context. But there are two aspects of her criticism that are significant. The more important has to do with the use of temple imagery to describe a community. We will examine the problem in detail in the next chapter. The other criticism has to do with the term ἀχειροποίητος. Interpreters have taken little trouble to examine the term carefully and have simply assumed that it means "spiritual." If the addition of the terms is important for the meaning of the charge in Mark, careful examination of the terms is necessary. At this point we are again not concerned whether the terms are added by Mark or were added at a prior stage of tradition. What is important is how they function in Mark, what they contribute to the meaning of the charge in its present context.

It is perhaps best to begin with Lohse's article on χειροποίητος in TWNT.[17] According to Lohse, the term presents few difficulties for interpreters. It has one principal meaning in Greek sources:

Das Adj χειροποίητος...ist seit Hdt belegt und hebt den Gegensatz des von Menschen gefertigten Werkes zum natürlich Gewordenen hervor.[18]

Its use in the LXX is also consistent:

In der LXX gibt χειροποίητος fast durchweg hbr אֱלִיל wieder und charakterisiert die Götzen als von Menschenhand gefertigt.[19]

The New Testament is no exception. The term has, according to Lohse, a consistent meaning wherever it is used:

Im Neuen Testament zeigt χειροποίητος an allen Stellen, an denen es verwendet wird, den Gegensatz des von

---

[15]Ibid., 124. [16]See chapter I, 25-29.

[17]E. Lohse TWNT 9, 424-26. [18]Ibid., 425. [19]Ibid., 426.

Menschenhänden Errichteten zum Werk Gottes an.[20]

He believes that the meaning of the opposite, ἀχειροποίητος, is appropriate for what is built by God. This is the meaning of the terms in Mk 14:58:

> Das Logion Mk 14:58 stellt den ναὸν τοῦτον τὸν χειροποίητον dem nicht mit Händen gemachten Tempel gegenüber...der binnen kürzester Frist errichtet werden soll.[21]

Lohse goes on to cite the other uses of the term χειροποίητος, assuming in each case that the use conforms to his distinction between what is accomplished by men and what is accomplished by God. He apparently believes that the use of the terms in Acts, where the statement is made twice that God does not dwell ἐν χειροποιήτοις (ναοῖς) (Acts 7:48, 17:24), and the use of the term in Hebrews, where the earthly sanctuary (σκηνή χειροποίητος or χειροποίητα ἅγια) is opposed to the heavenly (οὐ χειροποίητα ἅγια, σκηνή) in 9:11 and 24, are all equivalent to the usage in Mark.

That is, however, not obvious. In Stephen's speech and in Paul's Areopagos speech, the statement is made that God does not dwell in man-made structures. In Stephen's speech, Isa 66:1-2 is cited as proof. The text is cited also in Jewish tradition, where rabbinic commentators have noted a possible scriptural contradiction:

> In like manner you interpret: "And let them make Me a sanctuary, that I may dwell among them" (Exod 25:8). Why has this been commanded? Has it not been said: "The heaven is My throne...where is the house that ye may build unto me?" (Isa 66:1)? What then is the purport of the commandment: "And let them make Me a sanctuary"? To enable them to receive a reward for fulfilling it.[22]

The apparent contradiction is not solved in the same way by the author of Acts. From other passages in Acts and in Luke's Gospel, it would appear that the building of the Temple is not totally in contradiction to the will of God. But in Stephen's speech it is at least clear that Solomon's Temple is not to be viewed as the final stage in the fulfillment of God's promise for a place of worship (esp. the promise made to Abraham as cited in Acts 7:7).[23] According to Luke there will

---

[20]Ibid.   [21]Ibid.

[22]Mekilta on Exod 13:2. Translation from J. Lauterbach, Mekilta de-Rabbi Ishmael (Philadelphia: Jewish Publication Society of America, 1949), I, 131.

[23]On Stephen's speech, see Nils A. Dahl, "Abraham in Luke-Acts," Studies in Luke-Acts (ed. L. Keck and J. L. Martyn;

be a time when God is no longer worshipped in man-made structures.

The use of made with hands/not made with hands terminology in Mark is somewhat different from the usage in Acts 7.
The statement in Acts 7 that God does not dwell ἐν
χειροποιήτοις does not mean that he does dwell ἐν ναῷ
ἀχειροποιήτῳ . The statement means simply that God does not
dwell in buildings, in any structure. The meaning is even
clearer in Paul's speech in Acts 17. Especially in 17:24-25,
we can observe a familiar motif: God, as creator of heaven and
earth, is self-sufficient and needs neither earthly sanctuaries
nor sacrifices. The passage reflects a general polemic against
idol worship, found both in the O.T.[24] and in a variety of
first-century religious and philosophical traditions.[25] The
statement in 17:24 is clearly a polemic against the notion that
God dwells in buildings of any sort. The passage certainly does
not suggest that God does dwell ἐν ναῷ ἀχειροποιήτῳ, or that
such a "temple" is appropriate as a place of worhsip.

It should be clear that Lohse's definition of
χειροποίητος as man-made in contrast to God-made is not sufficiently precise as an interpretation of the term in Acts.
There is no contrast between a man-made and a God-made structure
in the two passages. The verses simply suggest that God does
not dwell in buildings of any sort. It is possible that the
term χειροποίητος in Mk 14:58 should be understood in light of
the passages in Acts. It may reflect the scriptural notion
(Isa 66) that God, as creator, inhabits all of creation and does
not require buildings, manufactured sanctuaries; it may also reflect the polemic against idol worship, which would imply a
rather radical view of the Jerusalem temple: According to Mark,
the temple in Jerusalem would be viewed as idolatrous, as one of
the many idol temples. Yet if this is the meaning of the

Nashville: Abingdon, 1966), 139-158, esp. 142-147; for the view
that a radical opposition to the temple is intended by Stephen's
speech, see A. F. J. Klijn, "Stephen's Speech--Acts 7:2-53," NTS
4 (1957), 25-31, and M. Simon, St. Stephen and the Hellenists
(London: Longmans and Green, 1958).

[24]H. D. Preuss, Verspottung fremder Religionen im Alten
Testament (Berlin: Kohlhammer Verlag, 1971).

[25]E. Haenchen, Die Apostlegeschichte (Meyer; 15th ed.;
Göttingen: Vandenhoeck and Ruprecht, 1968), on 17:24-25 (with
literature cited).

"temple made with hands," it is not at all clear how the phrase "temple not made with hands" is to be understood. The use of the term χειροποίητος in Acts suggests that no building is an appropriate place to worship God. Reference to another temple, even if built by God himself, is hardly anticipated.

Interpretation of χειροποίητος in Mark must begin with the recognition that it is paired with another term, ἀχειροποίητος. It is the second of the two that is the more unusual. The word does not occur in the Greek Bible. The only references included in Liddell and Scott are the occurrences of the term in the New Testament. Vincent Taylor has even suggested that the term was coined by Mark in this context.[26] It is reasonable, therefore, to begin the study of the two terms in Mark with the second, to determine, if possible, what "not made with hands" means in reference to a temple.

There is some evidence to support Lohse's suggestion that the terms point up the contrast between man-made and God-made. The evidence is even more attractive since the traditions to which reference will be made focus on the temple. There are Jewish exegetical traditions in which a man-made temple is contrasted to a God-made temple. The most obvious passage with which to begin is the midrash on Psalm 90:[27]

> "Let the grace of the Lord our God be upon us." The Holy One, Blessed be He, replied: Of yore, the Temple, having been built by the hands of mortals (נבנה... על ידי בשר ודם)was destroyed and is desolate because I removed My grace from the midst thereof, but in the time to come I Myself shall build it and cause My grace to dwell in the midst thereof, and it will never again be destroyed."

The midrash, as Braude indicates,[28] is actually commenting on the last half of verse 17: ומעשה ידינו כוננה עלינו. The contrast is made between the temple which has been destroyed (בית המקדש שנבנה על ידי בשר ודם) and the temple which God will build himself, the eschatological temple, which will never be destroyed. The comment provides an equivalent for the Greek χειροποίητος in the expression מעשה ידי בשר ודם , and although the text does not describe the new temple as made by God's hands, that specific terminology is familiar from other exegetical traditions. The passage thus provides a possible

---

[26] Taylor, Mark, 566.

[27] W. Braude, The Midrash on Psalms (Yale Judaica Series 13; New Haven: Yale University Press, 1959), II, 99.

[28] Ibid., 99, note 39.

meaning for the terms: made by man (מעשה ידי בשר ודם) as opposed to made by God. And both terms are used with reference to the temple. The tradition in the midrash on Psalms may certainly reflect the destruction of the second Temple in A.D. 70, but the reference to a temple of the future which God will build himself is much older. This image belongs to a special constellation of traditions dealing with Exod 15:17. The text from Exodus, part of Moses' Song, reads:

מקדש אדני כוננו ידיך

Professor Judah Goldin[29] has argued that the expression even in the original composition of the Song reflects an aware-ness of the contrast between a man-made and a God-made sanctuary. He has suggested that the phrase reflects a polemic directed at the Jerusalem Temple built by Solomon.[30] But we also know from rabbinic literature that the verse has been applied to a temple which God will build, the eschatological temple. The text in the Mekilta of R. Ishmael is perhaps the clearest example:

> "The sanctuary, O Lord, which thy hands establish:" How precious is the Temple in the sight of Him Who Spake and the World Came to Be! For when the Holy One, blessed be He, created His world, only with one hand did He create it, as it is said, "Yea, My hand hath laid the foundation of the earth" (Isa 48:13). But when He comes to build the Temple, it will be, as it were, with His two hands, as it is said, "The Sanctuary, O Lord, which Thy hands establish, when the Lord will reign." When will that be? When Thou shalt build it with Thy two hands![31]

The commentator is most interested in the use of the plural, ידיך. The building of the sanctuary with both God's hands makes this event most important in light of what Scripture says about God's hand. The same interest in the use of the plural is reflected in Pirke Aboth 6:10 and Aboth de R. Nathan 1. What is striking about the text from the Mekilta, however, is the application of the text to the eschatological temple, the temple which God will build.[32] And here there is a specific

---

[29] J. Goldin, Song at the Sea (New Haven: Yale University Press, 1971), 46ff.

[30] Ibid., 50-51.

[31] The translation is from Goldin, Song, 237-238.

[32] Goldin (Ibid., 237) translates וכשבא לבנות "But when he comes to build...." Lauterbach (Mekilta, II, 79) translates "But when He came to build the Temple...." The context, particularly the parable that follows the comment, supports the translation of Prof. Goldin.

reference to a temple built by God's <u>hands</u>. We have thus far
located a possible meaning for both terms in Mark, meanings
present in identifiable traditions with precise linguistic bases
for the Greek terms and both identified with temple traditions.
Made with hands is used to describe the temple(s) built by men
which have been destroyed; not made with hands means made by
God's hands (Exod 15:17), referring to the eschatological
temple. The next task is to determine if this tradition can be
dated prior to the destruction of the temple in A.D. 70.

Once again the Qumran material provides decisive evidence. The important text is found in 4QFlor:[33]

> [...] enemy [..."And] the son of wickedness [shall no more
> afflict] him as at first, and as from the day that [I
> commanded judges] (to be) over my people Israel" - that is
> the house which [...in] the end of days, as it is written
> in the book of [..."The sanctuary, O Lord, which] thy hands
> have [es]tablished. Yahweh will rule for ever and ever."

[...]ד אויב[...ולוא יסי]ף בן עולה
[לענות]ו כאשר בראישונה ולמן הים אשר
[צויתי שפטים] על עמי ישראל הואה הבית
אשר [...] ל[...ב]אחרית הימים כאשר כתוב
בספר [... מקדש אדני כ]וננו ידיכה
יהוה ימלך עולם ועד

This passage is discussed in detail elsewhere.[34] Whether
the passage is discussing the eschatological temple or is using
traditions about the eschatological temple to describe the
community itself, the passage from Exodus has been used in
traditions regarding the temple which God is to build in the
future. What is most interesting is that the tradition about an
eschatological temple predates the destruction of the second
temple. That would suggest that the views of Ms Linnemann and
others about the place of expectations of a new temple in Jewish
eschatology are over-simplified. Appeal is made in the Scrolls
to a tradition according to which the temple of the future is
to be built by God himself, the same tradition we find in later
Jewish literature. It is unnecessary at this point to explore
in detail the setting of such expectations within Jewish circles
prior to A.D. 70, since this will be done in the next chapter.[35]

---

[33]4QFlor I, 1-3. Text and translation are from DJD
V, 53-54.

[34]See below, 172-79.

[35]See below, 159-68, and esp the suggestions of D.
Flusser, 201.

It is conceivable that this exegetical tradition is behind the use of the terms in Mark. The traditions focusing on
Exod 15:17 would first provide evidence that in the case of
Mk 14:58, Lohse is correct. The terms could be understood to
mean man-made in contrast to God-made. The traditions would
provide precise linguistic equivalents for the two Greek terms
and evidence that the terms had already been employed to describe the eschatological temple in contrast to the existing
temple. Evidence comes from pre-70 as well as from later times.
The traditions would provide precise evidence for interpreting
the two terms in Mark. But such an equivalence of terminology
is unlikely.

The decisive difference is the identity of the builder
of the temple: in all of the traditions using Exod 15:17, it is
God; in Mark, the builder is Jesus. We have already examined
the charge within Mark and have suggested that the charge is
viewed as true at a deeper level, and further, that the identification of Jesus as the builder of the new temple is a reflection of messianic imagery; as builder of the new temple, Jesus
is the Messiah-King.[36] Not only do the traditions noted above
not suggest that the Messiah is the builder; there is also
indication in the midrash from the Qumran material that the
passage from Exodus can be used to rule out such a possibility.
It is certainly not accidental that the phrase from II Sam 7:13
("And he [the Son of David=Messiah] shall build a house for my
name") does not appear in the midrash.[37] The sectarian interpreters understood the text from II Sam as messianic, as referring to the coming King from the tribe of Judah. They have
therefore omitted the phrase from Nathan's oracle which suggests
that the Messiah will build the eschatological temple--since,
according to midrash, it is God who will build the temple at the
end of days (Exod 15:17). There is the possibility that the
text from Exod could be read in such a way that the "your"
(ידיך) might refer to someone other than God, but there is no
evidence in extant literature that the text has ever been read
in this way. It is also possible that Christians have interpreted the κύριος in the Greek translation of the Exodus text to
refer to Jesus, thus transferring scriptural statements about
God to the Lord Jesus. But there is little evidence of such
interpretations of Exodus tradition, and the interpretation

[36]See below, chapter 9.   [37]See below, 176-78.

requires too many assumptions to be convincing.

It would seem, therefore, that we have still not located any use of the two terms that provides a real clue to the precise meaning in Mark. The use of the term χειροποίητος in Acts does not adequately account for the use of άχειροποίητος in Mark. And the Hebrew equivalents of the Greek terms appear in Jewish exegetical traditions using Exod 15:17 to speak about the eschatological temple, as built by God. But in Mark, the contrast cannot be simply between man-made and God-made; the contrast is between a temple "made with hands" and a temple "not made with hands" that Jesus will build. That is the problem. Our concern here is to determine what the term άχειροποίητος contributes to the interpretation of the second half of the charge. The interpretation of the term will not solve all exegetical problems, but it may at least provide corroborative evidence for any interpretation of the "temple not made with hands" that is proposed. There is perhaps one more possibility for locating usage of the two terms that might shed light on their meaning in Mark: the use of the two terms as applied to circumcision in Col 2:11 and Eph 2:11 and the use of the terms as applied to the "heavenly" sanctuary in Heb 9:11, 23-24.

The same image is used in Ephesians and Colossians, with some slight variation. In Ephesians, the phrase περιτομή χειροποίητος is used to describe the former state of Gentiles; in Colossians, on the other hand, the phrase περιτομή άχειροποίητος is used to describe the present condition of believers. One thing is clear: the terms cannot be interpreted to mean "man-made" and "God-made" strictly speaking. The contrast is not between circumcision as performed by men and circumcision as performed by God, but between two different kinds of circumcision. In Ephesians the phrase έν σαρκί is added, with the obvious assumption that the new circumcision is not έν σαρκί. The image in Romans 2:29, περιτομή καρδίας, is also an equivalent. The image is clearly metaphorical. The use in Ephesians occurs in a passage where metaphorical use is also made of temple imagery (2:19-22). Imagery taken from the "old dispensation" is being used to describe the new situation of believers in Jesus Christ, and the "circumcision not accomplished with hands" is clearly not a physical sign of the same order as the old. The image is used to describe something of a different order, something "spiritual" as opposed to "fleshly." It is perhaps impossible to determine precisely what the term

ἀχειροποίητος contributes to the sense of imagery, but it is at
least clear that the term is not used with the exact meaning
of "God-made" as opposed to "man-made." The term seems to be
used as part of the contrast between two different orders, and
in this sense it is perhaps legitimate to argue that the term
is used as part of an attempt to "spiritualize" cultic imagery.

The term "spiritualize" is obviously being used in a
peculiar sense here. It does not mean a special relation to the
"Spirit," and Ms Linnemann's objection to the use of this term
to describe the image of a "temple not made with hands" is thus
hardly to the point. "Spiritual" suggests simply that, in the
case of circumcision imagery, the image is being used for something that is not circumcision. In the case of the temple
imagery in Mark, it would imply that building imagery is being
used for some reality that is not really a building. It seems
clear from the careful examination of the charge within the context of Mark that the "prediction" must point to a reality
termed "temple not made with hands" that Jesus will build--an
image that cannot refer to a building. In light of the use of
the term in Colossians, it is not impossible that the term is
being used by Mark in the same "spiritual" sense.

If this proposal is correct, if we can observe a rather
imprecise use of the term ἀχειροποίητος in Colossians in which
the term is used to describe a reality of a different order
(in contrast to what is purely human, fleshly), perhaps the use
of the term in Mark does not depend upon any specific prior
linguistic traditions (e.g. the use of the Hebrew ידי בשר ודם
as a conscious contrast to the ידי in Exod 15:17). Perhaps
the term has been coined specifically for this passage. There
is general agreement that the function of the terms in the
temple charge is to point in a specific direction. Our study
would suggest that the terms, particularly ἀχειροποίητος, reflect a struggle on the part of the interpreter to find language
appropriate to describe the Christian community by using temple
imagery. The term would suggest that the new "temple" is really
not a temple; it is a reality of a different order--corre-
sponding to the new character of reality subsequent to Jesus'
resurrection. The term χειροποίητος implies a value judgment;
it points to something inferior, something transcient with regard to the old temple. The precise view of this "inferiority"
can only be determined from the context. It is perhaps too much
to say that Mark views the Jewish temple as an idol temple among

other idol temples, although this use of the term would fit
with usage in the LXX and in Luke and would explain the opposition to the temple in Mark. It does seem apparent, however,
that the whole temple institution will be rejected according to
Mark. The new reality to which the saying in 14:58 refers may
be described as a "temple," but it is a temple of a different
order, a reality which is a temple only in a metaphorical sense.
In this sense, it can be said to be a "temple not made with
hands." And as a "temple not made with hands," it is as
superior to the old temple as the new order is to the old.

     The use of the term in Hebrews provides a final clue to
the sense of the term in Mark and perhaps indicates one reason
the terms have been chosen. In 9:11, Christ is described as
high priest of the good things to come, and his mission is
described in ritual imagery taken from the Day of Atonement
festival. Christ enters the tabernacle, but not the old tabernacle. He enters into the "greater and more perfect tent," one
not made with hands (οὐ χειροποίητος). The terms οὐ
χειροποίητος are defined by the parenthetical remark, "that is,
not of this creation." The term "made with hands" thus seems
to apply to something of this creation, of this order, earthly,
while "not made with hands" suggests something of a different
order. In 9:23-24, this tent (here the holy of holies) is
described as the heavenly sanctuary as contrasted with the
χειροποίητα ἅγια the "antitype of the true" (ἀντίτυπα τῶν
ἀληθινῶν). Here the term χειροποίητος seems to refer to something of this creation as contrasted with something heavenly.
Nevertheless, the use of χειροποίητος in 9:11 need not be
viewed as a precise phrase intended to suggest a contrast between earthly and heavenly. The expression "not made with
hands" still suggests a contrast between what is natural and un-
natural, between man-made and miraculous, between something of
this order and something of another order.

     The use of the terms in Hebrews confirms our findings in
Colossians and Ephesians but also suggests that the terms suggest a contrast between natural and miraculous. This particular
connotation would make the terms most appropriate in Mark's
account of the trial. It has already been suggested that the
meaning of the charge must be understood on two levels. The
false witnesses understand the charge as a threat against the
temple and as an impossible boast. The Christian reader is to
view the charge as a prophecy, as "true" in some sense at a

157

different level of meaning. The use of the terms "made with
hands/not made with hands" in Colossians, Ephesians, and Hebrews
suggests that they could serve to point to the different order
of the two "temples" referred to in the charge. The "temple
not made with hands" is a temple of a different order. But the
use of the terms in Hebrews to contrast natural with miraculous
would also make the use of the terms appropriate on the surface
level of the story. For Jesus' opponents, the terms would
simply add further mystery to the strange and impossible prediction about the temple.[38]

The interesting possibility is that the terms have been
chosen to retain some of the ambiguity present throughout the
story. Had Mark used a term like πνευματικός in the charge to
describe the new temple, presumably the Christian community,
the ambiguity would have been lost and the mysterious character
of the "prophecy" destroyed. The use of the terms "made with
hands/not made with hands" leaves the meaning open to some
doubt. The terms may simply suggest the contrast between
natural and supernatural, which would appropriately reflect the
meaning of the terms in the charge from the opponents' perspective. But the terms also point the Christian reader to a
different level of understanding: the new temple, in contrast
to the old, will be a temple of a different order, i.e.
superior. Whether or not Mark is responsible for the addition
of the terms, they function well in his account of the trial.

---

[38]The charge is reminiscent of the "impossible claims"
made by prophetic figures during the early part of the first
century mentioned in Josephus' works: Samaritan prophet (Ant
18:85-86); Theudas (Ant 20:97f); Egyptian (20:169); anonymous
γόης (Ant 20:188).

CHAPTER 8

COMMUNITY AS TEMPLE IMAGERY AT QUMRAN

One of the many criticisms Eta Linnemann advances against
the interpretation of "temple not made with hands" as a reference to the Christian community is that there is little evidence
of such application of temple imagery elsewhere. She does cite
the references to the Christian community in the New Testament
(I Cor 3:16, II Cor 6:16, and Eph 2:20-22), but she insists
that these few passages and the few other allusions to building
imagery do not suggest that the community-as-temple image is
firmly established in Christian tradition to the degree presupposed by those who insist that Mk 14:58 is to be explained
by such a tradition.[1] Her views are certainly debatable. The
evidence from the Gospel of Mark suggests that the building of
a "temple not made with hands" must be viewed as a prophecy.
There are few conceptual possibilities available for interpreting the strange expression, and the presence of a tradition in
the New Testament in which the Christian community is described
as temple is perhaps more noteworthy than Ms Linnemann believes.
Nevertheless, there are some difficulties involved in deriving
the imagery in Mk 14:58 from the references in I and II
Corinthians and Ephesians. Rather than reviewing the use of
temple-as-community imagery in Christian literature and attempting to work out some comprehensive history of tradition,
we shall examine the use of such imagery in the Qumran texts.
The Scrolls provide evidence of pre-Christian use of community-
as-temple traditions bound up with important scriptural texts
that enable us to understand Mk 14:58 without having to depend
upon a reconstruction of the history of Christian community-as-
temple traditions.

In 1932 Hans Wenschkewitz published a book entitled Die
Spiritualizierung der Kultbegriffe Temple, Priester und Opfer
im Neuen Testament.[2] In it he argued that the description of

[1]Linnemann, Studien, 122-124.

[2]H. Wenschkewitz, Die Spiritualizierung der Kultbegriffe
Temple, Priester und Opfer im Neuen Testament (Aggelos Beih. 4;
Leipzig: Pfeiffer, 1932).

159

the Christian church as "temple" in the New Testament could
only have developed on Greek soil. Parallel usage could only
be found in hellenized circles, under the influence, for example, of Stoic ideas (cf. esp. I Cor 6:9). Such usage of
temple imagery was not to be found in Jewish (Palestinian
Jewish) literature.[3] Similar observations were made by Phillip
Vielhauer in his dissertation, written in 1940, Oikodome. Das
Bild vom Bau in der christlichen Literature vom Neuen Teatament
bis Clemens Alexandrinus.[4] The derivation of such usage of
temple imagery does not account for some of the most characteristic usage in the New Testament, however, as Joseph Fitzmeyer
has pointed out.[5] The parallels from Stoic literature fit the
image of the individual as temple, but not the community. But
in II Cor 6:16, for example, Paul says: "For we are the temple
of the living God."[6] The discovery of the Qumran literature,
subsequent to the studies of Wenschkewitz and Vielhauer, now
provides the closest extant parallels to the use of temple
imagery to describe a group or community.[7]

A recent monograph by G. Klinzing has appeared in which
the author sets out to "supplement" the studies of Wenschkewitz
(and Vielhauer) by examining the use of temple imagery in the
Qumran literature.[8] He concludes from his study not only that
the usage of community-as-temple imagery in Qumran is closer to
the N.T. usage than Wenschkewitz's parallels, but that the
application of temple imagery to a community is borrowed by
Christians from Qumran, though he does not attempt to explain
how the contacts came about:

> Die christliche Umdeutung des Tempels wurde jedoch nicht
> aufs nicht aufs Neue und selbständig aus der jüdischen
> Hoffnung entwickelt, sondern als geprägte Vorstellung aus
> der Qumrangemeinde übernommen.[9]

His conclusion is perhaps less important than his careful

---

[3]Ibid., 113, note 3, and 116.

[4]Ph. Vielhauer, Oikodome. See chapter 5, note 23.

[5]J. Fitzmeyer, "Qumran and the Interpolated Paragraph
in 2 Cor 6:14-7:1," CBQ 23 (1961), 271-280.

[6]Ibid., 277-278.   [7]Ibid.

[8]G. Klinzing, Die Umdeutung des Kultus in der Qumrangemeinde und im Neuen Testament (Göttingen: Vandenhoeck and
Ruprecht, 1971).

[9]Ibid., 67-68.

study of the material. Klinzing is not the first to investigate
the use of temple imagery in Qumran. Bertil Gärtner's study
appeared in 1965.[10] But Klinzing's work represents a considerable advance over previous studies. He pays careful attention
to the Qumran texts and is concerned to work out the inner logic
of the texts before attempting a comparison with the New Testament. He has obviously been trained as a form critic, and he is
concerned to get back to original oral traditions that stand
behind the present written texts. His preoccupation with source
criticism sometimes stands in the way of appreciating the place
of individual verses in their present context, but this does
not diminish the overall value of his work. He is careful to
examine the relevant texts in light of the whole experience of
the Qumran sect and its unique composition, and he tries to
trace the development of the traditions in question with proper
recognition of this unique experience and situation. He avoids
simplistic harmonizations of traditions and over-hasty general-
izations.

Because such a careful study of the use of temple imagery
in Qumran has already been carried out, it is unnecessary here
to invest a great deal in an examination of the subject. Some
discussion of the material is necessary, but we will examine
only those aspects of the work that are immediately relevant.

The texts in which the community is most clearly characterized as temple are the following: IQS 8:4-7, 8:8-10, 9:3-6,
5:5-7; CD 3:18-4:10; IQpH 12:3.[11] Some comments on the most
important features of the texts are appropriate. First, we will
consider the texts from IQS.

In each of the four texts (or three if 8:4-10 is considered as a unit), the term "house" is used. As Klinzing
points out, "house" can be used as a designation of the temple
without further modification (Mic 3:12, Hag 1:8, Ps 30:1, Neh
11:12, I Chron 5:36, II Chron 23:7).[12] But the usage in the
Qumran texts is not uniform. The "house" in 9:6 ("a holy house
for Aaron" בית קודש לאהרון) would seem to be the clearest use

---

[10]B. Gärtner, _Temple and Community in Qumran and the New
Testament_ (NTSMS 1; Cambridge: Cambridge University Press,
1965).

[11]The list of texts from IQS , including the order,
reflects Klinzing's views as a form critic.

[12]Klinzing, _Umdeutung_, 62.

of "house" for temple; it is parallel to the "dwelling of
infinite holiness," (מעון קודש קודשים) in 8:8 and probably
parallel to the "most holy foundation for Aaron" (יסוד
קודש קודשים לאהרון) in 8:5.[13] Even in 8:5, the "holy house"
in Israel would seem to be a reference to the temple. But the
"house of perfection and truth in Israel" (בית תמים ואמת בישראל)
in 8:9, the "house of community for Israel" (בית יחד לישראל)
in 9:6, and "house of truth in Israel" (בית האמת בישראל) in
5:6 are by no means unambiguous references to the temple.
Klinzing himself believes that these usages of "house" appear
to have an origin independent of the usage in the statements
made with reference to Aaron.

Thus the presence of the term "house" as a characterization for the community in IQS does not prove that the community
is described as temple. There have been a variety of proposals
regarding the origin of the terminology.[14] In his article
"'Reign' and 'House' in the Kingdom of God in the Gospels,"
Sverre Aalen argues that there is evidence of a tradition derived from II Sam 7 and I Chron 17 in which house = family or
dynasty of David is applied to a group or a congregation. He
finds this to be the origin of the "house" terminology most
characteristic of Qumran:

> In these and in other related passages of the Qumran
> texts we can clearly observe how the 'house,' originally
> designating a family with its descendents, in Judaism be-
> comes a term for a community, a religious group or
> congregation.[15]

Klinzing insists, however, that the usage most characteristic of the Qumran sectarians in these passages is house =
temple. The most convincing proof is the repeated reference to
"atonement"; the verb כפר is used in each of the four sections.
The community is described as a "house" whose purpose is to
make atonement ("for the earth" 8:6; "for the earth" 8:10;
"expiate guilty rebellion and sinful infidelity" in 9:3--fol-
lowed by spiritualized sacrificial imagery). There can be
little doubt that the "house" imagery being applied to the
community in these passages means house = temple. And despite

---

[13]Klinzing's translation. For his reading יסוד instead
of וסוד, see 51, note 3.

[14]Ibid., 62.

[15]S. Aalen, "'Reign' and 'House' in the Kingdom of God
in the Gospels," NTS 8 (1962), 235.

the possibly independent origin of some of the "house" imagery,
even the statements made about the "house in Israel" should be
understood in these passages as references to "temple." It is
the whole community that offers atonement, not just the "house
for Aaron."[16] This also suggests that, although there may be
an independent origin for the elements from Isa 28:16 quoted
in IQS 8:7f, in the present context the "tried wall" and
"precious corner stone" probably refer to the temple. Later
Klinzing states: "Wenn auch kein genaues und als solches
eingeleitetes Zitat vorliegt, so kann doch kein Zweifel darüber
bestehen, dass man den Tempel als Erfüllung des Jesajawortes
verstanden habe."[17] The peculiar view of the temple as a place
of atonement and the preoccupation with atonement and purifica-
tion present in the Qumran literature is to be explained by the
unique composition and history of the community. The description of the community as a house whose function it is to offer
atonement is decisive evidence that the community conceived
itself as the temple.

In addition to the four passages from IQS, two others
deserve mention. The first is CD 3:18-4:10. The text speaks
about a "sure house in Israel" (בית נאמן בישראל) that God has
built. Again it is not immediately apparent that "sure house"
means temple. Aalen has argued that the "sure house" built by
God is a reference to II Sam 2:35 (the prophecy to Samuel), and
that echoes of Nathan's oracle are also present, especially in
the form of the prophecy in I Chron 17:10, where the verb בנה
is used with the בית God is to build for David.[18] The term
"house" would be equivalent to the usage in Enoch 53:6 ("House
of his congregation"). According to Aalen, the use of the term
in CD 3:19 belongs to the tradition of which the targums provide
evidence.[19] As in the case of the use of "house" in 4QFlor,
however, Aalen's proposal is not the only possibility.[20] But
whatever the origin of the terminology, in the present context
"sure house" must refer to the temple.

---

[16]Klinzing, Umdeutung, 62-63.   [17]Ibid., 150.

[18]Aalen, "'Reign' and 'House,'" 235.

[19]Especially prominent is the play on בית in II Sam
7:11, according to Aalen.

[20]See below, 177-78.

Nur wenn man das "Haus" in CD 3:18 als Tempel verstand, ist
der Anschluss des Zitats von Ex 44:15 sinnvoll: Die am
Haus festhalten (3:20) entsprechen denen, die den Dienst am
Heiligtum bewahrt haben (4:1f.). Im folgenden (4:2-6)
werden dann auch die im Zitat genannten Priester, Leviten
und Söhne Zadoks auf die Gemeindeglieder gedeutet.[21]

Finally, a brief comment should be made on IQpHab 12:3f,
in which the council of the community (עצת היחד) is identified
with "Lebanon" in Hab 2:17. In his well-known eassay "Lebanon"
in Scripture and Tradition in Judaism,[22] Geza Vermes argues
that this interpretation of the Qumran sectarians is intelligi-
ible only in light of a traditional interpretation according
to which Lebanon = temple. Vermes has traced the origin and
development of this tradition in the targums through rabbinic
literature, a tradition involving particularly Deut 3:25, Isa
60:13, and Ps 92:13-14.[23] According to a wide-spread tradition
of interpretation, Lebanon = temple. Among the sectarians at
Qumran, the belief is held that the community = temple. Based
on the belief of the sect and the traditional interpretation of
"Lebanon," the Qumran exegete is thus able to make the equation
Lebanon = community (here council of the community).

Klinzing has provided considerable substantiation for
the claim that within the Qumran literature, the community is
described as the temple. It is also clear, however, that this
is only one feature of a rather complex picture. The community
is described as temple only in certain of the Qumran documents:
IQS, CD, and IQpHab. More traditional expectations of a new or
restored sanctuary are found in other documents: IQM, IQpPs 37,
and 4QFlor, and in these texts the characterization of the
community as temple is absent. Neither is the characterization
found in IQH. On the other hand, there are no traditions about
a future temple in IQS, CD, and IQpHab. The two uses of temple
traditions are never found in the same document. And even among
those documents in which there are expectations of a future restored or new sanctuary there is no unanimity. 4QFlor seems to
point to a future sanctuary to be built by God himself; yet in
IQM, it appears that during the eschatological war, the sectarians expect to regain control of the present temple in

---

[21]Klinzing, Umdeutung, 78.

[22]G. Vermes, "Lebanon," Scripture and Tradition in
Judaism (SPB 4; Leiden: Brill, 1961), 26-39.

[23]Ibid., 28-35.

Jerusalem and officiate at services (IQM 2). The same hope of
a takeover of the temple seems to be present in 4QpPs 37:3, 10f.
To complicate matters further the Temple Scroll which Yadin is
expected to publish seems to envision a future temple to be
built by the sectarians.[24] The precise interrelationships
among the various motifs will probably not be worked out for
some time, certainly not before Yadin's publication of the
temple scroll. We should probably be suspicious of over-hasty
harmonization of the traditions:

> Fur uns ist schwer verständlich, wie nach der Entstehung
> der spezifischen Gemeindetheologie, die mit ihr
> unvereinbaren Vorstellungen weiter bestehen konnten und
> weiter überliefert wurden. Aber es wäre verfehlt, mit
> unserem Begriff der Unvereinbarkeit zu messen, was seinen
> Ursprung in einem Prozess der Entstehung und Überlieferung
> von Tradition hat. Wie im Alten und Neuen Testament gibt
> es auch in der Qumrangemeinde entegegengesetzte
> Vorstellungen, die geschichtlich verstanden werden müssen
> und nicht einfach miteinander ausgeglichen werden dürfen.[25]

The variety of temple traditions reflects the peculiar
composition of the sect and its history. The movement apparently began as a dispute over temple worship within the Jerusalem cult. Convinced that the present priesthood was corrupt,
a group of disenchanted priests broke of all contact with the
Jerusalem establishment and made provisions for its own worship.
The birth of the strange movement and the difficulties it faced
particularly in the early days seem to be reflected in IQpHab.[26]
Klinzing offers convincing evidence in his book that despite
the priestly character of the movement, the sect neither took
part in the worship of the Jerusalem cult nor did the sectarians
institute a rival sacrificial cult outside Jerusalem.

That meant, however, that the sectarians had to face a
difficult problem. According to their view, there was no place
where atonement was being made. The frequent reference to
atonement in the literature, often linked with sacrifice in the
material sense, indicates that the sectarians were not opposed
to sacrifice as such but to the present sacrificial cult.[27]

---

[24]Y. Yadin, "The Temple Scroll," BA 30 (1967), 135-139.

[25]Klinzing, Umdeutung, 93.

[26]The first two chapters of Klinzing's book are devoted
to the reconstruction of the history of the sect.

[27]Ibid., 93, 145-146; G. Vermes, Discovery in the Judaen
Desert (Paris: Desclee, 1956), 46, 212-213.

One response of the community was to rekindle hopes for a re-
newed or new sanctuary where legitimate sacrifices would once
again be offered.[28] But another response seems to have been
to reinterpret cultic imagery and to "spiritualize" sacrifice,
substituting proper obedience to the Law for bloody sacrifice.[29]
Part of this second response seems to have been the development
of the notion that the community was the temple, the place
where proper atonement could be made.

No easy harmonization of the traditions seems to be
possible. Attempts to arrange the traditions in chronological
order must remain conjectural. Klinzing's own attempt to explain the origin of the community as temple traditions represent
such conjecture, much of which is probably untenable. He argues
that the usage developed from the application of traditional
expectations about the eschatological temple to the community.
His principal evidence comes from 4QFlor. He must insist that
the exegetical traditions in this midrash pre-date the community
as temple traditions in IQS and CD, for which there is little
hard evidence. Some of his interpretations of the midrash on II
Samuel 7 in 4QFlor are questionable and in fact seem to reverse
the most intelligible process of development of the temple
traditions.[30] Some of the passages in which the community is
characterized as "house," particularly those like IQS 8:7f,
where a relationship to texts like Isa 28:16 is clear, cannot
easily be explained as derivations from expectations of an
eschatological temple, traditions deriving from a different set
of texts (Exod 15:7 and II Sam 7). It seems more probable
that the community as temple imagery is part of a rather complex
set of house/community/building images with various derivations.

The complexity of the imagery, however, does not obscure
the importance of the community as temple traditions for interpreting the New Testament. Whatever their derivation and relationship to other building imagery, such traditions are clearly
present, as Klinzing has demonstrated. This is what is important for the study of Mark. In a movement proximate to
Christianity in time and place, a community used temple imagery

[28]IQM, 4QpPs 37, 4QFlor.

[29]IQS 9:4f, CD 11:20f, 11QPs[a] 18:7. Klinzing, Umdeutung,
93-106.

[30]See the comments in the special study of 4QFlor, 172-
179 below.

as a self-designation. More important, temple imagery was used as a self-designation by a community that conceived itself as the congregation of the last days. Further, its use of such imagery is bound up with texts important to Christians in similar contexts.[31] Of these texts, II Sam 7 is certainly the most interesting for study of Mk 14:58, as we shall see below.

Klinzing's own suggestions for interpreting Mk 14:58 are perhaps not as valuable as his study of the Qumran material. As he notes himself, there are significant differences between the Qumran community and the author of Mark in the use of such imagery.[32] His arguments against Wenschkewitz and Vielhauer regarding hellenistic influences are strongest in the case of the epistolary literature. Although he believes that the "temple not made by hands" in Mark is derived not from Stoic imagery but from Qumran traditions, he admits that this presupposes a long period of development.[33] One chief difference is Mark's use of χειροποίητος, suggesting a basic opposition to the Jerusalem temple as such. Mark seems to view the Christian community as a replacement for the temple, and the contraposition of the two "temples" looks to Klinzing far more like traditional arguments against temple and sacrifice in hellenistic Judaism.[34] He is thus convinced that the tradition in Mk 14:58 is "late," that it could only have developed on hellenistic soil under the influence of hellenized Judaism.

Such views of the relationship between the Qumran and Christian literature and traditions are certainly oversimplified. There seems to be a very different logic behind Mark's use of temple imagery, which makes derivation from peculiarly Qumran traditions unlikely. The differences are more easily explained as modifications of common traditions, reflecting a different community with different beliefs and experiences. Although there seems to be little evidence for such common traditions, the use of similar texts in the context of discussions about the community as temple may provide important clues as to the existence of such traditions. As we shall see, 4QFlor provides evidence of traditions both about the Messiah and the temple that are decisive for interpreting Mark.

_____

[31]Isa 28:16 in IQS 8:7f; cf. Eph 2:20-22 and I Peter 2:4-8.

[32]Klinzing, _Umdeutung_, 203.   [33]_Ibid_.   [34]_Ibid_., 204.

In spite of certain weaknesses Klinzing's book is an important contribution to Qumran scholarship and provides convincing evidence that use of temple imagery to describe a community predates Christianity and to a certain extent parallels usage attested in Christian literature. The evidence lends greater probability to the view that "temple not made with hands" in Mk 14:58 is intended as a reference to the Christian community.

CHAPTER 9

From the evidence assembled in the previous three chapters we may state with some confidence that in Mark, the temple charge is to be viewed as true at a deeper level of the story. We have not yet determined the precise meaning of the charge, but several things have become clear. First, within the Gospel there are several statements about the temple that must be considered in the interpretation of 14:58. The context indicates that the charge represents a statement about the temple of decisive importance for the author. It is part of a broader conflict between Jesus and the Jewish religious leaders, but it must also be related to the statements and hints about the impending destruction of the temple from chapter 11 on. Its presence as one of the two charges at the trial suggests that it represents for Mark an important issue in the confrontation between Jesus and the religious leaders, between Christians and Jews. The charge indicates for Mark one of the two bases for Jesus' "rejection," and, at a deeper level of the story, one of the two bases for his vindication. The temple charge in 14:58 thus represents a "prophecy" the fulfillment of which is in some way bound up with Jesus' resurrection.

The evidence from Christian literature and from the literature of Qumran supports the view that the "temple not made with hands" is used by Mark as a reference to the Christian community, viewed as the replacement of the Jewish temple, the "temple made with hands." Although our study of the terms "made with hands/not made with hands" did not yield any absolutely convincing results, it did identify use of the terms that fits with the usage we have suggested for Mark. And the interpretation of the terms proposed here fits well both with the "temple not made with hands" as a reference to the church as well as with Markan style.

There remains one important feature of the charge yet to be explored: the characterization of Jesus as the destroyer of the old temple as well as the builder of the new. Some explanation for this characterization is important for several reasons.

Nowhere in Mark's Gospel does Jesus suggest that he will destroy the old temple, nor does he ever say anything about building a new temple. It may be, therefore, that the characterization has something to do with the "falseness" of the testimony.[1] More important, however, is the possibility that the statement about destroying and building the temple contains a veiled claim to be the Messiah. The suggestion has been made by numerous scholars and denied by numerous others.[2] No convincing answer has yet been given to the question whether the destruction and/or building of the temple was a task assigned to the Messiah. In this last section we will examine the question once again, seeking clues from the Gospel of Mark and reexamining the evidence in pre-Christian tradition for the existence of traditions about the Messiah and the temple.

Within the context of Mark's Gospel, there are some strong indications that the temple charge is part of the messianic imagery. The predominant theme throughout the passion story is the royal-messianic motif. Jesus is tried, mocked and executed as the Christ, the Son of God. This motif so completely dominates the account of the passion that even if there were no explicit evidence in the text, the possible relationship between the two charges would be worth exploring.

But there are some indications in the account itself that the temple charge and the question about Jesus' Messiahship are related. The question of the high priest in 14:61 follows Jesus' silence, his response to the previous charges (14:60). But after Jesus' silence, the high priest "again" (πάλιν) asks Jesus, "Are you the Christ," the Son of the Blessed?" The question seems completely unmotivated, unless the statement about the temple implies a messianic claim. This would also explain the "again" in the verse. Other translations are possible, such as "thereupon" or "further,"[3] and the verb ἐπερωτάω may be translated simply "questioned."[4] And since, as we have argued, Mark seems concerned not so much with the surface level of the

---

[1]Benoit, The Passion and Resurrection of Jesus Christ, 99.

[2]Those who have argued for messianic implications include Taylor, Schweizer, Blinzler, Lohmeyer, Klostermann; those who have denied such associations include Linnemann, Gaston, Donahue, Lightfoot, Nineham.

[3]Taylor, Mark, 567.

[4]Bauer, ἐπερωτάω

story as with its deeper dimension, it is not even necessary to
insist that there must be some motivation in the account of the
trial for the messianic question. Nevertheless, if there is
some relationship between the charges, some of the peculiarities of 14:60 would receive the most natural explanation. The
question is really whether the author intended the reader to
perceive any relationship between the two charges. The mention
of the lack of agreement between the witnesses in v. 59 and
Jesus' silence in v. 60 certainly introduces the messianic question as the decisive issue at the trial. But it is not obvious
that the verses are intended to dissociate the two charges.[5]

The temple charge points the reader to an important truth
about Jesus and the temple. It may also point to Jesus' identity as Messiah. The only way to substantiate such a claim,
however, is to examine messianic traditions to determine if the
Messiah and the temple could be related in a manner consonant
with Mk 14:58. We need to determine if the Messiah could be
expected to destroy and/or build the temple. The texts we will
examine have been studied before.[6] The only text unfamiliar to
Billerbeck is the eschatological midrash from cave 4 at Qumran,
and even this text has been subjected to careful scrutiny by
scholars.[7] The purpose of this examination of Jewish material
will thus not be to bring new evidence to bear on the text in
Mark but to reevaluate the evidence already available, to examine it from a different perspective.

The texts most important for the study of the temple
charge in Mark are those which have received perhaps the least
attention by Markan commentators: the midrash on II Sam 7:10-
14 in 4QFlorilegium and traditions found in the targums. These
texts provide the most important evidence about traditions involving the Messiah and the temple and will thus be studied in
some detail. Brief reference will be made to the tradition
common to Leviticus Rabbah (9:6), Numbers Rabbah (13:2) and
the Midrash on Song of Songs (4:16). Since there seems to be
less possibility of dating this tradition with any precision,

---

[5]Thus Bertram, Leidensgeschichte, 58; Lohse, History,
83; Lightfoot, History and Interpretation, 143.

[6]See Bill I, 1004-5 for the basic texts.

[7]In addition to the major studies, cf. the articles
cited in the bibliography on 4QFlor prepared by Fr. Fitzmeyer
(CBQ 31 [1969], 67-68).

however, it will be examined in less detail. After examining
the relevant texts, we will then review the evidence and conclude the chapter with a final proposal for the interpretation
of the temple charge in Mk 14:58.

I. Background
    A. 4QFlorilegium[1]
        Certainly one of the most intriguing as well as one of
the most elusive texts from Qumran is the midrash on II Sam 7:
10-14 from cave 4 (4QFlor). The text is being discussed in this
chapter because it provides unambiguous evidence that Nathan's
oracle was interpreted eschatologically as a messianic oracle
prior to the Christian era. That text is of particular concern
here because, in II Sam 7:13, it is promised that the seed of
David will "build a house for my name." It is also a text in
which the son promised David is called God's "son." The Qumran
text is also important because it provides possible corroborative evidence for use of temple imagery to describe a community.
        The manuscript itself, published by Allegro, has been
pieced together from twenty-six fragments. There are several
lacunae at crucial points in the midrash, which make interpretation precarious. The variety of proposals by experts for filling
in the lacunae and the importance of each decision for the interpretation of the midrash suggest that the text will not yield
all its secrets easily. Nevertheless much is clear, and the
midrash can provide valuable information for the interpretation
of Mark. None of the interpretations crucial for our purposes
depend upon reconstructions of the text.
        About one fact there can be little doubt: the midrash
regards Nathan's oracle from II Sam 7 as an eschatological
prophecy. The oracle, according to the interpreter, speaks a-
bout the "end of days" (באחרית הימים in lines 2 and 12).
Further, the oracle is viewed as a messianic prophecy: the
"seed" promised David is identified in line 11 as the "Shoot of
David" (צמח דויד), an expression used elsewhere in the scrolls

---

[1]Text and translation for 4QFlor are taken from the
critical edition, DJDJ V, 53-54. For alternative reconstructions of the text and different interpretations, see J. Strugnell, "Notes en marge du volume V des Discoveries in the Judean
Desert of Jordan," RQ 29 (1970), 220-22; and Y. Yadin, "A
Midrash on 2 Sam vii and Ps i-ii (4QFlorilegium)," IEJ 9
(1959), 95-98.

as a designation for the Davidic Messiah.[2] Gärtner's attempt to
apply the title to the community is unconvincing.[3] There is
widespread agreement that the comment beginning in line 10 interprets the oracle as a promise of the Davidic Messiah.[4]

What is interesting, if this is the case, is that no attempt is made to modify the father/son terminology in II Sam
7:14, a tendency clearly present in the targumic renderings of
this verse. The interpreter is not interested in this feature
of the text, but he also apparently feels no need to modify the
text to correct possible false impressions.[5]

If the midrash provides clear evidence of a pre-Christian
messianic interpretation of II Sam 7, it does not offer any con-
clusive evidence concerning the "spiritualization" of temple
imagery and its application to a community. Several commentators have argued that this is the case, that the בית about
which the midrash speaks is the community.[6] Others have argued
that the "house" is the eschatological temple.[7] Klinzing has
advocated the latter view most persuasively. He has observed
that the term מקדש is used elsewhere in the scrolls only of the
temple, whether the present temple in Jerusalem or the future
sanctuary.[8] His proposals for interpreting מקדש אדם as "sanctuary among men" are superior to any proposed thus far.[9]
Perhaps most important are his arguments that the phrase

_____

[2]IQpIsa, 4QPB. Cf. the use of the term in targumic
traditions, 182-83.

[3]Gärtner, Temple and Community, 35-39.

[4]L. Silberman, "A Note on 4Q Florilegium," JBL 78 (1959),
158-59; D. Flusser, "Two Notes on the Midrash on 2 Sam vii,"
IEJ 9 (1959), 104; Dupont-Sommer, Essene Writings, 313 and 315;
Michel-Betz, "Von Gott gezeugt," 10; Dahl, "Eschatology and
History," 16.

[5]See the excursus on Son of God, 182-83.

[6]Dupont-Sommer, Essene Writings, 311-312, esp. note 5 on
312; Michel-Betz, "Von Gott gezeugt," 8-10, esp. notes 34 and
35; Gärtner, Temple and Community, 30-42.

[7]Yadin, "A Midrash," 96; idem., "The Temple Scroll," 138;
Flusser, "Two Notes," 99-103; Klinzing, Die Umdeutung, 80-87.

[8]Klinzing, Die Umdeutung, 86--although his proposed
emendation of a text on 77-79 would result in the use of מקדש
for the community.

[9]Ibid., 82-83. The parallels cited are far superior to
those cited in Flusser, "Two Notes," 102, note 1.

באחרית הימים in the midrash must mean "last days" in the future sense. Although there may be some evidence that the
community believed that it was living in the last days, there
is no evidence elsewhere of a belief that the Davidic Messiah
had already come. It seems most probable, therefore, that the
"house" referred to in the midrash refers to the eschatological
sanctuary to be built at the end of days.

It is apparent, however, that the midrash does not
simply present a traditional picture of the eschatological temple. There are, as Klinzing has noted, striking similarities
between the description of the eschatological sanctuary and the
description elsewhere of the community. Klinzing believes this
is evidence that the midrash provides the missing link in the
development of community as temple traditions, implying that
the imagery developed from traditions about the eschatological
sanctuary.[10] But this is not the most natural way to explain
the differences between the traditional pictures of the eschatological sanctuary and the picture sketched in the midrash.[11]
It seems rather that the traditional imagery in II Sam 7 and
Deut 23 has been modified by a community that considered itself
the eschatological congregation.

Although the first lines of the midrash are missing, it
seems most likely that the interpretation begins with a comment
on II Sam 7:10: "And I will appoint a place (מקום) for my
people Israel." The text was presumably quoted through 7:11a,
though this is by no means certain.[12] The interpretation begins in line 2: "This is the house..." (הואה הבית). The
immediate question is where the "house comes from. It has not
been mentioned in the text from II Samuel thus far, and in the
text which is immediately quoted from Exod 15:17, the term בית
is not used. Further on in the midrash, however, there is
reference to a "house" that God will build (line 10). And in
the oracle from II Samuel, there are two references to "houses,"
one in 7:11 (presumably referring to David's dynasty), and one
in v. 13a (presumably referring to the temple David's seed is
to build). It appears, then, that the interpreter has related
the "place" in II Sam 7:10 to one of the two "houses" mentioned

_____

[10]Klinzing, Die Umdeutung, 87.

[11]The following comments were suggested to me by Professor Dahl.

[12]See esp. Strugnell, "Notes," 220.

in the oracle.

This house is then identified with the מקדש which, according to Exod 15:17, God is to build.[13] This verse is used elsewhere to describe the eschatological temple that God is to erect, and that seems to be the most likely meaning here. By appeal to Exod 15:17, therefore, the interpreter identifies the "place" in II Sam 7:10 and one of the two "houses" with the eschatological sanctuary.

The next comment begins in line 3b: "This is the house.." In this comment, the first part of which is obscured by a lacuna, rules for admission to the קהל יהוה from Deut 23 are applied to the "house" which God is to build at the end of days, with a term from Ezek 44:9 as well.[14] According to the interpreter, therefore, the eschatological sanctuary will not be the holy place to which the dispersed people of God will be gathered and to which all nations of the world will make pilgrimage. It is rather the place where the congregation of the pure will gather. The rules for admittance to the eschatological sanctuary thus reflect rules for admittance into the sectarian community (IQSa 2:3-9, IQM 7:4-5, IQH 6:27). The reason given for the rules of admission, כיא קדושי שם, whether the "holy ones" refers to members of the community ("saints") or to angels, reflects the particular beliefs of the sect (IQSa 2:8-9). The reference to מעשי תורה (or מעשי תודה)[15] seems to reflect the spiritualization of sacrificial terminology observed elsewhere in the sectarian literature. And finally, the interpretation of the "rest" promised in II Sam 7:11 is interpreted as a reference to the protection God will accord the "Sons of Light," the members of the community.

The passage does seem to refer to the eschatological sanctuary that God will build at the end of days, but the picture of that sanctuary is hardly typical. The midrash does not demonstrate how eschatological temple imagery has been applied to the community, as Klinzing has argued, but how eschatological traditions have been modified by the peculiar ideology and experiences of the Qumran sectarians.

---

[13] On Exod 15:17, see J. Goldin, The Song at the Sea, and the discussion of the text above, 230-31.

[14] Allegro's reading is supported by Strugnell, "Notes," 221.

[15] Ibid.

The section of the midrash most important for evidence of
messianic traditions, however, is yet to be discussed. As we
have noted, the oracle of Nathan is viewed by the interpreter as
an eschatological text, promising both the "Shoot of David,"
(lines 10-11) as well as a "house" to be built at the end of
days. The midrash is the only unambiguous piece of evidence
that this text has been so interpreted. But what is both
striking and at first glance disappointing is that the phrase in
II Sam 7:13a ("He shall build a house for my name"), the text
according to which the Messiah will build the eschatological
temple, is missing from the midrash. We must first determine if
this is accidental or intentional.

At first glance, it might seem that the scribe has simply
made an error in copying the text from Samuel. The last verb in
in v. 12 is הכינתי followed by את ממלכתו; v. 13c reads:
וכננתי את כסא ממלכתו   . The text from 4QFlor reads (line 10):
והכינותי את כסא ממלכתו   (omitting 13a). The phrases in vs.
12 and 13 are so similar that an error is conceivable.

Yet closer study of the text indicates that such an explanation is inadequate. There are several phrases omitted from
the text of II Sam 7:10-14, and none of the omissions is accidental. The first omission is in v. 12:

$$\text{כי ימלאו ימיך}$$
$$\text{ושכבת את אבתיך}$$

> ("Your days will be completed and you will
> sleep with your fathers")

The phrase is appropriate only to David's situation and
is unimportant in the commentary; it has nothing to add to the
picture of the future in which the interpreter is interested.
The second phrase to be omitted is in the same verse:

$$\text{אשר יצא ממעיך}$$

> ("who shall come forth from your body")

It is obvious that the phrase is appropriate for the
original statement, in which the reference is to Solomon. But
it is inappropriate in a midrash interested in the "seed" who is
to arise at the end of days. The third phrase to be omitted is
the   את ממלכתו   in 12c, and the reason for this omission is
probably that the phrase is redundant; it occurs again in 13b.

This would suggest that the omission of the statement in
13a, according to which it is the "seed" of David who will build

a house for God, is hardly accidental. The reason would seem
obvious: according to the first interpretive statement of the
midrash in line 2, the house to be built at the end of days
is to be built by God--as is stated in Exod 15:17:

מקדש אדני כוננו ידיך

It might seem strange that the interpreter would impose
such a view on a text which clearly states that it is the
Messiah who will build the temple. But in fact the text from
II Sam provides all the opportunity the interpreter needs. The
text mentions two "houses" which are to be built: the first, in
v. 11, is in the original text clearly the Davidic dynasty which
God will establish. The text in Samuel reads כי בית יעשה לך יהוה.
In the targumim, בית is translated מלכו to leave no doubt as
to the meaning. In the Qumran text, the verse is quoted in line
10 using the verb בנה. The second "house" in v. 13, as we have
already noted, is the "house" which David's son is to build for
God--in the original, the temple to be erected by Solomon. It
seems that the interpreter has chosen to read the first "house"
as "temple." If the term is read in this way, the verse
promises what is also promised in Exod 15:17: God will build a
"house" at the end of days ("sanctuary" in Exodus).

We have already referred in passing to the arguments of
Aalen regarding the interpretation of this passage in 4QFlor.[16]
He believes that the midrash provides clear evidence of the
process by which "house," originally designating dynasty, came
to be used for a community. This presumes, however, that "house"
in lines 2 and 10 refers to the community. As we have noted,
the citation of Exod 15:17 makes this improbable. The text of
the midrash seems to assume the meaning "temple" for "house"
in line 2. But this also seems to be the case in line 10. The
text from II Sam 7:11 reads כי בית יעשה לך יהוה. Instead
of the more neutral עשה, however, the midrash reads בנה. The
"house" to be "built" is clearly the temple, the sanctuary to
be built by God's hands. The interpreter seems thus to have
read the term בית in II Sam 7:11 as "temple."

If this is the case, it is not difficult to explain the
omission of v 13a. The text from II Samuel 7, according to the
interpreter, is a prophecy of the Davidic Messiah, the "seed of
David." But it is also a prophecy of the "house" which will be
built at the end of days. The oracle not only describes some-

---

[16]Aalen, "'Reign' and 'House'," 235; see above, 163.

thing about this "house" (identified apparently with the "place" in 7:10); it also indicates by whom it will be built. In fact, the oracle provides two possibilities: God (7:11, reading "house" as sanctuary or temple) or the Shoot of David (7:13a). The interpreter has chosen the first alternative and has omitted the second reference to the "house," obviously to avoid the potential contradiction within the oracle.

It seems unlikely that the interpreter has derived the idea that God would build the eschatological sanctuary from II Sam 7, although the statement in v. 11 does provide an opportunity for such an interpretation. The midrash does have to "force" its interpretation to some extent; the oracle from II Samuel could with far less effort be used as evidence that the Messiah would build the sanctuary. The midrash seems to represent the "inspired" interpretation characteristic of much of the Qumran exegesis. The widespread use of Exod 15:17 in discussions about the eschatological temple would make this verse the more likely origin of the tradition behind the interpretation. And although, as we have noted, there were scriptural possibilities for the view that the Messiah would build the eschatological temple (II Sam 7:13, Zech 6:12), the tradition that God would build the temple of the last days seems to have been far more common. Qumran traditions seem to represent no exception.

It is reasonable to assume that there would have to be some special reason for actualizing the tradition that the Messiah would build the temple, e.g. special interest in the image of the royal Messiah apparent in the Isaiah targum. It is not difficult to understand why that actualization failed to occur in Qumran. Although the expectation of the Davidic Messiah was an important feature of the sectarian eschatology, the image is largely traditional and mention of the royal Messiah is almost exclusively tied to traditional messianic texts, like Gen 49: 8-12, Num 24:15-17, Isa 11, and II Sam 7.[17] And although the Messiah ben David is expected to play a role in the last days, he is clearly subordinated to the priestly Messiah.[18]

The same tendency is present in our text. Line 10 reads:

----

[17]Dahl, "Eschatology and History," 16; van der Woude, Die messianischen Vorstellungen, 243ff.

[18]IQSa 2:11-17 and 19-21; cf. also the role of the priestly Messiah in the eschatological war (IQM 15:4-6), as compared with the brief mention of the "Prince" (IQM 5:1).

"This is the Shoot of David who will arise with the Interpreter of the Law..." The oracle is a prophecy of the Davidic Messiah, the royal figure. But the interpreter identifies this "Shoot of David" by relating him to the "Interpreter of the Law" (דורש התורה), most probably a reference to the priestly Messiah. The intrusion of this figure into a prophecy of the Davidic Messiah indicates his importance in the eyes of the sectarians. The precise inter-relationship among eschatological figures and the interpretation of traditional eschatological texts reflect the unique character and history of the Qumran movement.[19] Even reading the text from II Sam 7:10-14 as a messianic prophecy, there were good reasons for the interpreter to omit v. 13a. The midrash perhaps even reflects a conscious correction of a traditional view according to which the Messiah was expected to build the temple. In light of the special features of the sect's eschatological beliefs, it is not surprising that no attempt is made to increase substantially the stature of the royal Messiah by acknowledging his role as builder of the eschatological "house."

---

[19]Dahl, "Eschatology and History," 20-22.

174. FLORILEGIUM

(PL. XIX–XX)

(Already partly published in *JBL* lxxv (1956) 176–7; lxxvii (1958) 350–4.)

1–2

Col. I: Quotations from II Sam 7¹⁰⁻¹⁴ (I Chr 17⁹⁻¹³) Ex 15¹⁷⁻¹⁸ Amos 9¹¹ Ps 1¹ Isa 8¹¹ Ezek 37²³ (?) Ps 2¹ with *pešer*

```
]    ד אויֹבֹ[...ולוא יוסיֹ]ף בן עוׄלֹהֹ] לענות]וֹ כאשר בראישונה ולמן היום אשר   [...
[צויתי שפטים] על עמי ישראל הואה הבית אשר[ ... ]לֹ[...בֹ]אֹחרית הימים כאשר כתוב בספר
[... מקדש אדני כֹ]וׄנֹו ידיכה יהוה ימלוך עולם ועד הואה הבית אשר לוֹא יבוא שמה
[ ... ]           עד ]עׄולם ועֹמׄוני ומואבי וממזר ובן נכר וגר עד עולם כיא קדושי שם
יֹ]○[ׄהׄ]ׄ ... ]עֹולם תמיד עליו יראה ולוא ישמוהו עוד זרים כאשר השמו בראישונה   5
את מקדֹ[שׄ י]שראל בחטאתמה ויואמר לבנות לוא מקדש אדם להיות מקטירים בוא לוא
לפניו מעשי תורה ואשר אמר לדויד ו]הניחו[תי לכה מכול אויביכה אשר ינֹיֹחֹ להמה מכֹ]וׄל
בני בליעל הֹמכשילים אותמה לכלותמֹ[ה ... ]מה כאשר באו במחשבת ב]לֹ[י]ׄעל להכשיל בֹ[ני
אוֹ[ר]ׄ ולחשוב עליהמה מחשבות און למֹ[... נ]פׄשו לבליעל במשגת א]○[...]○ מה
וׄהֹ]גׄיֹד לכֹה יהוה כיא בית יבנה לכה והקימותי את זרעכה אחריכה והכינותי את כסא ממלכתו   10
[לעו]לֹ○ם אני אֹהֹיֹה לוא לאב והוא יהיה לי לבן הואה צמח דויד העומד עם דורש התורה אשר
[...]בצׄיׄ[ו]ן בא[ח]רית הימים כאשר כתוב והקימותי את סוכת דויד הנופלת היאה סוכת
דויד הנופל[ת א]שׄר יעמוד להושיע את ישראל
```

Col. I. '¹ . . .] enemy [. . . 'And] the son of wickedness [shall no more afflict] him as at firs and as from the day that [² I commanded judges] (to be) over my people Israel'—that is th house which [. . . in] the end of days, as it is written in the book of [³ . . . 'The sanctuary O Lord, which] thy hands have [es]tablished. Yahweh will rule for ever and ever.' That is th house 'where there shall never more enter [⁴ . . .] and 'the Ammonite and the Moabite' an 'bastard' and 'alien' and sojourner 'for ever,' for my holy ones are there. [⁵ . . .]ever, he sha be seen continually upon it, and strangers shall not again make it desolate as they desolate formerly ⁶ the sanc[tuary of I]srael because of their sin. And he purposes to build for him man-made sanctuary in which sacrifices may be made to him; ⁷ (that there may be) befor him works of the Law. And as he said to David, 'And I shall [give] thee [rest] from all thin enemies'—(meaning) that he will give rest to them from a[ll] ⁸ the sons of Belial who mad them stumble to destroy them [. . .] when they came with the device of [Be]lial to make th s[ons of] ⁹ Li[ght] stumble and to devise against them wicked imaginations, to [. . .] the [l]ife to Belial through their [. . .] error.

¹⁰ ['And] Yahweh tells you that he will build a house for you, and I shall set up your see after you, and I shall establish his royal throne ¹¹ [for eve]r. I shall be to him as a father, an he will be to me as a son.' He is 'the Shoot of David' who will arise with the Interpreter of th Law, who, ¹² [. . .] in *Zi*[*on* in the l]ast days; as it is written, 'And I shall raise up the tabernac of David that is fallen.' That is 'the tabernacle of ¹³ David that is fal][len' is he] who wi arise to save Israel

II Sam 7:13-14

הוא יבני ביתא לשמי ...
אנא אהוי ליה כאב
והוא יהי קדמי לבר

He will build the house for my name . . .
I will be like a father to him
And he will be like a son before me.

I Chron 17:12-13

הוא יבנה לי בית מקדשא לשמי ...
אנא אחבב יתיה כאבא לבריה
והוא יהי חביב קדמי כברא לאבא

He will build for me the temple for my name . . .
I will love him as a father his son
And he will be beloved before me as a son
   to his father.

Zech 6:12

ותימר ליה למימר
כדנן אמר יוי צבאות למימר
הא גברא משיחא שמיה
עתיד דיתגלי ויתרבי
וריבני ית היכלא דיוי

And you shall say to him,
"Thus says the LORD of hosts,
This man, Messiah is his name.
He will be revealed and will be exalted,
And he will build the temple of the LORD."

Isa 53:5

והוא יבני ביה מקדשא
דאיתחיל בחרבנה
אתמסר בעויחנה

He will build the temple
Which was profaned because of our transgressions
And delivered up because of our sins.

B. Evidence from the targums[20]

The Targums provide no evidence of traditions that the
Messiah would destroy the temple at his coming, nor that he would
destroy the existing temple and build a new one. The only
"messianic" task in the targums is the building of the eschatological temple. The most direct evidence for such a belief comes
from the targums to Isaiah and Zechariah (Targum Jonathan). Included at the conclusion of this section are the readings from
the two relevant passages in the targums opposite the readings
from the MT.[21] The targumic versions of Nathan's oracle (both
II Sam and I Chron) are only slightly less important. These
texts will also be discussed, and the readings from the targums
and MT have been included as well.[22]

The Zech targum is the most straightforward. The Hebrew
text says that the man whose name is the Branch (or Shoot; צמח)
will build the temple of God. The targumist simply interprets
for his readers the term צמח ; he translates it משיחא. As
we shall see, he was not the first to understand צמח as a
designation for the Messiah.[23] By the translation of the one
term he has made the messianic reference explicit. Thus the
text in the targum now says that the Messiah will build the
temple of God.

The Isaiah targum is by far the more striking, because
the phrase about building the eschatological temple is so
clearly an insertion of an entirely new idea into the text and

---

[20]For general introduction to the study of the targums
and proper methodology: R. Bloch, "Note methodologique pour
l'etude de la litterature rabbinique," RSR 43 (1955), 194-225;
J. Bowker, The Targums and Rabbinic Literature (Cambridge:
Cambridge University Press, 1969); R. McNamara, The New Testament and the Palestinian Targum to the Pentateuch (AnBib 27;
Rome: Pontifical Biblical Institute, 1966); G. Vermes, Scripture
and Tradition in Judaism (SPB 4; Leiden: Brill, 1961). For
more specific background on the targum to the prophets: P.
Churgin, Targum Jonathan to the Prophets (Yale Oriental Series,
14; New Haven: Yale University Press, 1927); J. F. Stenning,
The Targum of Isaiah (Oxford: Clarendon Press, 1949).

[21]The texts are taken from the critical edition of the
targums by A. Sperber, The Bible in Aramaic: II The Former
Prophets according to Targum Jonathan; III The Latter Prophets
according to Targum Jonathan; IVa The Hagiographa.

[22]See the discussion of 4QFlor above, 172-79.

[23]See below, 183-84.

not simply a translation. We shall have to examine the text
carefully to determine what possible motivation the targumist
could have had for the insertion, but at this point we can at
least observe the mechanics of the insertion. What makes it
possible is the reading of the participle מחלל to mean
"profaned" instead of "pierced" or "wounded."[24] Thus the הוא
in the text refers not to the servant, but to the temple which
has been "polluted" or "profaned." The rest of the verse is
appropriately referred to the destruction of the temple, not the
mishandling of the servant. The rebuilding of the temple by the
Messiah ("my servant the Messiah" in 52:13) is not derived from
the text but is inserted into the verse as something entirely
new.

It is not surprising that the targum to Isa 53 has received the most attention from commentators interested in finding evidence for a tradition in Jewish eschatology about the
Messiah and the temple of the last days. The passage has been
important for other reasons, and the phrase about the Messiah
and the temple is one of the few unambiguous pieces of evidence
about such an expectation. And the striking manner in which
the phrase is inserted into the verse makes it no less impres-
sive. The targum has been cited by several commentators on
Mark,[25] perhaps most recently by Edw. Schweizer, who says that a
messianic claim could be inferred from the saying in Mk 14:58
"without any question being asked, since according to a Jewish
paraphrase of Isa 53:3...the Messiah was to rebuild the temple
which had been profaned by the guilt of the people."[26] The quotation from Schweizer is perhaps a caricature, but it is not
atypical of most commentators who cite evidence from the targums.
Little attention is paid to the problem of dating the material
and to the kind of evidence it can provide about first century
traditions.

---

[24] It is probably not even necessary to repoint the participle מחלל as suggested by Brown, Driver and Briggs. For a
discussion of the problem, see H. Hegermann, _Jesaia 53 in
Hexapla_, _Targum_ und _Peschitta_ (Gütersloh: Bertelsmann, 1954),
79, note 3.

[25] Klostermann, _Mark_, 155; Taylor, _Mark_, 567; Lohmeyer,
Mark, 327; W. Grundmann, _Das Evangelium nach Markus_ (Berlin:
Evangelische Verlagsanstalt, 1965), 301.

[26] Schweizer, _Mark_, 32.

Thus the criticism voiced by Eta Linnemann[27] is understandable. She insists that those using targumic material for
understanding Mark must recognize real problems, the foremost of
which is dating the traditions.[28]   There is little doubt that
the targums contain old traditions, but there is just as little
doubt that the translations evolved over several centuries,
assuming their final form perhaps as late as the seventh century.[29]   There has been a recent tendency to view the targumic
techniques as early,[30] and M. McNamara has attempted to demonstrate the antiquity of the targums as a whole.[31]   Independent
scrutinizing of individual traditions cannot be avoided, however. Wherever individual traditions from the targums are to be
used as evidence of specific first-century beliefs, the traditions must be studied independently and corroborative evidence
sought from other Jewish sources.

This is particularly true when dealing with traditions
involving the temple. The disastrous wars with Rome initiated
an extremely fruitful period in the development of haggadah and
of the targumic tradition,[32] certainly most evident with respect
to the temple. One need only glance through the targum to
Isaiah to observe how profoundly the destruction of the temple
has influenced the interpretation of passages. Ms Linnemann
concisely summarizes a crucial problem:

_____

[27]Linnemann, Studien.   [28]Ibid., 125-27.

[29]Churgin (Targum Jonathan to the Prophets, 29) favors
the more usual dating of the final redaction of the targum prior
to the invasion of Babylonia by the Arabs in 640-41. He argues
that for the editor, the fall of Babylon is still a fervent expectation; its overthrow is not yet on the horizon. More recently, S. Levy ("The Date of Targum Jonathan to the Prophets,"
VT 21 [1971], 186-96) has argued that the final redaction of
the targum must be dated subsequent to the Arabian conquest.

[30]Cf. the articles by R. Bloch and G. Vermes already cited.

[31]McNamara, The New Testament and the Palestinian Targum
to the Pentateuch. His work is not concerned specifically with
the targums to the prophetic books.

[32]Vermes, Scripture and Tradition, 229: "Further doc-
trinal readaptation was inevitable as a result of the struggle
against Hellenistic infiltration in the second century B.C.
and the two wars against Rome in the first and second centuries
A.D. with their far reaching consequences for Judaism as a
nation and a religion."

In the targum to Isa 53:5, it is expected of the Messiah
that he will build the sanctuary. Yet here also it is
presupposed that it is already destroyed, for otherwise
not only the building of the (new) sanctuary would have
to be mentioned, but also the removal of the (old), profaned sanctuary, handed over to the Gentiles. The destruction of the temple, which in Mk 14:58 is attributed
to Jesus, thus has in this passage no parallel.[33]

The targum to Isaiah 53 is not a clear parallel to Mk
14:58. Yet that may not be as decisive as it appears. We must
determine with some care what we are attempting to find in
Jewish literature. One would hardly anticipate finding a tradition that the Messiah is to destroy the temple made with hands
and in three days build another not made with hands. The relationship between destroying and rebuilding deserves careful
attention, as does the possible modification of Jewish traditions in light of Christian experience. It will hopefully become clear that the conditions Ms Linnemann lays down for citing
material relevant for understanding Mark 14:58 are too restric-
tive and reflect insufficient appreciation of the way Christian
tradition developed.

Let us now proceed to each of the four targums.

II Sam 7:13-14 There is no unambiguous evidence that
this passage has been interpreted by the targumist to refer to the
future Son of David, the Messiah. Nevertheless, it seems highly
probable. We know from the New Testament[34] and from Qumran[35]
that the oracle of Nathan has been interpreted to refer to the
Messiah. There is no clear evidence in the targum that the
targumist agrees with such a reading of the text, but more im-
portantly, there is no suggestion that he does not accept its
messianic significance and is attempting to historicize the text.
He simply renders the text in Aramaic, following the Hebrew
quite literally. In v. 14, however, there are indications that
the targumist is more concerned about careful translation. His
translation makes quite clear that the father/son language is
purely symbolic, that the Son of David is not literally God's
son.[36] The passage has been noted by many scholars and is sometimes cited as proof that in Jewish expectation, the Messiah is

---

[33]Linnemann, Studien, 126.

[34]E.g., Lk 1:32-33, Jn 7:42, Acts 2:30, Heb 1:5, etc.

[35]4QFlorilegium. Cf. 172-73.

[36]Cf. the text to the targum on the appended sheet.

a human figure, not God's Son.[37] We have dealt with this question above.[38] It seems reasonable to infer from the obvious sensitivity reflected in the translation that the passage has traditionally been taken to refer to someone other than Solomon. This is a strong indication that the passage has been important in messianic discussions. (It was productive for Christian exegetes.)

I Chron 17:12-13 Once again the targum seems to view the text as messianic. The modifications in the translation are slight. The targumist uses the more common בית מקדש for בית , and he has attempted to include both the reading from II Sam and the reading from I Chron (both לי and לשמי). Verse 13 is evidence that the version of Nathan's Oracle in Chronicles has not escaped the attention of the careful translator. Here he is even more careful to demonstrate the purely figurative character of the father/son imagery. As in the case of Tg II Sam 7:14 the sensitivities suggest that the text is messianic in the mind of the targumist.

Zech 6:12 There are several interesting changes to be observed in the targum, although none of them are major. The most obvious change, as well as the most important, is the translation of צמח (shoot or branch) with משיחא (the Messiah). The same translation occurs in 3:8, where the expression עבדי צמח (my servant the branch) is rendered עבדי משיחא (my servant the Messiah).[39] In the next line the targumist adds עתיד ד־ , making certain that the events to be described are understood as future. He translates the strange expression מתחתיו יצמח (shall grow up from his place) [in his place-- RSV][40] with two verbs, the first (יתגלי , be revealed) being considerably more than a mere translation.[41] The passage is

---

[37]Schweizer, *Mark*, 325; E. Haenchen, *Der Weg Jesu*, 514; E. Lohse, *History*, 85 (using Psalm 2 as his example).

[38]Cf. 108-14 above.

[39]This text has probably been the source of the "servant" tradition, in which passages speaking about "my servant" (עבדי) are interpreted to refer to the Messiah. Cf. P. Seidelin, "Der 'Ebed Jahwe und die Messiasgestalt im Jesajatargum," ZNW 35 (1936), 194-231, esp. 226-228, and p. 196 below.

[40]"from his place": Brown, Driver, Briggs, on תחת, II, 2a.

[41]The word seems to be a technical term for the appearance of the Messiah. For a discussion, cf. McNamara, *New Testa-*

clearly messianic. It describes events which are to take place
in the future, the most important of which will be the revealing
of the Messiah and his building the temple of the Lord
(היכלא דיוי).[42]

Isa 53:5 The most significant change, as has already
been noted, is the insertion of יבני בית מקדשא ("he shall build
the temple"), made possible by reading מחלל to mean "profaned"
instead of "pierced" or "wounded." The following two phrases
are altered accordingly (the verse is referred to the temple
by means of the relative ד).

It would be useful at this point to consider briefly some
of the objections that have been raised against the use of the
Isaiah Targum for interpreting the New Testament.[43] Lloyd
Gaston is perhaps the most recent scholar to insist that the
phrase והוא יבני בית מקדשא in v. 5 is simply a gloss from
the Zechariah Targum and thus merits no consideration as a separate indicator of old traditions.[44] He appeals for support to
a book by Harald Hegermann,[45] an outgrowth of a dissertation
written in 1951 by a student of J. Jeremias. Hegermann, however, provides no real evidence for his contention that the
phrase is taken from the Zech targum and simply refers the
reader to a statement by Gustav Dalman that the phrase is "an
old gloss."[46] Dalman's statement is simply an assertion, however, with no evidence offered.

---

ment and Palestinian Targum, 249 and the literature there cited.
The same expression is used of the appearing of the Messiah in:
TJI Gn 35:21; PT Ex 12:42; Tg Jer 30:21; Tg Zech 3:8. The verb
רבה (in Zech 6:12) is used of the Messiah also in Tg Isa 11:1.

[42]There is some indication that the following verse is
also part of the picture of the eschatological future (esp the
כהין רב).

[43]We have already noted the objections of Eta Linnemann
against the use of the targum (Studien, 126).

[44]L. Gaston, No Stone on Another. Studies in the Significance of the Fall of Jerusalem in the Synoptic Gospels
(Leiden: Brill, 1970), 149, note 1.

[45]Hegermann, Jesaia 53, 79.

[46]G. Dalman, Armäisches Dialektproben (Leipzig:
Hinrichs, 1896), 10, note 25 (the work is appended to the first
edition of Grammatik des jüdisch-palästinischen Aramäisch
[Leipzig: Hinrichs, 1896]).

188

The contention that the phrase in the targum to Isa 53:5 is a gloss from Zech 6:13 is unsupportable. The translator is in every case faithful to the Hebrew original when rendering the word "temple." When the Hebrew term is היכל, the targumist always translates (היכל א); when the Hebrew term is בית, he always uses (בית (מקדשא. There are no exceptions.[47] The clearest example of the consistency can be found in Zech 8:9 and Isa 6:2-4, where both בית מקדשא and היכל are used, following exactly the Hebrew text. The point is simply that the phrase in Isa 53:5 is the common בית מקדשא, while the term used in Zech 6:12-13 is rather היכל. Unless we are to assume that the insertion is capricious and completely out of character with the rest of the targum, the phrase will have to be viewed as something more than a gloss from Zech. Even a late redactor would not have been so insensitive about such an obvious characteristic of targumic usage. If we are looking for exact linguistic parallels to the phrase in Isa 53:5, the most obvious passage would be II Sam 7:13 (or the parallel version in I Chron 17:12). For here the exact phrase (בית (מקדשא is used (מקדשא occurs only in the targum to Chronicles). The passage is all the more attractive as a candidate when it is observed that in Qumran the whole Oracle is viewed as referring to the Messiah.[48] It would be difficult to press the argument, however. The use of (בית (מקדשא with בנה is not unexpected enough to be used as decisive evidence for the derivation of the imagery from the targum to II Samuel. But if the exact scriptural origin of the expression cannot be demonstrated, it is at least clear that the phrase is more than a gloss. It represents conscious use of traditional messianic imagery. The imagery may be scriptural, but its use in the targum indicates that it has been assimilated, that it has already become part of a definite picture of the end time. And the boldness with which the phrase is interjected

---

[47]For use of היכל in Tg Isa, cf. 6:1, 4; 44:8, and 66:6; for (בית (מקדשא cf. 2:2, 3; 6:4; 37:1, 14; 38:20, 22; 56:5, 7; 60:13; 63:18; 64:10-11; 66:20. For use of היכל in Tg Zech, cf. 6:12, 13, 14, 15; 8:9; for use of (בית (מקדשא cf. 1:16; 3:7; 4:9; 8:9; 9:8; 14:20, 21. It is clear that in both targums, the more common term is בית מקדשא. Whenever the term "temple" is added in the translation (with no corresponding term in the Hebrew original), בית מקדשא is used; cf. Tg Zech 8:3, 11:13; Tg Isa 5:2, 22:22, 24:16, 28:10, 12, 13, 30:20, 29, 32:14, 33:16, 38:11, 52:11.

[48]See above, 172-73.

into the verse would suggest that the imagery is not unique to
the targumist. He can simply say "he [the Messiah] will build
the temple" because his readers already know about such things
and will not be taken totally by surprise. Gaston's pronounce-
ment ("Never is the Messiah expected to build the temple"[49]) is
thus incorrect.

Thus far we have established that at some point in the
development of the targumic tradition, it became customary to
refer the prophecy in Zech 6:12-13 to the Messiah, and that at
some point the phrase was added to Isa 53:5, reflecting the
belief that the Messiah would rebuild the fallen temple. The
task now remains to locate these traditions more precisely in
time.

The task is somewhat easier with respect to the prophecy
in Zech. The targum is in this case principally a translation,
emphasizing what is already explicit in the text. We can learn
from other sources a) how widely צמח was regarded as a designation for the Messiah and b) what evidence there is that this
particular passage from Zech was recognized as messianic. Such
information can help locate the particular targumic tradition
in time.

a) Use of צמח as a designation for the Messiah
   1) Qumran
      a) 4QFloreligium I, II: (comment on II Sam 7:
         11-14): "He is the Shoot of David (צמח דויד)
         ...."[50]
      b) 4QPatriarchal Blessings 3-4 (commenting on
         Gen 49:10): "Until the Messiah of Righteous-
         ness comes, the Branch of David (צמח דויד)
         ...."[51]
      c) 4QpIsa (commenting on Isa 11:1ff): "The
         explanation of this concerns the Shoot of
         David who will arise at the end of days...."[52]
   2) Usage elsewhere in the targum (translated with
      משיחא everywhere the term occurs: Isa 4:2;

---

[49]Gaston, No Stone on Another, 149.

[50]The text and translation are from DJD V, 53-54.

[51]Translation in A. Dupont-Sommer, The Essene Writings
from Qumran (tr. G. Vermes; New York: Meridian Books, 1961),
315; Hebrew text in JBL 75 (1956), 174-76.

[52]Translation, Dupont-Sommer, Essene Writings, 274-75;
text, JBL 75 (1965), 177-82, plates 2 and 3. The צמח is
not visible on the manuscript, but it is a highly probable
reconstruction.

Jer 23:5, 33:15; Zech 3:8) (related: Isa 11:1).

b) Specific reference to Zech 6:12f

1) Lam R 1: 51: (Discussion about the name of the Messiah): Rabbi Joshua ben Levi said: His name is 'Shoot'; as it is stated 'Behold, a man whose name is Shoot, and who shall shoot up out of his place, and build the temple of the Lord' (Zech 6:12)."[53] (The same quotation appears in Berakoth II, 5a top, but the quotation ends with "out of his place, etc.")[54]

2) Numbers R. 18, 21: (Speculation on letters מ נ צ פ כ   of the Heb. alphabet) "The double ẓade is hinted at in the verse 'Behold a man whose name is the shoot (ẓemaḥ) and who shall shoot up (yiẓmaḥ), etc.' (Zech 6:12). This refers to the Messiah, of whom it also says 'I will raise unto David a righteous shoot (ẓemaḥ zaddik), and he shall reign as king and prosper ....'[55]

3) Pirke de Rabbi Eliezer 48: (Discussion of same letters of Heb. alphabet) "With 'Zaddi' 'Zaddi' the Holy One, blessed be He, in the future will redeem Israel from the oppression of the kingdoms, and He will say to them, I have caused a branch to spring up for you, as it is said, 'Behold, the man whose name is (Zemach) the Branch; and he shall grow up (yizmach) out of his place, and he shall build the temple of the Lord' (Zech 6:12)."[56]

What we can observe from the passages cited above is first of all that the term צמח has been understood as a designation of the Messiah since before the Christian era. The authors of the Qumran material use the term as an accepted messianic designation. One can only speculate regarding the scriptural origin of the term among the sectarians, but the phrase "Branch of David" would seem closest to the usage in Jeremiah.[57] By the principle of analogy, however, the passage in Zech must certainly have been considered messianic. The earliest attestation we have for the use of the Zech passage itself is the early third century (if we can trust the attribution of the quotation of Zech. 6:12 to Joshua ben Levi in the Palest. Talmud and in Lam. R.). Even then, however, it is clear that the text is not

---

[54]Talmud Yerushalmi: תלמוד ירושלמי או תלמוד המערב ריש קורין לו תלמוד ארץ ישראל (Jerusalem: Israel-American Offset, 1960).

[55]Midrash Rabbah: Numbers, 2, 734.

[56]Pirke de Rabbi Eliezer (tr. G. Friedlander; New York: Bloch Publishing Co., 1916), 384.

[57]Cf. Dupont-Sommer, Essene Writings, 313, note 1.

cited as proof that the Messiah is to build the eschatological temple. But that is not surprising, since the idea is hardly a major feature of eschatological imagery in any of the Jewish sources we possess. It is interesting to observe that there seems to be no hesitation in the sources about continuing the quotation of 6:12 to include the building of the temple. We know that Rashi and Ibn Ezra were quite concerned to point out that the "Branch" referred to in the text was Zerubbabel and that the building of the temple was an historical reference. Thus it is not unimportant that none of the scholars quoting the text from Zech feel compelled to exclude the building of the temple by the Messiah from the rest of a text that clearly speaks of the eschatological future. This is hardly convincing proof that the Messiah was expected to build the eschatological temple in the first century, but it is at least indirect evidence that the option was available for those whose experiences or interests might lead them to expect that such a task would fall to the Messiah.

The Isaiah targum would seem to indicate that there was such a group for whom it seemed particularly appropriate that the Messiah should build the temple. There were obviously those for whom it seemed more appropriate that God should build the temple.[58] Pinkhos Churgin, in his book on the targum to the Prophets, suggests that an expectation like that expressed in the targum to Isa 53:5 would be most appropriate during the time of the Bar Kochba revolt ("V. 5 points clearly to Bar Kochba.")[59] It is not difficult to imagine how in such a situation the song of the suffering servant in Isa 53 could be transformed into a description of the victorious servant-Messiah, and how the expectation could arise that this national hero would rebuild the temple destroyed by the hated Romans.[60] This is, of course, only a conjecture, and it is certainly not original. But it is conceivable, and it would help to explain the predominant tendency in other literature to leave the building of the eschatological temple to God. Experiences with would-be Messiahs were sobering. Such experiences--and not simply anti-Christian polemics--might also be responsible for the paucity of references in the first centuries of the Christian era to this whole

[58]See the texts in Bill I, 1004.

[59]Churgin, _Targum Jonathan_, 26.   [60]_Ibid_.

chapter from Isaiah:

> Is the sparseness of Jewish concern with the chapter at a
> popular level an accident, or has Jewish address to it been
> inhibited by historical factors, internal or extraneous?
> If--as seems more probable--historical circumstance has to
> be taken into account, the reason may not solely be the
> emphasis placed upon this text by Christianity and the con-
> sequent anti-Jewish animus with which the Church harnessed
> it. Hesitations might also have sprung out of Jewish dis-
> illusionment with apocalyptic; for although Isaiah 53 does
> not belong to the same literary genre as Daniel or 4 Ezra,
> in the decades that succeeded Bar Kokhba's rising it could
> well have been the case that the description of the
> dazzling career of the once despised and rejected servant
> as set forth in this chapter seemed too potent a draught
> for healthy consumption by the folk who flocked to the
> synagogues.[61]

Unfortunately such historical conjecture is the only external means available for locating the targumic tradition in
time. The insertion is unique. But if external criteria are
lacking, it is possible to examine the phrase within the context of the targum to determine whether it fits with the traditions about the Messiah and the temple elsewhere. It is possible
to get an impression of the messianic expectations of the targum
as a whole and to compare them to what we know from other
sources. It is thus useful to know whether the phrase in 53:5
accords with the targumic traditions generally or is clearly a
later development. The following observations may be made:

> 1) The passage from 52:13-53:12 is messianic; the tar-
>   gumist applies the entire passage to the Messiah. The
>   key to the interpretation is the term עבדי in 52:13.
>   As Seidelin has argued,[62] the use of עבדי as a
>   designation for the Messiah probably derives from Zech
>   3:8, where the phrase עבדי צמח appears. We have
>   already noted above that צמח was understood to be
>   a designation for the Messiah; in the targum, the
>   passage reads עבדי משיחא . By the principal of
>   analogy (gezera shewa), it may be inferred that the
>   term עבדי in 52:13 may also be understood as applying
>   to the Messiah (as also the same term in 42:1 and 43:
>   10). The "servant" described by the text is thus
>   understood to be the Servant-Messiah.

---

[61]From p. 19 of the Prolegomenon by Raphael Loewe to the
new edition of S. R. Driver and A. Neubauer, The Fifty-Third
Chapter of Isaiah according to the Jewish Interpreters (New
York: KTAV, 1969). The work was first published in 1877.

[62]Seidelin, "Ebed Jahwe," 226-228.

2) To a degree unparalleled elsewhere in the targum, the sense of the original passage is consistently reversed in the translation. The picture of the suffering servant is transformed into a picture of a victorious figure, of extraordinary appearance, who delivers his people from bondage, punishes the wicked, and makes intercession for the sins of the people. The suffering imagery is either transformed or transferred to the opponents of the servant. What makes the passage unusual is not the imagery, but the cost at which such an interpretation has been purchased. The translation completely alters the sense of the original, and it does so consistently in this passage.

3) As has been noted, however, the messianic imagery is not unusual. It fits with the characteristics of the Messiah described elsewhere in the targum and in other Jewish literature.[63] The picture seems to accord well with perhaps the most typical messianic passage in Jewish literature, the 17th Psalm of Solomon.[64] The details should not be pressed. The point of the comparison is to indicate that the picture of the Messiah in the targum to Isa 53 is unusual only because it purports to be a translation of Isa 53. This is important in determining the stage in the development of the targum at which the interpretation in 53:5 occurred. J. Jeremias and his student, H. Hegermann, have argued that the insertion of the phrase "he shall build the temple" is late, part of a concerted effort to obscure the more traditional image of the suffering servant-Messiah.[65] They argue that the translation of מחלל as "profaned" or "polluted" instead of as "pierced" or "wounded" precedes the transferral of the imagery to the temple.[66] But the passage would then

---

[63] For a detailed comparison, Ibid., 222-224.

[64] For a detailed comparison, Ibid., 224-225.

[65] H. Hegermann, Jesaia 53, 79-80; J. Jeremias, TDNT 5, 696-697.

[66] The evidence cited by both men is the reading in the Armenian version of the Testament of Benjamin and in the translation of Aquila (βεβηλῶμενος); and in both of these translations "profaned" is applied to the Messiah (Hegermann, Jesaia 53, 79-80; Jeremias, TDNT 5, 689-90). It is interesting to note,

194

make less sense, and most important of all, it would
present an image of the Messiah unique in the whole
targum. There is no indication that the servant is
expected to suffer, and he certainly is not expected
to die.[67] Seidelin's observations regarding the verse
are worth quoting:

> Die Worte über den Temple, die von Dalman
> gestrichen werden, könnten freilich als eine
> Einschaltung anmuten; aber beim näheren Zusehen
> muss man sie doch wohl zu dem ursprünglichen
> Text rechnen. Inhaltlich sind sie einwandfrei;
> dass der Messias den Temple wieder aufbauen
> sollte, wusste man schon von der Weissagung
> Sacharjas (6:12f), und diese Weissagung ist von
> dem Sacharjatargum wieder aufgenommen worden.
> Ausserdem ist der Sinn, der durch die Streichung
> entsteht, kein glücklicher, weil das Entweihtsein
> und das Übergebensein sich dann auf den Messias
> bezieht, was sonst sorgfältig vermieden wird.[68]

4) The phrase would thus seem to fit the general messianic concerns present in the rest of the targum.[69]
But it also squares well with the obvious concern for
the temple observable in the rest of the targum. The
phrase presupposes the destruction of the temple. It
is clear from the numerous insertions of "the temple"
into the text in the rest of the targum that this is a
major concern for the targumist and his audience.[70]

however, that in previous editions of Kittel, Jeremias' article
had included a section on the Testament of Benjamin, but in the
latest edition the section has been dropped on textual grounds
(cf. 687, note 241).

[67]On the interpretation of the expression הערה למות
נפשו , cf. among others Seidelin, "Ebed Jahwe," 215; Loewe,
Fifty-Third Chapter, 19.

[68]Seidelin, "Ebed Jahwe," 212-223.

[69]It is impossible within the scope of this dissertation
to rehearse all of the attempts to explain the unique feature of
the targum in chapter 53. The reader is referred to the works by
Jeremias, Hegermann and Seidelin noted above. It is important to
observe, however, that the insertion of the phrase about building
the temple is more than an attempt to cover up a more traditional
rendering of the verse. It represents one facet of a fairly coherent interest in the Messiah and the temple found elsewhere in
chapter 53 and in the targum as a whole.

[70]For the addition of the term "temple" in the targum,
cf. note 28 above.

The targumist is constantly searching for texts that
will help his audience understand the destruction of
the temple as well as its place in the age to come.
The idea that the temple was destroyed because of the
sins of the people is not unique to 53:5,[71] nor is it
unique to the targum of Isaiah. What is novel in the
passage is the notion that the fallen temple would be
rebuilt by the Messiah. And as we have already seen,
there were messianic passages in Scripture where such
an idea could be found (Zech 6:12, II Sam 7:13 and
I Chron 17:12).

It might be possible to pin down more exactly the situation in which such traditions about the temple could have found
their way into the targumic tradition. But such an attempt is
beyond the scope of this study. It is conceivable, though hardly
demonstrable, that the concerns reflected date from the century
following the destruction of the temple. There are phrases that
seem clearly to reflect that era (e.g. Tg Isa 25:2: "an idol
temple of the nations shall never be built in Jerusalem"
[בית דחלת עממיא בקרתא ירושלם לעלם לא יתבני]--especially interesting in light of the construction of Aelia Capitolina by
Hadrian in 130--on the old site of the temple). But even such
clues do not provide proof of dating.

The study of the targums does provide us with important
information, however. We can learn, particularly in the Isaiah
Targum, how a community faced with the destruction of the temple
tried to pick up the pieces of its shattered tradition and put
them back together in a meaningful way. The targum, of course,
is a translation of Scripture, not a homily or a legal treatise.
It can be expected to provide only traces of underlying traditions, only certain kinds of information. But we can observe
in the targum the correlation between Scripture and experience.
We can observe how the experience of the community has influenced translations and where the text has been used to shed
light on experience. We learn from the Zechariah Targum and

---

[71]The idea is encountered in the Song of the Vineyard in
5:2ff, the imagery of which is explicitly interpreted in the
targum to refer to the temple (temple = watchtower; altar = wine
vat). (See above, 136-137.) The same is true in 28:9-13, where
the obscure Hebrew provides an opportunity for the targumist to
interject themes important to himself and his audience. The
translation speaks about the House of Israel's disregard of the
law (v. 10), its lack of respect for the temple (10 and 12),
and the resultant punishment (v. 13).

the targums on II Samuel and I Chronicles that the building of
the temple by the Messiah was a possibility; the notion appears
in a passage that is clearly messianic. We learn from the
Isaiah Targum that for one community this possibility was
actualized. From the manner of the insertion of the phrase "he
will build the temple," it is clear that the targumist is not
simply translating or citing Scripture. He is giving expression
to an actual belief which he presumes to share with his audience. And because the belief is present in the targum, it must
be viewed as more than a private opinion. The evidence, far
from being unimportant, suggests that the building of the
eschatological temple was a fixed part of the constellation of
messianic traditions.

    C.   Leviticus Rabbah 9:6 (parallels in Numbers Rabbah 13:2
        and Midrash on Song of Songs, 4:16)

לכשיתעורר המלך המשיח שנתון בצפון יבוא
ויבנה את בית המקדש שנתון בדרום
הה"ד העירותי מצפון ויאת ממזרח שמש

> Or, the Messianic King whose place is in the
> north will come and rebuild the Sanctuary which
> is situated in the south. This is [indicated by]
> what is written: "I have roused up one from the
> north, and he is come" (Isa. 41:25).[73]

In each of the commentaries, the text appears as one of
a number of interpretations of the phrase "Awake, O north wind,
and come, O south wind!" from Song of Songs 4:16. The presence
of the interpretation in Leviticus and Numbers Rabbah indicates
that this is part of a traditional constellation of interpretations on the verse from Song of Songs. The interpretation has
nothing to do with the particular verses in Leviticus and
Numbers on which the initial comment, with the reference to Song
of Songs 4:16, has been made.

    The mechanics of the interpretation of the phrases from
Song of Songs are rather obvious. The verb עור appears also
in Isa 41:25, and in both Song of Songs 4:16 and Isa 41:25, the
verb is used with the term צפון. The verse in Isaiah has been
interpreted as a reference to the Messiah in the north and has
been used to interpret the terms in Songs of Songs. The

---

[72] כדרש ויקרה רבה   (ed. M. Margulies; Jerusalem: Ameri-
can Academy for Jewish Research, 1953).

[73] Midrash Rabbah 4: Leviticus (ed. H. Freedman and M.
Simon; London: Soncino Press, 1939).

reference to the temple in the south perhaps reflects an interpretation of the "garden" in Song of Songs 4:16 as a reference
to the temple. It is clear, however, that the building of the
temple (rather, the rebuilding) is not derived from the verse
in Song of Songs nor from the verse in Isaiah. As in the case
of the phrase in TgIsa 53:5, the statement about the Messiah
as the (re)builder of the temple at the end of days has been
imposed on a text. Further, the precise wording indicates that
the phrase about building the temple is not a direct quotation
of a scriptural passage like Zech 6:12 or II Sam 7:13. This
suggests, then, that as in the case of the comment in the Isaiah
Targum, potential traditions according to which the Messiah would
build the eschatological temple have been actualized in the community from which this comment derives. Traditional messianic
imagery has been used to interpret the verse from Song of Songs,
and part of that traditional imagery is the belief that the
Messiah will build the temple at the end of days. The suggestion about the rebuilding of the temple by the Messiah is
clearly imposed on the verse, which simply indicates the currency of this tradition. The possibility of dating the tradition seems somewhat remote, but the text does provide another
example of an actualized tradition according to which the
Messiah is to be the builder of the temple at the end of days.

II. Destruction and (Re)Building in Mk 14:58

          We are concerned in this chapter with the charge in Mk
14:58 as part of the messianic imagery at the trial. We have
now surveyed the relevant texts from Jewish sources and are ready
to examine the charge in Mark in light of these texts. Scholars
have studied carefully most of the texts cited and have examined
Mark in light of the traditions known from the Jewish circles
from which the literature derives. Apart from a few observations on the texts, the principal value of this section will be
to reconsider the relationship between Christian and pre-Christian expectations regarding the Messiah and the temple. Most of
the studies of Mark, including the study by Ms Linnemann, take
an oversimplified view of this relationship that often precludes
the possibility of real insight.

          First, there is no evidence for an expectation according
to which the Messiah will destroy the temple when he comes.
That is hardly surprising. The closest approximation to such an
expectation is found in PsSol 17:33: "And he shall purge

198

Jerusalem, making it holy as of old." The text says nothing
about destroying the temple, but it is possible that what is behind the charge in Mark is a messianic tradition according to
which the Messiah will purify the temple when he comes. Such a
possibility is particularly attractive in Mark in view of the
account of the cleansing in chapter 11. If this view is correct,
the statement about destroying the temple in 14:58 would not be
meant literally; it would refer to the eschatological purifica-
tion that the Messiah was expected to carry out. The charge
would imply a "messianic" claim, assuming the currency of a
tradition like that found in Ps Sol 17, and it would also provide a link between the cleansing in chapter 11 and the trial.

As we have already observed, however, this approach to
the charge in Mark cannot be defended. The charge in 14:58 cannot be interpreted by 11:15-17. In fact, the situation would
appear to be the reverse: the account of the cleansing is
probably to be interpreted by the charge at the trial, at least
with regard to the statement about destruction. There is no
hint in Mark's account of the trial that the witnesses refer to
anything but a prediction of destruction. And even in the
account of the cleansing, there seems to be a veiled reference
to the coming destruction of the temple. The cleansing is sandwiched between the cursing of the fig tree. And the quotation
from Jeremiah is most intelligible if the author has in mind
the actual destruction. And even if the cleansing is related
to the charge at the trial by means of the (impending?) destruction of the temple, the three statements about the temple in the
passion story (ναός; 14:59; 15:29, 38) have a relationship to
one another that is not shared with other temple statements in
the last chapters of the Gospel. Perhaps the best way to view
the relationship between the cleansing and the charge in 14:58
is to view the cleansing as a prophetic anticipation of the impending destruction of the temple.

The second observation that can be made about the Jewish
texts is that the Messiah can be described as the (re)builder of
the temple. First, there are scriptural possibilities for the
development of such a tradition in II Sam 7:13 and Zech 6:12.
We know that both of these texts were viewed as "messianic," as
referring to the coming Messiah-King.[74] The Jewish texts also
suggest, however, that the potential tradition has been actual-

[74]See above, 185-86.

ized rarely. The only evidence for such actualized tradition
is post-70; and the tradition of the Messiah as the builder of
the eschatological temple had to compete with traditions
according to which God himself would build the temple in the
last days. Traditions about God as builder, appealing to such
texts as Exod 15:17, appear to have been more widespread. Where
we do have clear evidence of beliefs about the eschatological
temple prior to 70 (Qumran), it is God who is expected to build
the temple--despite the messianic interpretation of II Sam 7
in 4QFlor.[75]

Despite the lack of definite traditions about the Messiah as the builder, however, the literature does provide important evidence. Among traditional messianic texts were two (II
Sam 7:13 = I Chron 17:12 and Zech 6:12) in which the statement
is made that the future king will build the temple. Although
there were other possibilities for eschatological traditions
(Exod 15:17), we have evidence that at least for some, this
potential task of the coming Messiah was actualized.[76] There
were Jews who believed that the Messiah would build the temple
at the end of days.

The real difficulty, as Ms Linnemann and others have
pointed out, is that in Mk 14:58 Jesus is charged with having
made a statement about destroying the present temple as well as
a statement about (re)building. And a survey of the Jewish texts
provides no evidence that the Messiah would destroy the existing
temple as well as rebuild it (or build a new one). The single
text cited to support such a tradition is Enoch 90:28-29, and
even a cursory reading of the text indicates that it is of
little help in establishing messianic traditions. The "Lord of
the Sheep" is obviously God, not the Messiah. The Messiah,
assuming the reference in 90:37ff is to the Messiah, does not
appear until after the judgment described in 90:20-27 and until
after the old "house" is folded up and the new house is brought
by the Lord of the Sheep. God is viewed as the "builder" of
the eschatological temple in Enoch and, if the removal of the
old house is to be viewed as part of the judgment scene, as the
destroyer of the old temple.[77] Even if the text provides no

---

[75] See the discussion of 4QFlor.

[76] TgIsa 53:5, above, 191-195; LevR 9:6 (and parallels),
above, 196-197.

[77] The "they" in the text (90:28) "are God's agents."

evidence of messianic expectations, however, it is interesting
to observe that the old "house" the author seems to view as
corrupt[78] must be removed before the new house is "built." This
should probably be viewed less as an example of a fixed tradition
than as a modification of traditional expectations in light of
special concerns and circumstances. It is at any rate apparent
that Enoch tells us little about what was expected of the coming
Messiah.

From our survey of destruction and building imagery in
Jewish literature, we are left with two problems:

1. Most, if not all traditions about the building of an
   eschatological temple, are found in literature written
   or edited after A.D. 70, after the actual destruction
   of the Second Temple.
2. In none of the messianic texts is the Messiah expected
   to destroy the temple, even as a prelude to the building of a new temple.

We will deal first with the problem of temple traditions
in general, with special attention to the problems posed by the
destruction of the Second Temple in A.D. 70. The crisis of 70
was not unique in the history of Israel. Once before the temple
had been destroyed and Jews had been forced to take a new look
at themselves and their religion. That crisis left its mark on
Jewish literature written long after the event. But the First
Temple was rebuilt, even if the building constructed by the returned exiles was a poor imitation of the original (Ezra 5:63-
65, Haggai 2:3). These events became particularly meaningful
for those who witnessed the destruction of the temple in 70.
They were able to make sense of their present experience in
light of their past. As the Temple of Solomon had been destroyed because of the sins of the people, so the second temple was
destroyed because of Israel's sins (Tg Isa 53:5; Enoch 89-90?;
Jos Ant VIII, 126ff). But just as the First Temple was rebuilt,
so will the Second Temple be rebuilt--but more splendid even
than the First (Midr Ps 22:9; Midr Ps 90:19; Sifre Deut 33:12).

What is difficult to know is what expectations about a
future temple were held among diverse Jewish groups between the

---

[78]"And they began again to build as before, and they
reared up that tower, and it was named the high tower; and they
began to place a table before the tower, but all the bread on it
was polluted and not pure" (89:73).

two crises. Many, including Ms Linnemann,[79] have assumed that
once a new temple was built, expectations about a future temple
would have died out. The only real motivation for the reactual-
ization of such traditions could have been the events of 70.
What makes the question about eschatological temple traditions
in the early first century difficult to answer is that all of
the literature written subsequent to 70 bears the indellible
stamp of current events. Even literature containing traditions
prior to 70 that has been edited subsequent to the destruction
of the Second Temple can be used only with great care to reconstruct earlier beliefs. Yet there is evidence that even among
Jews for whom the temple was a reality, even Herod's impressive-
ly remodeled version, expectations of a future temple to be rebuilt by God himself or, less frequently, the Messiah, did not
die out. It is not clear to what extent expectations of the
destruction of the temple were current, but hopes for a new
temple were certainly present.

Such hopes did not necessitate dissatisfaction with the
present cult. David Flusser, in his article on 4QFlor cited
above,[80] has argued that even with the building of the Second
Temple by the returned exiles expectations of a future temple
developed. The temple built after the exile was hardly equivalent to the magnificent temple built by Solomon as it had been
idealized in the memory of the community (Ezra 5:63-65; Haggai
2:3). Flusser argues that even then, men began to look to the
future when God would build the temple with all its former
splendor (or an even greater splendor).[81]

But there were also those for whom even Herod's temple was
unacceptable. For groups like those from which Enoch and the
Qumran literature derive, the problem was that the present
temple was corrupt. At least one response to such a situation
was to look to the future, when a new purified temple would replace the old corrupt one. This hope appears to be present in
Enoch. And among the diverse expectations of the sectarians at
Qumran, there are hopes for a new temple at the end of days to
be built by God himself (whatever that meant with regard to the
present temple).

---

[79]Linnemann, Studien, 126-127.

[80]Flusser, "Two Notes on the Midrash on 2 Sam vii."

[81]Ibid., 99-100; Haggai 2:49, Tobit 14:4-5, Enoch 90:29,
Midr Ps 90:19, etc.

The common feature among such temple traditions from Ezra
through the middle ages is the expectation of a future temple,
a temple built by God, or, less commonly, by the Messiah. But
if there are common features, there are also great differences,
as one would expect. We should not anticipate exact similarities among traditions regarding the temple to be built at the
end of days, particularly not among those separated by the destruction of the Second Temple in 70. Traditional imagery has
been modified in light of actual events. The expectations of
the community at Qumran were not shaped by the destruction of
the Second Temple; they were developed in response to a crisis
that resulted in the severance of all ties with the present
temple establishment in Jerusalem. They were conditioned by the
peculiar composition and experience of the group. It is not
surprising that traditions were reshaped and modified in light
of the community and its unique history and experience.[82] The
version of the expectation of a new temple in Enoch has been
modified by a view of the present temple as corrupt. The arriv-
al of the new house necessitates the removal of the old. However the text in Enoch is to be dated and interpreted in detail,
it at least provides another set of circumstances in which
traditions about a future temple and hope for the replacement of
the present temple could be combined prior to A.D. 70.

What we can learn from study of literature written after
A.D. 70 is how Jews, faced with the fact of the destroyed
temple, were able to redo their eschatology. When describing
the future in light of their unique experience, they were unable
simply to reproduce traditional ideas. They had to take a new
look at tradition. The Isaiah Targum is an excellent example of
such a rethinking of tradition. For the targumist, one given
fact is the destruction of the temple. The participle מחלל in
Isa 53:5 provides the opportunity for the targumist to relate
this catastrophic experience to Scripture, to a text that provides some means of understanding the event.[83] He also, however, relates this experience to traditional expectation by
adding a reference to the rebuilding of the temple to be carried
out by the Messiah when he comes. The result is a new tradition,
new because traditional imagery has been modified in light of

---

[82]Dahl, "Eschatology and History in the Light of the
Dead Sea Scrolls."

[83]See above, 187.

new events and problems. The tradition is messianic because the
rebuilding of the temple is viewed as one of the tasks of the
Messiah when he comes. But the Messiah is not expected to destroy the temple, since it is already in ruins.

Such reinterpretation of traditional material also occurred within early Christianity. To argue that Mk 14:58 can be
"messianic" only if a pre-Christian text can be found in which
the Messiah is expected to destroy and rebuild the temple is to
fail to appreciate the interplay between history and eschatology.
We can hardly expect to find such a tradition after 70, since
the destruction of the temple was already an accomplished fact.
For such a tradition to be possible prior to 70, we should expect to find some opposition to the present temple such as we
find in Qumran or in Enoch. We cannot expect in advance that
the Messiah will appear as the builder of the eschatological
temple in all pre-Christian literature. We have already observed that there were options, one of which was that God himself would build the temple at the end of days. The apparent
dominance of this tradition in extant literature does not mean
that the Messiah could not be viewed as the builder of the
eschatological temple. The lack of such a tradition in Qumran,
where we even find a messianic interpretation of II Samuel 7,
suggests that there has been an interplay between tradition and
the history and experience of the community.[84]   Perhaps the
most we can do is to suggest what traditional options were
possible to early Christian interpreters by surveying the way
traditions about the Messiah and the temple have been related
to current events and experiences in other circles, then to examine Mk 14:58 to determine to what extent messianic traditions
are present and to what extent they have been modified by the
unique experience of early Christians. Having completed our
survey of Jewish texts, we are now ready to focus on the close
examination of Mark.

Many Old Testament texts and images have become "messianic"
when applied to Jesus Christ by Christian exegetes. But in Mk
14:58 it is possible to recognize messianic imagery in the more
traditional sense. Within extant Jewish literature, there are
at least two explicit references to the Messiah as builder of

---

[84]See above, 172-79.

the eschatological temple.[85] There are two scriptural texts
(II Sam 7:13 = I Chron 17:12 and Zech 6:12), both of which were
considered messianic in pre-Christian Jewish circles, according
to which the Messiah-King will build the temple when he comes.
We know from other New Testament literature that II Sam 7 has
been extremely important in the development of Christology.[86]
If Jesus is tried, according to Mark, as "Christ, the Son of
the Blessed," it seems highly probable that it is as Messiah
that he will build the "temple not made with hands."

The difficulty is the charge that Jesus will destroy the
present temple. As we have observed, nowhere do we find evidence of a tradition according to which the Messiah will destroy
the present temple before building a new one. It is not difficult to understand how Jesus could be viewed as the builder of
the eschatological temple, particularly if the image of the
temple and temple worship had already been spiritualized and
applied to the Christian community. It is more difficult to
understand how Jesus could be characterized as the destroyer of
the present temple. Here we will attempt a solution to this
problem within a limited scope. A thorough solution would require a reconstruction of the history of the tradition of 14:58
as well as consideration of the probable origin of the statement
about destruction, its dating, and its possible currency in
anti-Christian circles. Here we shall confine our remarks to
Mark, to determine if possible what the statement about destruction means in Mk 14:58 and how it is related to the more traditional "messianic" statement about building the new temple.

We should first observe that the characterization of the
present temple as one "made with hands" and the comparison to a
superior temple "not made with hands" is not out of place in
Mark. In chapter 11, Jesus "cleanses" the temple, insisting
that it no longer functions as God intended.[87] The account is
interpreted by Mark by the cursing of the fig tree, with the
obvious implication that the present religious establishment
will be rejected, cursed, because of its failure to bear fruit.
This account is followed by a controversy section which includes
both the parable of the wicked husbandmen and the statement in

---

[85]TgIsa 53:5, Lev R 9:6 (and par).

[86]See esp the excursus on Son of God, 108-114.

[87]See above, 129-136.

12:33 that the command to love is "greater than all burnt
offerings and sacrifices." In 13:2, Jesus predicts that the
temple will be destroyed. And at the climax of the passion
story, Mark reports that the temple curtain was torn from top to
bottom (15:38). At least with regard to Mark's view of the
events, there is strong evidence to support Lohmeyer's suggested
anti-temple-cult bias.[88]

It is still difficult, however, to understand how Jesus
can be viewed as the destroyer of the temple as well as the
builder of its replacement. Many have argued that Jesus could
never have made such a statement. The question we must answer
is what the statement means for Mark, if, as seems probable, he
views the statement as true in some sense. It is conceivable
that this is the sense in which the statement can be described
as "false testimony": Jesus never made such a statement; he
never predicted that he would destroy the temple. But if our
view of the double level of the story is correct, if the charge
is to be viewed as ironically true at a deeper level, this cannot be the solution to the problem. It is possible, however,
that Mark may still view the charge as "true" at a deeper level
while also recognizing that Jesus could never have made such a
statement. We must return to the text for the clues the author
provides.

The two facts in the passion story that provide the most
important evidence for the author's interpretation of the statement about destruction are the mention of "three days" in the
charge and the reference in 15:38 to the tearing of the temple
curtain at the moment of Jesus' death. As we have already noted,
the reference to "three days" in 14:58 must be understood by the
reader as a reference to the resurrection.[89] If the term is
used also as a widespread designation for a short period of time,
that simply provides the possibility for misunderstanding on the
part of Jesus' enemies. The result of the resurrection will be
the erection of a new temple not made with hands, i.e., the
Christian church. As the "rejected stone" of Ps 118:22, Jesus
has become the "head of the corner"; as the Messiah, he is the
builder of the new temple. But his death and resurrection also
affect the old religious establishment. At the moment of his
death, the "destruction" of the old order occurs. As he dies,

---

[88] Esp. Lord of the Temple; see above, 138-39.

[89] See above, 143-44.

the temple curtain is torn from top to bottom. Whatever interpretation be preferred for the tearing of the veil,[90] the event
is for Mark the fulfillment of the "prophecy" made in 14:58 and
15:29. With Jesus' death, the old religious order comes to an
end; those who have rejected Jesus, the religious leaders, have
now been rejected by God. The old temple made with hands has now
been replaced by a new temple not made with hands. Jesus is the
destroyer of the temple in a figurative and in an ironic sense:
its destruction is a result of his death, brought about by those
in charge of the temple worship. The imagery would be most
pointed at a time when the author and his audience know that the
Jewish temple is in ruins. Mark makes no explicit attempt to describe the (impending?) destruction as God's punishment for
having put Jesus to death, but such a view is not totally out of
accord with what we find in his Gospel.

This suggests that the charge in 14:58 can be both "false
testimony" (Jesus never threatened to destroy the temple) and
"prophetic" (as a result of his death the old religious order
symbolized by the temple comes to an end). It does seem, however,
that Mark's interpretation of the charge is more intelligible as
interpretation of current tradition than as the creation of such
tradition. One might ask if Mark would have characterized Jesus
as destroyer of the temple, even in an ironic sense, if traditions about such a statement of Jesus were not current in his
day. Other Christians were apparently sensitive about such a
charge. According to Matthew, Jesus said, "I am able to destroy
..." (26:61). Luke does not include the charge in his account of
the passion. He does include a version of the charge in the
statement made by false witnesses against Stephen (Acts 6:14),
but it is clear from Stephen's speech that Luke is unwilling to
view Jesus as one who intended to "destroy this place the change
the customs delivered to us by Moses."[91] In the Fourth Gospel,
the saying has been interpreted as a reference to the destroying
and raising of Jesus' body (Jn 2:19-21). It is unnecessary to
answer the question whether or not the threat to destroy the
temple goes back to Jesus himself; perhaps the question cannot be
answered. It is at least clear that if the charge was somewhat
embarrassing to Christians, they were unable to dismiss it out of
hand. If Mark is not totally out of touch with such sensitivities,
it is easier to understand his interpretation of the charge as

---

[90]See above, 140-42.   [91]See above, 148-49.

interpretation of current tradition.

There is also some question whether the saying about destroying and building pre-dates Mark. No real attempt will be made to answer this question here. At least for Mark, the charge seems to reflect knowledge of the actual destruction of the temple, whether impending or already an accomplished fact. The rejection imagery in 11 and 12, the prediction of the destruction of the temple in 13:2, and the preoccupation with the temple in chapters 14 and 15 would seem most understandable for an author and audience living immediately before or soon after the catastrophic events of 66-70. But our interpretation of the charge does not depend upon such dating of the Gospel, which can probably be argued only by appeal to temple traditions. Even prior to the destruction of the temple it was possible for Christians as well as Jewish sectarians to describe their communities as a temple.[92] The awareness of a contrast between the two "temples" in Mark does not necessarily presuppose the destruction of the old temple, and it is thus conceivable that the saying about destroying and rebuilding may pre-date Mark.

It is not clear what the charge might have meant in a pre-Markan form, first of all because the charge in Mk 14:58 has almost certainly been modified by Mark. Commentators have argued that the pre-Markan form of the charge looked more like 15:29 than 14:58.[93] It is not obvious how the history of such a tradition could be written, or what answers could be given to questions about its probable origin or possible messianic overtones. Solution of that problem is not necessary for interpreting Mark, however.[94] Even if the two versions of the charge in 14:58 and 15:29 are to be explained as versions of prior tradition, the charge and its restatement in 15:29 within the context of Mark provides the evidence necessary for determining Mark's view of the charge. The relationship between the two versions of the charge must be understood in light of the two-level narrative, as well as the use of misunderstanding and irony. V. 14:58 provides clues for the reader to the real meaning of the statement,

---

[92] II Cor 6:16. See above, 159-68.

[93] See above, 123-24.

[94] Even with respect to the pre-Markan tradition of the temple charge, it is difficult to imagine how the reference to the (re)building of the temple could have been conceived as anything but a "messianic" act.

208

while 15:29 suggests how the charge has been misunderstood by
Jesus' opponents.[95] They view the statement as a threat against
the present temple and as an impossible boast by one who cannot
even save himself--the would-be Messiah who dies on a cross.
Mark, on the other hand, suggests that the statement, even if
never made by Jesus, does point to truth at a level beyond the
comprehension of Jesus' enemies: Jesus' death will mark the
end of the temple establishment, and the new temple he will
"build" will succeed the old temple as the real place of worship.
And as the "builder" of this new temple, Jesus is revealed to be
the promised Messiah.

What is decisive for interpreting Mark is the distinction
between the two "temples" in 14:58. This is where Mark provides
his interpretation of the charge. The Christian community is
the temple not made with hands, the successor to the old temple.
And Jesus is the builder of this new temple. From our survey
of messianic expectations and of traditions about the eschatological temple, we have observed that there are only two possible builders of the temple at the end of days, God or the
Messiah. Ms Linnemann has objected that there is no evidence
that the building of the temple is "messianic."[96] In light of
our study, we might argue precisely the opposite in regard to
Mk 14:58. There would seem to be no other conceptual possibilities available within Jewish eschatology for describing builders
of the eschatological temple. Jesus is either being described
as God, which seems highly improbable, or he is being described
as Messiah. If we have correctly interpreted the function of
the charge in Mk 14:58, the most reasonable explanation of the
charge is that it identifies Jesus as the Messiah who will build
the temple at the end of days.

What we find in Mark is not a simple reproduction of
standard Jewish messianic tradition, if such pure tradition,
unaffected by the experience of the groups within which traditions circulated, ever existed. The statement in 14:58 includes
mention of the destruction of the temple by Jesus. The origin
of this statement should be sought not in standard Jewish messianic expectation but within the experience of the Christian
church, perhaps in the context of Jewish-Christian polemics.
The reference to three days also points to Christian experience

[95]See above, 124.
[96]Linnemann, *Studien*, 125-127.

of Jesus' resurrection and reflects traditions like those found
in I Corinthians 15 and in the passion predictions in Mark.
The temple to be built is not simply the temple, but a
"spiritual" temple identified with a community of believers.
Some of the imagery, particularly the three days and the mention
of the destruction of the temple, has perhaps become "messianic"
by virtue of its application to Jesus. But the statement about
rebuilding the temple (or building the new temple) in Mark points
to traditions according to which the Messiah will build the
temple. If Christians have actualized such traditions attested
in few other sources, the reason is to be sought in the unique
experience of those who confessed Jesus as "the Christ, the Son
of God." Messianic traditions had a special attraction for
followers of the crucified and risen Messiah.

CHAPTER 10

We have now completed our study of the trial within Mark's
passion story. It has been argued that the trial scene is best
approached on the literary level; it should be studied within
the context of the passion story and the Gospel as a whole. Any
interpretation of the trial proposed must be able to explain its
function within the story. Approaching the trial from this
perspective, we have seen that in Mark, the trial is the place
chosen by the author to introduce themes of particular importance in the account of Jesus' death which follows. There are
also indications that these themes are of decisive religious
significance for the author; they represent the real meaning of
Jesus' "rejection," predicted by Jesus himself in 8:31 and
prophesied in Scripture in Ps 118:22. This theme of rejection
is bound up with the corresponding theme of vindication, related
particularly to the resurrection and introduced in the three
passion predictions as well as in the citation of Ps 118:22 in
12:10-11. At the trial, specific charges are made on the basis
of which Jesus is rejected. But by the use of a two-level narrative, Mark suggests that these charges also provide the basis
for Jesus' vindication and thus represent the real meaning of
Jesus' trial and death.

For Mark, the true meaning of the passion can only be
understood in terms of the confession of Jesus as Messiah, Son
of God. The use of the titles in the Gospel as a whole but
particularly within the passion story suggest that they represent for the author the fundamental Christian confession. Mark's
use of "Christ" does not reflect a desire to avoid traditional
royal imagery in describing Jesus. His use does indicate, however, that he is aware of contrasting messianic conceptions. In
Peter's confession in 8:29-31 and especially within the account
of the trial and passion, it is clear that Mark is aware of another conception of Messiah that Jesus does not fit. One of the
purposes of Mark's story seems to be to prove to his readers
that, contrary to all appearances and despite the obvious
differences between Jesus and the image of the Messiah in

211

popular expectation, the crucified Jesus is the Messiah, the
Son of God. In composing his Gospel, Mark was certainly interested in doing more than correcting false conceptions of
Christology. Chapters 8-10 would suggest that the issue of
discipleship is as important as proper Christology, or rather,
that what Christians think of Jesus has some bearing on how they
understand themselves. The preoccupation with the temple in the
last chapters of the Gospel suggests that the Jew/Christian
problem is important for the author. Nevertheless, the attempt
to explore the nature of Jesus' Messiahship is one of the
important concerns visible in the story, particularly in the
last chapters of the Gospel, and some tension between proper and
improper conceptions of the Messiah is present. The concern to
present a proper view of Jesus Christ, the Son of God is thus an
important aspect of the author's overall purpose in the story.

The trial introduces the royal motif in Mark's passion
story. Jesus is formally rejected by the Jewish religious
leaders as "the Christ, the Son of the Blessed," to be tried before Pilate, mocked and crucified in the next chapter as "the
King of the Jews" and "the Christ, the King of Israel." At a
deeper level of the story, however, Mark intends the reader to
appreciate the irony of the drama. It is the Jewish leaders who
will be rejected. And it as "the Christ, the Son of God" that
Jesus will be vindicated by God.

The trial also introduces a second theme of considerable
importance to the author. The first charge in 14:58 is part of
a broader concern with the temple beginning in chapter 11 and
culminating with the tearing of the temple veil in 15:38. Mark's
use of this temple theme in the last chapters of his Gospel indicates his concern to link the "rejection" of the Jewish religious leaders with the destruction of the temple. The interpretation of the charge in Mark is not dependent upon the dating
of the work, but the author's concern makes most sense if he is
writing at a time soon after the destruction of the temple. The
destruction of Jerusalem and its temple was dramatic evidence
for Christians that God had rejected the temple establishment,
indeed the whole Jewish nation. There is reason to avoid
speaking about the "rejection of Israel" in Mark's Gospel. The
author restricts the remarks about rejection to the religious
leaders, the elders, the chief priests and the scribes. Jesus'
use of the Shema and the ensuing discussion in 12:29-34 reflect
a positive attitude toward some aspects of Jewish worship. The

silencing of the Sadduces in 12:18-27 need mean nothing more than that followers of Jesus, like Pharisees, believe in the resurrection. The concern for Gentiles that many have observed in Mark does not necessarily imply a negative view of Jews. Nevertheless, the "rejection" theme is present in Mark, particularly in the parable of the wicked husbandmen in 12:1-11. The destruction of the temple demonstrates that God has rejected at least one segment of the Jewish community. Mark's concern with the trial and his apparent attempt to heighten the responsibility of the Jewish leaders in Jesus' death are part of this concern. The temple charge suggests that Jesus' death not only brings about the birth of a new community but the rejection and destruction of another. The "temple not made with hands" is a replacement for the old "temple made with hands."

But the temple charge seems to have still another function within the account of the trial in Mark. It provides further insight into Jesus' Messiahship. He is the Messiah who will build the new temple. If, as has been argued, Mark has inserted the temple charge into a traditional account of the trial whose point is that Jesus was condemned for his messianic claim, the insertion is most understandable if the temple charge was understood by Mark as "messianic" in the proper sense. Its insertion into the trial not only provides important clues for the Christian reader about the relationship between Christianity and Jewish temple religion; it also provides another clue to Jesus' identity as Messiah.

If the interpretation of the trial suggested here is correct, there are several further questions that may be asked. The focus of the trial and passion story on Jesus as Messiah-King suggests that the history of the passion tradition may deserve closer scrutiny. It may well be, as Prof. Dahl has suggested, that the starting point for the tradition is the inscription "the King of the Jews."[1] If that is the case, it may be that from the outset, the account of Jesus' death was an account of the death of the hidden Messiah. The interpretation of the trial also raises interesting questions about the setting and date of the Gospel of Mark. There is strong evidence for a date immediately subsequent to the destruction of the temple, as well as for a setting within a community for whom Jewish Scripture, Jewish messianic conceptions and Jewish worship are of

---

[1] Nils A. Dahl, "Der gekreuzigte Messias."

considerable significance. The space devoted to the trial and its importance within the structure of the Gospel suggest that in Mark's church, questions about the relationship between Christian/Jew or between the church and Israel are by no means settled or peripheral.

But perhaps the most immediate implications of this study are methodological. It should be obvious that the approach to the trial here is somewhat different from what has been typical of most recent studies. Most studies of the Gospels begin by separating tradition and redaction, with the understanding that the interpretation of the author's views will focus principally on his additions to or modification of tradition. Many who employ such methods of study approach the Gospels as part of a wider concern to write a complete history of early Christian tradition. Schreiber, Linnemann and Donahue all attempt to explain the trial in Mark by relating it to tradition; they seem to assume that a passage has been interpreted only when its place in the history of tradition has been precisely fixed.

Within these various studies of the trial in Mark, many of the same questions we have asked are asked, many of the same observations are made. This is perhaps least true of Eta Linnemann's work. She is preoccupied with source reconstruction and reflects little interest in broader literary questions. There are, however, a good number of similarities between the approach I have followed and that of John Donahue. One reason is that Donahue is interested in more than separating tradition and redaction. His approach to the Gospel reflects an appreciation for the literary character of Mark's work. A second reason is that his instincts as a redaction critic interested in Mark's use of tradition would lead him to some of the same problems we have studied. The differences between 14:58 and 15:29, for example, can be viewed as evidence of reworking of traditional material. If 15:29 seems to be the more primitive version of the saying, a redaction critic would focus on those features peculiar to 14:58 as particularly suggestive of the author's interpretation of the saying--the terms "made with hands/not made with hands" and the distinction between the two temples.

Yet reconstruction of the history of this tradition and isolation of Markan additions cannot solve the crucial problems of interpretation. Redaction critics who agree about Mark's additions and modifications cannot agree on the interpretation of the passage in its present context. And one cannot help but

be impressed by the degree to which interpretation of Mark is
made to depend upon the meaning of verses in pre-Markan tradition and the precise determination of the author's additions and
modifications, much of which is highly conjectural. And if there
is no way to distinguish precisely between tradition and redaction, if there is no absolutely reliable criterion for determining what Mark has added to his sources and how he has modified
them, if there is simply insufficient data for reconstructing
the history of a particular tradition, one would have to assume
that interpretation of that text in Mark is impossible.

The advantage of the approach I have followed is that interpretation begins with basic literary questions that can be
answered without knowing the prior history of tradition or the
precise delineation of tradition and redaction, and that must be
answered even when such information is attainable. Reconstructing the history of gospel tradition is an important facet of
biblical studies. But one of the primary goals of biblical
studies must be to interpret the individual books that comprise
the respective testaments. As has been suggested for some time,
the interpretation of books may require some adjustment in
approach.

Whatever the meaning of the temple charge in pre-Markan
tradition, whatever its ultimate origin, whatever features of the
charge are to be attributed to the author's editing, the meaning
of the charge in Mark can only be determined by study of the
verse within its context. Interpretation of the charge in Mark
is possible even if the mysteries of the temple charge in pre-
Markan tradition are never solved; it is possible even if no two
redaction critics ever agree on precisely what Mark has done with
his traditional material. To account for certain features of the
trial narrative in Mark, it is perhaps necessary to view the
author as an interpreter of tradition rather than as a creator.
But to understand Mark, it is necessary to come to grips with
his work as a piece of literature. For such study, the present
models of "literary" interpretation of the New Testament are
in need of revision.

BIBLIOGRAPHY

I. Texts and translations

The Babylonian Talmud. Edited by I. Epstein. London: Soncino
    Press, 1935-53.

Charles, R. H. Aprocrypha and Pseudepigrapha of the Old
    Testament. Oxford: Clarendon Press, 1913.

Danby, H. The Mishnah. Oxford: Clarendon Press, 1933.

Discoveries in the Judean Desert of Jordan I: Qumran Cave 1.
    Edited by D. Barthelemy and J. T. Milik. Oxford:
    Clarendon Press, 1955.

Discoveries in the Judean Desert of Jordan V: Qumran Cave 4.
    Edited by John Allegro. Oxford: Clarendon Press, 1968.

Driver, S. R. and Neubauer, A. D. The Fifty-third Chapter of
    Isaiah according to the Jewish Interpreters. New York:
    KTAV, 1969 (reprinted).

Dupont-Sommer, A. The Essene Writings from Qumran. Trans. by
    Geza Vermes. New York: Meridian Books, 1967.

Goldin, J. The Fathers according to Rabbi Nathan. Yale
    Judaica Series 10. New Haven: Yale University Press,
    1955.

Goldin, J. The Song at the Sea. New Haven: Yale University
    Press, 1971.

James, M. R. The Biblical Antiquities of Philo. New York:
    KTAV, 1971.

Kisch, G. Pseudo-Philo's Liber Antiquitatum Biblicarum. South
    Bend: Notre Dame Press, 1949.

Lauterbach, J. Mekilta de-Rabbi Ishmael. Philadelphia: Jewish
    Publication Society of America, 1949.

The Midrash on Psalms. Trans. by W. Braude. Yale Judaica
    Series 13. New Haven: Yale University Press, 1959.

Midrash Rabbah. Trans. and edited by B. A. Freedman and M.
    Simon. London: Soncino Press, 1939.

Midrash Rabbah: Leviticus מדרש ויקרה רבה . Edited by M.
    Margulies. Jerusalem, 1953.

Midrash Tehillim מדרש שוחר טוב על תהלים . Jerusalem: "Midras,"
    1960.

Pirke de-Rabbi Eliezer. Trans. by G. Friedlander. New York:
    Bloch Publishing Co., 1916.

Rabin, Chaim. The Zadokite Documents. Second revised edition.
    Oxford: Clarendon Press, 1958.

Sperber, A. The Bible in Aramaic. Leiden: Brill, 1959-68.

Stenning, J. F. The Targum of Isaiah. Oxford: Clarendon
    Press, 1949.

218

Strugnell, John. "Notes en marge du volume V des Discoveries in the Judean Desert of Jordan." RQ 29 (1970), 163-276.

Talmud Yerushalmi תלמוד ירושלמי או תלמוד המערב ויש קורין לו תלמוד ארץ ישראל. Jerusalem: Israel-American Offset, 1960.

Thackeray, H. and Marcus, R. Josephus. Loeb Classical Library. Cambridge: Harvard University Press, 1927-67.

Yadin, Y. "A Midrash on 2 Sam vii and Ps i-ii (4Q Florilegium)." IEJ 9 (1959), 95-98.

II. Reference works

Bauer, W. A Greek-English Lexicon of the New Testament and Other Early Christian Literature. Trans. and revised by W. Arndt and F. W. Gingrich. Chicago: University of Chicago Press, 1957.

Blass, F. and Debrunner, A. A Greek Grammar of the New Testament and Other Early Christian Literature. Trans. and revised by R. Funk. Chicago: University of Chicago Press, 1961.

Brown, F., Driver, S., and Briggs, C. A. Hebrew and English Lexicon of the Old Testament. Oxford: Clarendon, 1907.

Dalman, G. Aramäisches Dialektproben. Leipzig: Hinrichs, 1896.

Idem. Aramäisch-Neuhebraisches Handwörterbuch zu Targum, Talmud, und Midrash. Hildesheim: G. Olms, 1967.

Idem. Grammatik des jüdisch-palästinischen Aramäisch. Leipzig: Hinrichs, 1896.

Jastrow, M. A Dictionary of the Targumim, the Talmud Babli and Yerushalmi, and the Midrashic Literature. New York: Pardes, 1950.

Kittel, G. and Friedrich, G. Theological Dictionary of the New Testament. Trans. by G. Bromiley. Grand Rapids: Eerdmans, 1968.

Liddell, H. and Scott, R. A Greek-English Lexicon. New edition revised by H. S. Jones. Oxford: Clarendon Press, 1961.

III. General works and commentaries

Aalen, S. "'Reign' and 'House' in the Kingdom of God in the Gospels." NTS 8 (1963), 215-40.

Auerbach, E. Mimesis: The Representation of Reality in Western Literature. Trans. by W. Trask. Princeton: Princeton University Press, 1953.

Baumgarten, J. "Sacrifice and Worship among the Jewish Sectarians of the Dead Sea (Qumran) Scrolls." HTR 46 (1953), 141-159.

Benoit, P. The Passion and Resurrection of Jesus Christ. Trans. B. Weatherhead. New York: Herder and Herder, 1969.

Bertram, G. Die Leidensgeschichte Jesu und der Christuskult. Göttingen: Vandenhoeck and Ruprecht, 1922.

Best, E. The Temptation and the Passion: The Markan Soteriology. NTSMS 2. Cambridge: Cambridge University Press, 1965.

Betz, O. and Michel, O. "Von Gott gezeugt." Judentum, Urchristentum, Kirche, BZNW. Berlin: Töpelmann, 1960, 1-23.

Beyer, H. βλασφημία. TDNT 1, 621-25.

Bickermann, E. "Utilitas crucis. Observations sur les recit du proces de Jesus dans les Evangiles canonique." RHR 112 (1935), 169-241.

Blinzler, J. The Trial of Jesus. Trans. by I. and F. McHugh. Westminster, Md.: Newman Press, 1959.

Bloch, R. "Note methodologique pour l'etude de la litterature rabbinique." RSR 43 (1955), 194-227.

Borgen, P. Bread from Heaven. Leiden: Brill, 1965.

Bornkamm, G., Barth, C., and Held, H. D. Tradition and Interpretation in Matthew. Trans. by P. Scott. Philadelphia: Westminster, 1963.

Bowker, J. The Targums and Rabbinic Literature. Cambridge: Cambridge University Press, 1969.

Brandon, S. G. F. Jesus and the Zealots. Manchester: Manchester University Press, 1967.

Idem. The Trial of Jesus of Nazareth. London: Batsford, 1968.

Büchsel, F. "Die Blutgerichtsbarkeit des Synedrions." ZNW 30 (1931), 202-10.

Idem. "Noch einmal: Zur Blutgerichtsbarkeit des Synedrions." ZNW 33 (1934), 84-87.

Bultmann, R. History of the Synoptic Tradition. Trans. by J. Marsh. New York: Harper and Row, 1963.

Burkill, T. A. "The Condemnation of Jesus: A Critique of Sherwin-White's Thesis." NovT 12 (1970), 321-42.

Idem. Mysterious Revelation. Ithaca, N.Y.: Cornell University Press, 1963.

Idem. "St. Mark's Philosophy of the Passion." NovT 2 (1957), 245-271.

Idem. "The Trial of Jesus." VC 12 (1958), 1-18.

Catchpole, D. The Trial of Jesus. SPB 18. Leiden: Brill, 1971.

Churgin, P. Targum Jonathan to the Prophets. Yale Oriental Series 14. New Haven: Yale University Press, 1927.

Cohn, H. The Trial and Death of Jesus. New York: Harper and Row, 1967.

Conzelmann, H. The Theology of St. Luke. Trans. by G. Buswell. New York: Harper and Row, 1961.

Dahl, Nils A. "Abraham in Luke-Acts." Studies in Luke-Acts. Edited by L. Keck and J. L. Martyn. Nashville: Abingdon, 1966. 139-158.

Idem. "Eschatology and History in the light of the Qumran Scrolls." The Future of Our Religious Past. Edited by J. M. Robinson. New York: Harper and Row, 1971. 9-28.

Idem. "Der gekreuzigte Messiah." Der historische Jesus und der kerygmatische Christus. Edited by H. Ristow and K. Matthiae. Berlin: Evangelische Verlagsanstalt, 1960. 149-69.

Idem. "New Testament Christology." Unpublished lectures delivered at the Yale Divinity School in 1968-69.

Idem. "Die Passionsgeschichte bei Matthäus." NTS 22 (1955-56), 17-32.

Idem. "The Purpose of Mark's Gospel." An unpublished translation of "Markusevangelietssikte," SEA 22-23 (1957-58), 32-46.

Danby, H. "The Bearing of the Rabbinical Criminal Code on the Jewish Trial Narratives of the Gospels." JTS 21 (1919-20), 151-76.

Danker, F. W. "The Demonic Secret in Mark: A Reexamination of the Cry of Dereliction (15:34)." ZNW 61 (1970), 48-69.

Dibelius, M. From Tradition to Gospel. Trans. B. Woolf. New York: Scribners, 1935.

Donahue, J. Are You the Christ? The Trial Narrative in the Gospel of Mark. SBLDS 10. Missoula: SBL, 1973.

Esh, S. הקב"ה "Der Heilige - sei er gepriesen;" Zur Geschichte einer nachbiblisch-hebräischen Gottesbezeichnung. Leiden: Brill, 1957.

Fitzmeyer, J. "Qumran and the Interpolated Paragraph in 2 Cor 6:14-7:1." CBQ 23 (1961), 271-280.

Flusser, D. "Two Notes on the Midrash on 2 Sam vii." IEJ 9 (1959), 99-109.

Gärtner, B. The Temple and the Community in Qumran and the New Testament. NTSMS 1. Cambridge: Cambridge University Press, 1965.

Gaston, L. No Stone on Another: Studies in the Significance of the Fall of Jerusalem in the Synoptic Gospels. NovTSup 23. Leiden: Brill, 1970.

Glasson, T. F. The Second Advent. London, 1945.

Goldin, J. "The First Chapter of the Abot de Rabbi Nathan." Mordecai M. Kaplan: Jubilee Volume on the Occasion of his Seventieth Birthday. New York: Jewish Theological Seminary of America, 1953. 263-280.

Grob, R. Einführung in das Markus-Evangelium. Zürich: Zwingli Verlag, 1965.

Grundmann, W. Das Evangelium nach Markus. THNT 2. 3rd edition. Berlin: Evangelische Verlagsanstalt, 1965.

Gutbrod, W. Ἰσραήλ. TDNT 3, 369-91.

Haenchen, E. Der Weg Jesu. 2nd edition. Berlin: de Gruyter and Co., 1968.

Hegermann, H. Jesaia 53 in Hexapla, Targum und Peschitta. Gütersloh: Bertelsmann, 1954.

Hill, H. E. "Messianic Expectations in the Targum to the Psalms." Unpublished PhD dissertation submitted to Yale University, 1955.

Hooker, M. Jesus and the Servant. London: S.P.C.K., 1959.

Iersel, B. M. F. van. Der Sohn in den synoptischen Jesusworten. NovTSup 3. Leiden: Brill, 1961.

Jeremias, J. ABBA: Studien zur neutestamentlichen Theologie und Zeitgeschichte. Göttingen: Vandenhoeck and Ruprecht, 1966.

Idem. "Zur Geschichtlichkeit des Verhörs Jesu vor dem Hohen Rat." ZNW 43 (1952), 145-50.

Idem. Jerusalem at the Time of Jesus. Trans. by F. and C. Cave. Philadelphia: Fortress, 1969.

Idem. παῖς. TDNT 5, 677-717.

Juster, J. Les Juifs dans l'empire Romain. Paris: Guethnen, 1914.

Kilpatrick, G. The Trial of Jesus. Oxford: Clarendon Press, 1952.

Klijn, A. F. J. "Stephen's Speech - Acts 7:2-53." NTS 4 (1957), 25-31.

Klinzing, G. Die Umdeutung des Kultus in der Qumrangemeinde und im Neuen Testament. Studien zur Umwelt des Neuen Testaments 7. Göttingen: Vandenhoeck und Ruprecht, 1971.

Klostermann, E. Das Markusevangelium. HNT 3. Tübingen: Mohr, 1950.

Kürzinger, J. "Das Papiaszeugnis und die Erstgestalt des Matthäusevangeliums." BZ, n.f. 4 (1960), 19-38.

Kuhn, K. Ἰσραήλ. TDNT 3, 359-69.

Idem. Konkordanz zu den Qumrantexten. Göttingen: Vandenhoeck und Ruprecht, 1960.

Le Deaut, R. "Actes 7:48 et Matthieu 17:4 (par) a la lumiere du Targum palestinien." RSR 52 (1964), 85-90.

Levy, S. "The Date of Targum Jonathan to the Prophets." VT 21 (1971), 186-96.

Lietzmann. H. "Der Prozess Jesu." Sitzungsberichte der preussischen Akademie der Wissenschaft, Phil-Hist Klasse (1931), 313-322.

Idem. "Bemerkungen zum Prozess Jesu I." ZNW 30 (1931), 211-15.

Idem. "Bemerkungen zum Prozess Jesu II." ZNW 32 (1932), 78-84.

Lightfoot, R. H. The Gospel Message of St. Mark. Oxford: Clarendon Press, 1950.

Idem. History and Interpretation in the Gospels. New York: Harper Bros., 1934.

Lindars, B. New Testament Apologetic. London: SCM Press, 1961.

Linnemann, Eta. Studien zur Passionsgeschichte. Göttingen: Vandenhoeck und Ruprecht, 1970.

Linton, O. "The Trial of Jesus and the Interpretation of Psalm 110." NTS 7 (1961), 258-62.

Lövestam, E. Son and Savior. Trans. M. Petry. Lund: Gleerup, 1961.

Lohmeyer, E. Das Evangelium des Markus. Meyer, 17th edition. Göttingen: Vandenhoeck und Ruprecht, 1967.

Idem. Lord of the Temple. Trans. by S. Todd. Richmond: John Knox Press, 1962.

Lohse, E. History of the Suffering and Death of Jesus Christ. Trans. by M. O. Dietrich. Philadelphia: Fortress, 1967.

Idem. συνέδριον. TDNT 7, 867-68.

Idem. υἱός. TDNT 8, 357-62.

Lohse, E. χειροποίητος. TWNT 9, 425-26.

Marxsen, W. Mark the Evangelist. Trans. by D. Juel et al. Nashville: Abingdon, 1969.

Maurer, C. "Knecht Gottes und Sohn Gottes im Passionsbericht." ZTK 50 (1953), 1-38.

Idem. "Das Messiasgeheimnis des Markusevangeliums." NTS 14 (1967-68), 515-25.

McKelvey, R. The New Temple: The Church in the New Testament. Oxford: Clarendon Press, 1969.

McNamara, M. The New Testament and the Palestinian Targum to the Pentateuch. AnBib 27. Rome: Pontifical Biblical Institute, 1966.

Meeks, W. The Prophet-King. Leiden: Brill, 1967.

Michel, O. ναός. TDNT 4, 880-90.

Moule, C. F. D. "Sanctuary and Sacrifice in the Church of the New Testament." JTS, n.s. 1-2 (1950/51), 29-41.

Mowinckel, S. He That Cometh. Trans. by G. W. Anderson. Nashville: Abingdon, 1954.

Nineham, D. E. Saint Mark. Pelican Gospel Commentaries. Baltimore: Penguin Books, 1963.

Perrin, N. "The Creative Use of the Son of Man Traditions in Mark." USQR 23 (1967-68), 357-65.

Idem. "Mk 14:62: The End Product of a Christian Pesher Tradition?" NTS 12 (1966), 150-55.

Idem. What is Redaction Criticism? Philadelphia: Fortress Press, 1969.

Preuss, H. D. Verspottung fremder Religionen im Alten Testament. Berlin: Kohlhammer, 1971.

Quesnell, Q. The Mind of Mark: Interpretation and Method through the Exegesis of Mark 6:52. AnBib 38. Rome: Pontifical Biblical Institute, 1969.

Robinson, J. A. T. Jesus and His Coming. Nashville: Abingdon, 1958.

Schmidt, K. L. Der Rahmen der Geschichte Jesu. Berlin: Trowitzsch, 1919.

Schneider, C. καταπέτασμα. TDNT 3, 628-30.

Schreiber, J. "Die Christologie des Markusevangeliums." ZTK 58 (1961), 154-183.

Idem. "Der Kreuzigungsbericht des Markusevangeliums." An unpublished PhD dissertation submitted to the U. of Bonn, 1959.

Idem. Theologie des Vertrauens. Hamburg: Furche Verlag, 1967.

Scroggs, R. et al. "Reflections on the Question: Was there a pre-Markan Passion Narrative?" Report prepared by the Markan Task Force for the 1971 meeting of the Society of Biblical Literature. Seminar Papers II, 503-565.

Schweizer, E. "Anmerkungen zur Theologie des Markus." Neotestamentica et Patristica. Zürich: Zwingli Verlag, 1963. 35-46.

Schweizer, E. The Good News According to Mark. Trans. by D. Madvig. Richmond: John Knox Press, 1970.

Idem. υἱός. TDNT 8, 363-92.

Seidelin, P. "Der 'Ebed Jahwe und die Messiasgestalt im Jesajatargum." ZNW 35 (1936), 194-231.

Sherwin-White, A. N. Roman Society and Roman Law in the New Testament. Oxford: Clarendon Press, 1963.

Simon, M. "Retour du Christ et reconstruction du Temple dans la pensee chretienne primitive." Aux source de la tradition Chretienne. Paris: Delachaux et Niestle, 1950, 247-57.

Idem. St. Stephen and the Hellenists. London: Longmans and Green, 1958.

Smith, M. "'God's begetting the Messiah' in IQSa." NTS 5 (1959), 218-24.

Stauffer, E. Jesus and His Story. Trans. by R. and C. Winston. London: SCM, 1960.

Stendahl, K. "Prayer and Forgiveness." SEA 22/23 (1957-58), 75-86.

Streeter, B. H. The Four Gospels. London: Macmillan, 1964.

Suhl, A. Die Funktion der alttestamentlichen Zitate und Anspielungen im Markusevangelium. Gütersloh: Gütersloher Verlagshaus, 1965.

Taylor, V. The Gospel according to St. Mark. London: Macmillan, 1963.

Vermes, G. Discovery in the Judean Desert. Paris: Desclee, 1956.

Idem. Scripture and Tradition in Judaism. SPB 4. Leiden: Brill, 1961.

Vielhauer, Ph. "Erwägungen zur Christologie des Markusevangeliums." Zeit und Geschichte. Edited by E. Dinkler. Tübingen: Mohr, 1964. 155-69.

Idem. Oikodome. Das Bild vom Bau in der christlichen Literatur vom Neuen Testament bis Clemens Alexandrinus. Karlsruhe: Durlach, 1940.

Weeden, T. "The Heresy that Necessitated Mark's Gospel." ZNW 59 (1968), 145-58.

Idem. Traditions in Conflict. Philadelphia: Fortress, 1971.

Wellhausen, J. Das Evangelium Marci. Berlin: Reimer, 1909.

Wenschkewitz, H. Die Spiritualizierung der Kultbegriffe Temple Priester und Opfer im Neuen Testament. Aggelos Beiheft 4. Leipzig: Pfeiffer, 1936.

Wilson, W. R. The Execution of Jesus. New York: Scribners, 1970.

Winter, P. On the Trial of Jesus. Berlin: Gruyter, 1961.

Woude, A. S. van der. Die messianischen Vorstellungen der Gemeinde von Qumran. Aasen: van Gorcum and Co, 1957.

Wrede, W. Das Messiasgeheimnis in den Evangelien. Göttingen: Vandenhoeck und Ruprecht, 1901.

Yadin, Y. "The Temple Scroll." Ba 30 (1967), 135-39.